For my much missed friend and former Canberra pilot, Tim Garden

ANDREW BROOKES

CANBERRA BOYS

FASCINATING ACCOUNTS
FROM THE OPERATORS OF
AN ENGLISH ELECTRIC CLASSIC

GRUB STREET | LONDON

Published by

Grub Street

4 Rainham Close

London

SW11 6SS

Copyright © Grub Street 2017

Copyright text © Andrew Brookes 2017

A CIP record for this title is available from the British Library

ISBN-13: 9-781-910690-33-8

Cover and Book Design by Daniele Roa

Printed and bound by Finidr, Czech Republic

PUBLISHER'S NOTE

The reader will note that there are two styles to the text layout in this book. Indented and full out.

Indented text indicates when a contributor is speaking, whereas full out text signals the words of Andrew Brookes. ▪

ACKNOWLEDGEMENTS

For all the Canberra old and bold who gave of their reminiscences and tales of derring-do unstintingly and without whom this book would never have achieved lift-off.

CONTENTS

FOREWORD

In *Canberra Boys*, Andrew Brookes weaves together reminiscences from hundreds of Canberra aircrew into a collection of narratives. Deftly, he brings the story of this remarkable machine and the men who flew it together to life. The reader is reminded of the amazing versatility by role and mission type of over 20 marks and variants, the spirit of innovation by the men that flew the aircraft and maintained it and the genuine sense of affection that crosses the generations. Coupled with high loss rates, which to the contemporary eye, looks shocking.

I was posted to Canberras in 1979 flying, as a navigator, the Canberra PR7 out of Wyton in the photographic-reconnaissance role almost all over the globe (we could not cross the Pacific). And I led the fond farewells to the PR9s of 39 Squadron in 2006. Therefore I connect with this volume of well-written recollections and anecdotes and reflect that, in the history of air power, few other aircraft can match the record of the Canberra. But that is to miss the point. The point is this book reflects the worldwide sense of spirit, leadership and adventure by the men who flew them and I commend it to the general and specialist reader alike.

Air Chief Marshal Sir Stuart Peach GBE KCB ADC DL
UK Chief of Defence Staff

CHAPTER 1
IN THE BEGINNING

BOB FAIRCLOUGH joined English Electric as an apprentice in 1960. He was co-author of the English Electric volume in Putnam's company histories series.

During the 1930s, English Electric (EE) made electrical products at five main factories, ranging from small electrical items to the heaviest power station generation plant. One factory was at Strand Road, Preston, its main products being tramcars and tramway electrical equipment. In 1938, as part of the huge re-equipment programme for the RAF, EE received contracts to build bomber aircraft. These were allocated to the Preston factory, and were initially for the Handley Page Hampden medium bomber. After 770 had been completed, production switched to the Halifax heavy bomber. Between 1941 and 1945, 2,145 Halifaxes were produced; always at a higher rate than the minimum specified in the contract, and at a lower cost than any comparable factory. Quality was also high, in spite of the works staff increasing in number from under 1,000 in 1938 to over 14,000 in 1944, and the factory doubled in size over the same period. In addition, a new flight test airfield with three hard runways and five hangars was built at Samlesbury, a few miles from the Preston factory.

In 1944, the company decided that it would stay in aircraft work at Preston after the end of the war. However, it was obvious that post-war contracts would not be available to build other company's aircraft; EE would have to design and build their own aeroplanes, in competition with the older established manufacturers. EE therefore needed to create a design team with suitable staff and facilities, and the first steps in that direction were taken in 1944. That year, the Air Ministry decided that EE should receive contracts to build the new De Havilland Vampire jet fighter; the first was completed in 1945, and in the period to 1951, 1,369 were delivered. After Halifax production ceased in 1945, Vampire work provided valuable continuity of aircraft work for the Preston factory, until EE's own design could enter production.

TEDDY PETTER

Probably the most critical step in setting up EE's new design team was the selection of the leader, who would have to form the team and conceive the first new design. At the right time, in 1944, a suitable man became available. He was William Edward

Willoughby Petter (known as Teddy) who was, at the time, technical director/chief designer at Westland Aircraft. His father was the founder of Westland, but the company was controlled by major shareholders. By mid-1944 Petter had conceived the basic design for a fighter-bomber that was regarded as a jet replacement for the Mosquito. The Air Ministry showed real interest in the proposal but the board of Westlands decided that they should proceed with the design of a strike fighter for the Royal Navy. This was to be propeller-driven and regarded as a lower risk; it became the Wyvern and had very limited success. Teddy Petter did not agree with this decision, and he resigned from Westland. Probably through the Air Ministry, he was contacted by EE and in July 1944 he joined the company as chief engineer of the aircraft division at Preston. At that time he was 35 years of age.

As the founder member of the design team, Petter's first task was to recruit the key senior members of the new team. His first recruit, in March 1945, was F. W. (Freddie) Page, who was to have a critical role in the future of the Canberra. He soon effectively became Petter's deputy. The team's home was a building occupied by EE in Corporation Street, Preston, about a mile from the Strand Road factory. These premises were controlled by the Ministry of Labour, and had been used as a training centre for building workers. They were officially known as the 'government training centre' or GTC; during EE's occupancy this was shortened to just 'TC'. The TC building had been built in the 1930s for Barton Motors, a large firm of car dealers, and had spacious showrooms, offices and workshops. EE occupied the building initially for overflow work from the Strand Road factory, but in 1944 most of the building became the home of the new design team and other technical support functions, plus the development workshops.

While Petter was leaving Westland, he had obtained their agreement that he could take with him the embryonic ideas for his jet fighter-bomber. As these ideas had already received favourable comment from the Air Ministry, it was potentially EE's first new and original project. The first important task for Petter and Page, therefore, was to prepare a brochure describing their ideas for the new aircraft for submission to the ministry so that funding could be obtained for a full study of the proposed jet bomber. This brochure was submitted in May 1945, and a study contract, valued at £1,000, was received on 13 June. This enabled more staff to be recruited, which Ministry of Labour regulations would not permit unless there was a contract to prove they were necessary. The contract was for work on a high-speed, high-altitude jet bomber to specification E3/45.

EVOLUTION OF THE BASIC CONFIGURATION

The aircraft described in the May 1945 brochure was to have one large centrifugal compressor engine in the centre fuselage. This engine was to be basically a scaled-up Rolls-Royce Nene with 12,000-lb thrust. It had wing-root intakes, and an exhaust through the rear fuselage. A centrifugal engine of this large size was rather ambitious, and its position in the centre fuselage was right where the fuel and bomb load wanted to be! Therefore, when Petter and Page heard from Rolls-Royce that they were considering a much more compact axial flow engine with 6,500-lb thrust (the AJ65, later to become the Avon), they produced a revised proposal for the ministry. This was submitted in July 1945. The modified layout had one of the proposed AJ65s in each wing root, leaving the fuselage clear for fuel and bomb load. At about this time information was starting to become available on the benefits of swept wings for jet aircraft.

The aircraft in the July brochure was shown with 30° of sweep-back, but after considering the benefits and penalties, the brochure concluded that swept wings were 'not yet considered essential or desirable'. Both brochures had the large radar for navigation and bomb aiming (the H2S Mk 9) in the lower part of the nose. In the following months the configuration was further revised, the engines being moved out of the wing roots and placed in separate nacelles in the wings. The first version of the E3/45 (E for English Electric) high-altitude bomber was designated the 'A1'. Previously usually known within EE as the 'HAB', the aircraft now became generally known as the A1. In official and ministry circles it was usually referred to as the E3/45. The layout defined in December 1945 proved to be the final iteration, as it remained unchanged for the rest of the aircraft's life. This layout was the subject of a revised proposal to the ministry (by now the Ministry of Supply). This was accepted and a formal contract to complete detail design and build four prototypes was received by EE on 15 January 1946. Still a two-seater with a radar in the nose, but, in most other respects, the Canberra. The serial numbers of these prototypes were to be VN799, VN813, VN828 and VN850.

Shortly afterwards the experimental specification number of E3/45 was changed to the definitive B3/45, which defined the requirements for the initial production standard of the aircraft. Thus the new design team (which had started with just three men at TC) had gone from initial proposal to prototype contract in only nine months.

EMERGENCE OF THE PROTOTYPE

During 1946 and 1947 detail design work proceeded at TC, where full-scale mock-ups were built of the nose and cockpit areas, and also of the complete aircraft. Recruitment of staff was also in progress, and a wide variety of skills and levels of experience was acquired. The basic design point of the aircraft was a still air range of 1,400 nm at a cruising speed of Mach 0.75, at 45,000 ft with 6,000 lbs of bombs. In 1946 these requirements were a major challenge. There were to be two crew plus the large and complex H2S Mk 9 navigation and blind-bombing radar. The parts for the prototypes were made in the Strand Road factory, and assembly was done at both Strand Road and TC. From the start TC had been regarded as an interim home for the design team, and a suitable flight test airfield was required. Samlesbury airfield would be satisfactory for production test flying, but would not be suitable for experimental work. EE therefore looked for a new design and flight development centre.

The chosen site was at Warton, about five miles west down the Ribble Estuary from the Strand Road factory. Warton had been a major USAAF maintenance base during WW2, but by 1947 it was only used by the RAF as a storage unit. EE arranged to lease

a hangar and an office block, and use the large airfield, which was eminently suitable for development as a flight testing centre. During 1947 EE designed and built a large low-speed wind tunnel and a structural test rig, both being housed in the large No. 25 hangar at Warton. During 1948 testing of A1 models and major structural assemblies started in 25 hangar, and in September the design team (by now about 100 strong) moved from TC to the L Block office at Warton. By this time EE had recruited a chief test pilot, Roland (Bee) Beamont, who was based at Warton. Early in 1949 assemblies for the first A1, VN799, began to arrive at 25 hangar, the front part of which was used as the prototype flight hangar.

While the basic aircraft was making good progress in 1947 and 1948, the radar bombing system and the AJ65 Avon engine both ran into serious problems. The H2S radar, which was being developed by an electronics company, was proving to be a much bigger and more complicated task than expected. The project was running several years late, and the number and size of the equipment items to be installed in the aircraft had exceeded that possible in the A1. Accordingly, in 1947, the decision was made by EE and the ministry that the A1 would not have a radar bombing system; instead it would have a visual bombsight in the nose and an updated wartime navigation system. A third crew member was added to operate the revised equipment fit. To reflect these changes, the B3/45 specification was superseded by B5/47, although the four prototypes already on order would continue to be built to B3/45. These prototypes would be used to test and evaluate the basic aircraft; in March 1948 further prototypes were ordered to reflect the provisions of B5/47.

The problem with the AJ65 engine, by now designated the Avon RA1, was persistent surging during test bed running. This threatened to delay the availability of flight-cleared engines for the A1. To avoid delays to initial flight testing, it was decided that the second A1 prototype would be fitted with two well-proven Rolls-Royce Nenes. Accordingly, this aircraft, VN813, was built with rather fatter engine nacelles to contain the bulky centrifugal Nene engines. The necessary design and engineering work was undertaken while construction of the first four prototypes was underway and as work began on the design of the photo-reconnaissance (PR) and trainer variants of the basic A1 that were expected to be ordered in addition to the basic bomber version.

COMPLETION AND FLIGHT TESTING OF THE PROTOTYPES

By the spring of 1949, the first A1, VN799, was being assembled in 25 hangar at Warton and it was rolled out for first engine runs at the beginning of May. Taxi trials started on 7 May, and Beamont took VN799 off the ground on the 9th for a short 'hop' to check unstick speed and low-speed control feel. A few more hops were made before, on Friday 13 May, VN799 was cleared for flight. Beamont took off at 1046 for a 30-minute flight. After the flight he recorded in his logbook, 'Satisfactory, overbalanced rudder'. This was a very low-key way of recording a very successful flight; the remark about the rudder was not serious, as it was known to be difficult to get the size of the horn balance correct before flight testing. To facilitate adjustment, if any should be needed, the top of the rudder was made of wood, so that it could be easily changed. Before the second flight, the top of the rudder was cut down, altering the fully rounded tip to a more flat-topped shape. This was the shape featured on all subsequent aircraft. By the end of May Beamont had made ten flights, totalling just over 17 hours.

Freddie Page later wrote, 'thus started one of the most straightforward and successful flight test programmes in post-war history'. By the end of 1949 all four A1 prototypes had flown, and the aircraft obviously had no significant faults. Any snags found were minor, and readily rectified. The first assessment by the customer, the A&AEE at Boscombe Down, had been completed with VN799, and was 'extremely satisfactory'.

PREVIOUS PAGE: Canberra 'leading lights' at Warton, May 1949. L-R: Don Crowe (chief structure designer), Dai Ellis (chief aerodynamicist), 'Harry' Harrison (chief draughtsman), A. Ellison (chief designer), Teddy Petter (chief engineer), Bee Beamont (chief test pilot), D. Smith, Freddie Page (chief stress-man), H. Howatt. The underlying English Electric design philosophy was said to be an aircraft at 'the extreme in adventurous conventionalism'. (Peter Green Collection)

BELOW: The first A1, VN799, just before its initial flight. (Peter Green Collection)

Up to now it had been policy to name RAF bombers after 'an inland town of the British Commonwealth or associated with British history'. Soon after the first flight, Australia showed an interest in acquiring the new aircraft and the EE chairman, Sir George Nelson, proposed that the A1 should be named 'Canberra', after the Australian capital city. Officialdom agreed and the first four prototypes became the Canberra B1 to be followed by the operational three-crew B2. The main difference over the B1 was the visual bomb-aiming station through the glazed nose, while fitment of the RA3 engine added 500 lbs of thrust. The B2 was built in larger numbers than any other variant. In the UK there were four manufacturers – English Electric, Short Brothers, Handley Page and Avro, although all export models were built by EE.

In 1949 Teddy Petter, father of the Lightning supersonic interceptor as well as the Canberra, had fallen out with the EE hierarchy and ridden off to design the Gnat for Follands. Freddie Page, who was just 32 years old at the time, became the new chief engineer and he was to guide the Canberra through its long and varied career for most of the next 20 years.

Australian Prime Minister Robert Menzies officially names the Canberra at Biggin Hill, 19 January 1951. WD929 was used for the ceremony. (Peter Green Collection)

TEST PILOT VIEW

The Canberra flying controls were smooth and straightforward though some muscle power was required above 350 kts. 40,000 ft was exceeded (to 42,000 ft) on 11 August 1949 and Mach 0.80 was achieved the following day. On 31 August the initial design speed of 470 kts was flown at 4,500 ft, giving the required margin of 20 kts over the proposed initial service limit of 450 kts IAS.

In 2000 BEE BEAMONT, he disliked the name Roly, was interviewed on his recollections at the Newark Air Museum.

English Electric was tasked with designing the twin-engined bomber roughly cast as a Mosquito replacement, and my task was to take charge of the test flying programme from its first flight onwards. I'd done a lot of experimental flying on Typhoons and Tempests during the war, many hundreds of sorties in quite critical flight testing conditions, so as far as experience was concerned, I felt ready to do this. But there were some people about, saying this is this country's first jet bomber, how come it's being done by a pilot who's never done a prototype's first flight in his life? That didn't worry me, and it didn't seem to worry my boss, Teddy Petter. When this aeroplane came to flight status, I had been working round it for a couple of years and I flew it very well. I had a strong feeling of confidence that it was going to be a fine aeroplane, based on the fact that it was going to have Rolls-Royce's second generation of jet engine. A lot of people thought that combining a brand new engine design with a brand new airframe design was a recipe for disaster, but Rolls-Royce were confident with their Avon engine and Teddy Petter and the team were confident with their design.

It surprised even me, on my first flight – this aeroplane was not an aeroplane that was going to turn round and bite or be a struggle to assess and find out about. It flew as if it had been flying for a hundred hours – it came off the ground at exactly the predicted speed with exactly the predicted stick forces, it was controllable with the fingertips, no muscle force and right from the first take-off, it was a delightful flying experience. One could talk about this for hours – we were at the breakthrough there, at the beginning of a new era. It started as it went on, to be a most exceptional aeroplane. We are talking about May 1949 and it's now the year 2000 and there are Canberras in the RAF today that will still be in service until 2005, I'm told. This is the first time the air force has had a type in service for fifty years, quite extraordinary!

We took that aeroplane to Farnborough in September 1949 and by that time I'd got one or two things up my sleeve, because I realised we had a bomber here that could do all the manoeuvres that a fighter could, and more. In some aspects we could actually out-manoeuvre the jet fighters of the day and we were damn near as fast as the fastest of them. So we broke into the Farnborough display scene with a display that I had worked out privately, out of sight of anybody up in Lancashire and nobody knew what was coming – they saw this bright blue-painted, twin-engined bomber tearing around the airfield, inside the perimeter track, in vertical banked turns, pulling up into rolls off loops, coming down the runway doing rolls like a fighter and they were absolutely astonished.

As *Flight* magazine put it, a new aircraft had 'never been more convincingly demonstrated'.

Bee Beamont (left) with Wally Sheen (station commander) and Pat Connolly (OC Flying) after delivering the RAF's first production Canberra B2 to Binbrook, 25 May 1951. WD936 is painted in Bomber Command colours, black on the bottom and light grey on top. (Peter Green Collection)

CHAPTER 2
EARLY DAYS

The RAF Air Staff did not expect the Canberra to cover the whole bomber spectrum. 'Our intention,' wrote AVM John Boothman to C-in-C Bomber Command on 29 March 1946, 'is to provide two types – a long-range bomber, the primary feature of which will be long range at very high cruising speed, and a much smaller bomber with a relatively modest range but a very high cruising speed.' The former would be the V bombers and EE's high-speed creation was seen as a tactical and technical jumping off point for its larger brethren.

'Rags' Barlow, Hamish Mahaddie and John Brownlow – the first station level aircrew to convert to the Canberra. (John Brownlow)

Commenting after a meeting at HQ Bomber Command in late January 1951, ACM Sir Ralph Cochrane told CAS that, 'There was...a tendency to look upon the Canberra as a long-range, high-flying bomber, and to press for equipment to enable it to undertake this role. At the end, however, it was generally accepted that the Canberra is a short-range tactical bomber, that there is no equipment which will enable it to hit a small target from 45,000 ft, and that it must therefore come down to a height from which it can achieve results....' Consequently, the radar bombing system was replaced with a visual bombsight in the nose together with an updated wartime Gee-H Mk II navigation system.

JOHN BROWNLOW joined the RAF in 1947 and flew as a Canberra navigator with 12 and 101 Squadrons and as a pilot with 103 and 213 Squadrons before attending the Empire Test Pilot School in 1958.

In 1950 I was serving at Binbrook as a member of 12 Squadron which was equipped with Lincolns. As well as squadron flying, I was deputed, together with Flt Lt R. A. G. Barlow of 101 Squadron, to fly with our Wing Commander Flying, Hamish Mahaddie, a highly-decorated Pathfinder pilot. 'Rags' Barlow, as he was known, was an experienced wartime navigator and, as the junior boy in the crew, I was more or less taken along to make sure the transport arrived on time and to carry the bags.

Flying with Hamish, we led the Bomber Command King's Birthday Fly-past down the Mall to Buckingham Palace on 8 June 1950, and the RAF Display Fly-past at Farnborough on 7 and 8 July. Good fortune flew with us and we managed to get to the palace and to Farnborough on time – without the aid of GPS, I might add. Strange though it may seem, I think these flights eventually led to Rags and I becoming members of the first station-level Canberra crew. Hamish always led from the front, so he and Sqn Ldr Ernest Cassidy, OC 101 Squadron, were the first station pilots to convert. Rags and I joined them as the first two navigator/bomb aimers then serving in operational squadrons to train as Canberra aircrew. As you can imagine, as a mere pilot officer, in the midst of all this seniority and experience, I was expected to be first in line to buy the beer if we were diverted. None of us had flown in a jet aircraft before. Some ground and flying training was obviously in order, so we travelled to Farnborough to spend a few days with the Institute of Aviation Medicine. They provided lectures on hypoxia along with practical experience of the rigours of the decompression chamber, including explosive decompression from, I seem to remember, 25,000 ft to 45,000 ft, plus familiarisation with use of the pressure waistcoat and the Canberra's oxygen system. In order to acquire some initial jet experience, we also flew in a Meteor 7 with Wg Cdr Ruffell-Smith, a well-known aviation specialist medical officer/pilot at the time.

My own Meteor flight was on 10 September 1950. Compared with the Lincoln, we all found this first jet flight a revelation in terms of speed, rate of climb, smoothness, low noise level and high-cruising altitude. We were then detached to English Electric at Warton, on an opportunity basis, for conversion to the Canberra under the super-vision of the chief test pilot, Wg Cdr 'Bee' Beamont and his team. Bee's team included Johnny Squier and Peter Hillwood, both of whom had been sergeant pilots in the Battle of Britain, and the company's navigator, Dennis Watson. Flight instruction was given from the Rumbold seat.[1] Ground school was largely confined to briefings at the aircraft and self-study. Personally, I first flew in a Canberra on 17 October 1950. This was with Hamish Mahaddie at Warton during his type conversion. The aeroplane was WD929, the first of an initial production batch of 132 Canberras, which had made its first flight just nine days earlier on 8 October. Later, a Jet

Unusual shot of Hamish, Rags and John Brownlow taken from outside the cockpit. (John Brownlow)

---

1. The Rumbold seat (aka the rumble seat) was a col-lapsible seat that was restrained against the starboard cabin wall to allow the rear crew to enter and exit their dark domain. It was to the right, slightly aft and below the pilot's ejection seat. Anyone sitting on it was sup-posed to roll out of the door in an emergency. It was said that the only good thing about the Canberra T4 was that it lacked a Rumbold seat.

Conversion Flight was formed at Binbrook to convert squadron aircrew, first to the Meteor and then the Canberra. This flight was up and running by mid-1951 as an integral part of 101 Squadron. It was commanded by Flt Lt Bill Morley, an experienced jet QFI, assisted by Flt Lt Debenham and Fg Off Young, also jet QFIs.

There was considerable concern at the time about the ability of the bomb aimer to get back from the nose and strap into his ejection seat in an emergency. Rags and I spent quite a lot of time during 1950 and early 1951 practising this move and timing how long it took to strap in. Our conclusion was that it was very difficult to do rapidly, especially, as was very likely to be the case, if any 'g' was being pulled (or pushed). We recommended that easy-to-release clips should be fitted to the sides of ejection seats so that the parachute and seat straps could be left lying open, instead of in a heap, thus minimising strapping-in time. This modification was eventually incorporated. The only navigation aid, other than VHF bearings, and Rebecca, was Gee, and, of course, an air position indicator. The Gee box was the universal indicator, allowing Gee or G-H to be selected. The controls and CRT display were mounted on the left-hand side of the navigator's seat, about level with his left thigh. This positioning made the box awkward to operate and one often developed a painful crick in the back and neck during longish trips. It also made it impossible for the Gee box to be operated by the navigator in the right-hand seat, which was a significant limitation. The Gee indicator and controls were eventually moved to the central navigation panel. At the time, Bomber Command navigators were trained to stick to track and take a Gee fix every six minutes. This basic procedure was no more difficult in a Canberra than in a Lincoln, and generally it was easier to track accurately because of the higher speed and smaller drift angles when the first aircraft, WD936, was delivered to 101 Squadron.

From the start, navigators were responsible for maintaining the Howgozit graph, taking periodic fuel readings and plotting them against planned time, predicted fuel remaining and distance. The published fuel consumption figures for the Canberra were, incidentally, very accurate, which was just as well, as the fuel reserve margins were much lower than those to which we were accustomed in the Lincoln, and at that time the aircraft were not fitted with tip tanks. The B2 received its release to service in the spring of 1951 and Bee Beamont delivered 101 Squadron's first aircraft to Binbrook on 25 May. Perhaps inevitably, there were considerable delays in delivery of new aircraft to the squadron, so Canberra flying was rather spasmodic during 1951. Concentration was obviously on conversion of crews and it was not until March 1952 that we

took part in an Exercise Bullseye – a Bomber Command high-level cross-country exercise – and routine bombing practice started in earnest. The T2 bombsight was very similar, if not the same, as in the Lincoln, and both visual and G-H bombing soon became the norm, using 25-lb practice bombs on the East Coast and Wash ranges. During these early days the motorised Alvis bomb-loading trolleys, which were tailor-made for the Canberra and featured an hydraulically-operated means of lifting bombs into the bomb bay, were found to be unable to cope with repeated long-distance journeys to and from the bomb dump. The consequent bombing-up problems were solved largely through modifications and procedures devised by Binbrook's senior armament officer, Sqn Ldr Ken Wallis. In essence, he had loaded Type F bomb trolleys pre-positioned at the dispersals, from which bombs could then be easily transferred to the Alvis trolleys for loading into the aircraft; once relieved of its load, the more robust Type Fs could be shuttled back to the dump to collect another batch of bombs. Ken Wallis deserved, and eventually received, considerable credit for the solutions he proposed which were rapidly introduced to service. He also played an important part in investigating the cause of a number of early Canberra accidents by eliminating the possibility of inadvertent detonation of the explosive collar in the elevator circuit that was required to allow the control column to go forward before pilot ejection. The cause of these accidents was eventually determined to be loss of control following a runaway of the pitch trim actuator. Much later, Ken Wallis became well-known for his work on autogyros, and his contribution to the James Bond film You Only Live Twice.

Early in 1952 I was posted to HQ 1 Group at Bawtry as ADC to the AOC, AVM Dermot Boyle. The AOC converted to the Canberra at Binbrook with the Jet Conversion Unit, and I flew with him throughout his conversion, and regularly during 1952. This included our unofficial record flight from Binbrook to Malta and back on 25 September 1952. Our total flying time was six hours ten minutes. Sgt Tommy Cramp from 12 Squadron was the second navigator. Coincidentally Tommy and I had been on the same navigators' course at No. 1 ANS at Topcliffe in 1947-49. On this flight our navigation aids were Gee, VHF bearings and map-reading.

Meanwhile, during 1952, the Canberra Wing at Binbrook was building up. 101 Squadron was joined by 617 Squadron in January, 12 Squadron in March, 9 Squadron in May, and 50 Squadron in August. As an indication of training priorities, the records show that in August, 12 Squadron dropped 200 25-lb practice bombs – 140 of them by G-H and 60 visually. By this time 231 Operational Conversion Unit (OCU) at Bassingbourn had been established and the first formal Canberra conversion course began in May 1952. About 50 per cent of student aircrew going through the OCU at this time were National Servicemen. ▦

TOP: Canberra B2 WD951 with Meteors of the Jet Conversion Flight at Binbrook in December 1951. (Peter Green Collection)

BELOW: Sgt Tommy Cramp, AVM Dermot Boyle and John Brownlow immediately after landing at Binbrook following a return flight to Malta on 25 September 1952. (John Brownlow)

CHAPTER 3
THE LIGHT
BOMBER FORCE

On 5 July 1951, WD938 suffered the first RAF Canberra accident. After an electrical power failure during a practice overshoot, resulting in the loss of both engines, Flt Lt Thomas managed to make a wheels-up landing on the airfield and neither he nor Ernest Cassidy, who was instructing him, nor the navigator Sgt Dix were injured – WD938 flew again on 24 July.

101 Squadron retired its last Lincoln during July 1951 but monthly Canberra B2 production was only one or two in the first half of the year, rising to six by December. Authorised to have ten B2s, 101 Squadron only had nine by the end of 1951 when it was still the only Canberra squadron in Bomber Command. Many early Canberras were allocated to experimental flying but 1952 saw a rapid increase in the size of the force to eight (seven bomber and one PR) squadrons.

101 Squadron not only absorbed the first operational Canberra crews but it was also made responsible for Canberra intensive flying trials (IFT), which covered the complete operational range and performance of the aircraft together with testing an entirely new range of flying clothing. Once the squadron had received its full complement of aircraft and crews, the Air Ministry organised a press visit to Binbrook after which *The Aeroplane* reported on 18 January 1952:

> 'The introduction of the Canberra is more than a re-equipment programme, and marks the start of the general expansion of Bomber Command. Selected crews from existing Lincolns and Washingtons will convert onto Canberras to form new squadrons, but the piston-engined bombers will remain in service with Bomber Command until the introduction of the Vickers Valiant multi-jet bomber. In the case of 101 Squadron, commanded by Sqn Ldr Ernest Cassidy DFC … it is flying at two or three times the intensity of normal peacetime squadron routine. When an aircraft is in large-scale production, it is preferable that any changes found necessary under intensive operations should be incorporated as soon as possible on the production line, rather than made retrospectively on a large number of aircraft in general squadron service. IFT should assist in accelerating the re-equipment of RAF squadrons with aircraft ready for immediate and effective operational employment.'

Binbrook became the first station in Bomber Command to house four Canberra squadrons – 101, 617, 12 and 9 Squadrons – with administration of the Jet Conversion Flight becoming the responsibility of 617 Squadron until 231 OCU was established on 1 December 1951 with the task of 'training pilots, navigators and radar operators to reinforce PR and light bomber squadrons at home and overseas'.

The first 231 OCU Canberra course, totalling five crews, passed out on 26 August 1952 and by July 1953, the OCU had 30 Canberra B2s plus a T4, together with 10 Meteor T7 trainers. The flying task hammered the ground crews who, according to an *Air Clues* article published in 1977, were 'largely National Service and poorly paid, worked in primitive conditions from unheated, poorly lit and unsanitary dispersal huts. They were under constant pressure to produce serviceable aircraft for the intensive flying effort... Shortage of components and inadequate stock control necessitated frequent "robbing" of items from one aircraft to make another serviceable for the flying programme. Bomb racks were so scarce that if an aircraft became unserviceable before flight, the crew had to wait for a second aircraft to be armed from scratch with the bomb rack from the first.'

A fifth Binbrook squadron – 50 Squadron – formed during August 1952 with its first Canberra B2 arriving on 18 August. Thus by the end of 1952, Bomber Command's Canberra force consisted of five main force light bomber squadrons, two marker squadrons and the beginnings of a Canberra PR squadron. Official totals at the end of the year were 70 B2s authorised and 48 in service, plus eight PR3s authorised and one delivered. The official return for Oct-Dec 1952 reported that 'the five Binbrook and two Hemswell squadrons

Canberra B2 WH640 of 109 Squadron at Boscombe Down, February 1953.
An Avro York and Shackleton are behind. (Peter Green Collection)

were now equipped to eight UE (Unit Establishment) and that some of the 139 Squadron crews were still undergoing conversion training by the Jet Conversion Flight'.

A Canberra policy meeting held on 9 January 1951 was briefed that 'the Canberra B2 is designed as a short-range day bomber. Owing to its navigation limitations it cannot effectively be operated outside Gee cover except in visual conditions. Its role in Bomber Command has therefore been defined as bombing in support of the land battle within 250 miles of the front line.' The brief stressed the importance of marking targets which were beyond the range of ground-based aids. 'From high altitudes, target identification makes visual day bombing difficult. For accurate bombing therefore, there is a continuing need both by day and by night to be able to mark targets accurately. There will therefore be a requirement for an aircraft to mark visually for a medium-range Canberra force.' The implication was that, provided the Canberras operated over Europe where they could use Gee, they could bomb effectively. Outside of Gee cover they needed a target marker force.

C-in-C Bomber Command, Air Mshl Sir Hugh Lloyd, expected to have ten Canberra squadrons by the end of 1952 but in the event he had 101, 617, 12 and 9 (formed in that order) at Binbrook; 109/105 at Hemswell and 50 Squadron at Binbrook in August 1952; 139 Squadron at Hemswell in November 1952 and the eighth, 540(PR) Squadron at Benson which received its first PR3 in December 1952. Under Plan H, Sir Hugh Lloyd was also to have ten Lincoln and eight Washington squadrons by December 1952 and in a directive from CAS dated 20 March 1950, the C-in-C had been told: 'Your principal effort is likely to be directed against targets within 250 miles of the Rhine so that full advantage can be taken of maximum bomb loads and navigational aids to bombing.' Another note from CAS dated 1 March 1952 on British bomber policy stated that 'the ultimate build-up of the bomber force under Plan H aims at the provision of 560 light bombers and 152 medium bombers. All the light bombers are committed to the support of Supreme Allied Commander Europe (SACEUR) and in fact constitute the main part of his striking force.' The primary task of the Canberra force when it was being built up was to help halt a Soviet advance into West Germany.

The terms 'light' and 'medium' conformed with USAF terminology which was based on radius of action rather than all-up-weight: 'light' meant less than 1,000 nm and 'medium' 1,000-2,500 nm. CAS described the Canberra as 'a good modern light bomber for tactical use at night and in bad weather against airfields, communications, etc.' The Chiefs of Staff, in their 12 October 1950 report on the 'Size and Shape of the Armed Forces over the Three Years beginning 1951/52', said that most of Bomber Command's 36 front-line squadrons by the end of 1953/54 would be equipped with the Canberra 'which can only carry 6,000 lbs over a radius of 500 miles; and its hitting power will be small in relation to its commitments in support of the defence of the UK and the land battle in Europe.'

Thus from its inception, the RAF Canberra light bomber force (LBF) was committed to the defence of Europe – 'The light bomber component of your force will be operated wholly in support of SACEUR, and controlled by you on his behalf', wrote CAS (Air

Chf Mshl Sir William Dickson) to C-in-C Bomber Command (Air Mshl Sir George Mills) on 13 May 1953. Initially Mills' main force squadrons were based in the UK and it was not until August 1954 that the first Canberras deployed to Germany, and even then, they were still operationally controlled by Bomber Command. 'Although the Canberra light bomber force is part of RAF Bomber Command,' wrote VCAS to the defence minister on 20 January 1956, 'it is wholly assigned to SACEUR except for the marker squadrons. The medium bomber force is retained under HMG's control but the Minister of Defence agreed on 17 December 1953 that one of its primary tasks in war would be retardation operations designed to assist SACEUR.'

1953 saw the re-equipment of B-29 Washington squadrons with Canberras. 44 Squadron was the first to start conversion training, followed by 149, 57 and 15 Squadrons. At the beginning of the year 10 Squadron, whose previous existence had been flying Halifaxes in the transport role, was re-formed at Scampton. Its ORB recorded that the squadron commander, Sqn Ldr Donald Howard, was posted in from RAF Binbrook where he had completed a tour of duty as flight commander on 101 Squadron.

By the end of 1953, there were 17 Canberra bomber and three Canberra PR squadrons. By the end of 1954, there were 24 squadrons in the UK and three in Germany, the latter being 'under overall policy control of Bomber Command but under day-to-day operational control of 2nd TAF'. The Canberra LBF reached its zenith at the end of April 1955, with 390 aircraft equipping 27 squadrons. The UK had met the RAF bomber rearmament programme instituted after the North Atlantic Council meeting in December 1950. As the V bombers that could reach deep into the USSR entered service, they were manned by Canberra men like 'Podge' Howard who was selected to be the first Vulcan squadron commander. Truly, the Canberra LBF was in the van of jet bomber expertise.

B2s of 27 Squadron at Scampton in June 1954, prior to departing on a European tour. (Peter Green Collection)

Squadron	Formed	Date	Previous Aircraft
101	Binbrook	May 1951	Lincoln B.2
617	Binbrook	January 1952	Lincoln B.2
12	Binbrook	March 1952	Lincoln B.2
9	Binbrook	May 1952	Lincoln B.2
109	Hemswell	August 1952	Mosquito B.35
50	Binbrook	August 1952	Lincoln B.2
540(PR)	Benson	December 1952	Mosquito Mk 34A
10	Scampton	January 1953	Dakota
149	Coningsby	March 1953	B-29 Washington
44	Coningsby	April 1953	B-29 Washington
57	Honington	May 1953	B-29 Washington
15	Coningsby	May 1953	B-29 Washington
27	Scampton	June 1953	Dakota
18	Scampton	August 1953	Dakota
21	Scampton	September 1953	Mosquito VI
40	Coningsby	October 1953	York
139	Hemswell	October 1953	Mosquito B.35
76	Wittering	December 1953	Dakota
58(PR)	Wyton	December 1953	Mosquito PR.35
82(PR)	Wyton	December 1953	Lancaster B.1
90	Marham	January 1954	B-29 Washington
199	Hemswell	January 1954	Lincoln/Mosquito
115	Marham	February 1954	B-29 Washington B.1
207	Marham	March 1954	B-29 Washington B.1
100	Marham	April 1954	Lincoln B.2
35	Marham	April 1954	B-29 Washington B.1
61	Wittering	July 1954	Lincoln
102	Gütersloh	October 1954	Liberator VI/VIII
103	Gütersloh	December 1954	Lancaster VIII
104	Gütersloh	March 1955	Lancaster VII
213	Ahlhorn	July 1955	Vampire
542	Wyton	November 1955	Spitfire XIX
88	Wildenrath	January 1956	Sunderland GR.5
59	Gütersloh	August 1956	York
32	Akrotiri	January 1957	Venom FB.1
73	Akrotiri	March 1957	Venom FB.1
6	Akrotiri	July 1957	Venom FB.4
249	Akrotiri	August 1957	Venom FB.4
45	Changi	December 1957	Venom FB.1
69(PR)	Laarbruch	May 1954	Mosquito XVI
31(PR)	Laarbruch	May 1955	Devon
80(PR)	Laarbruch	June 1955	Hornet F.3/4
17(PR)	Wahn	June 1956	Beaufighter TT.10

CHAPTER 4
GEARING UP

DEREK TUTHILL joined the RAF in 1951 and trained as a navigator on Wellingtons during the Korean War expansion period.

I went to Lindholme in the summer of 1953 to practise visual bombing from Lincolns, which were flown by Czechs and Poles. We dropped 25-lb practice bombs. In those days the UK was full of bombing ranges. There was an inland range near Lindholme; two in a Suffolk forest; one north of Oxford and the coastal ranges. There was a T2 bombsight in the great big glass house at the front of the Lincoln. Then I went to Bassingbourn on No. 38 Long Bomber Course – the short course was for those with jet experience.

Everyone on my course went to 40 Squadron then forming at Coningsby. Four months later the squadron moved to Wittering where we watched 100 Squadron's Lincolns fly out to be scrapped.

A Canberra crew consisted of one pilot and one nav in those days. I did both plotting and bomb aiming but after a year, a third guy was brought in for safety reasons – he specialised in working Gee and also visual bomb aiming. We worked that way for the rest of my tour.

The Canberra emitted a series of pulses which triggered ground beacons to transmit a corresponding series of pulses. The delay between transmission and reception of the transponded pulse from the ground was directly proportional to the range of the aircraft from the beacon. By measuring the distance to the ground station, the bomber was able to navigate along a circular arc in the sky, dropping its bombs when it reached a pre-computed distance from another station. The accuracy of fix depended on the angle at which the two range vectors intersected, being greatest when they intersected at right angles.

Derek Tuthill (far left) after his 40 Squadron Canberra tour as a nav plotter on Valiants. (Derek Tuthill)

23

Transmitters in the Canberra operated in the 20-80 Mc/s band and used a pulse recurrence frequency in the neighbourhood of 100 c/s. The time taken by the beacon to receive a pulse, send out the response and return to the receiver was about 100 microseconds. With a pulse recurrence frequency of 100 c/s a beacon would be busy for 10,000 microseconds in any one second dealing with the enquiries of one aircraft. It would therefore have 990,000 microseconds free in each second in which to respond to other aircraft, giving a theoretical maximum handling capacity of 100 aircraft. In practice, the aircraft could not be expected to phase their pulses as to make the best possible use of the beacons and therefore a handling capacity of 70 to 80 Canberras was the sensible limit. The basic Gee-H concept remains in use today as the civilian DME system.

It was relatively easy to jam a pulsed navigation system like Gee simply by sending out additional pulses on the same frequency, cluttering up the display and making it very difficult for the operator to read the signal. With Gee-H, each aircraft had its own unique timing and therefore there were dozens of such transmitters so the magnitude of the jamming problem became considerably more difficult. Moreover, as the Gee-H system used existing Gee equipment, simply turning off the transmitter turned it back into a normal Gee unit which could be directly read on a map and was therefore useful for navigation over NW Europe in peacetime.

DEREK TUTHILL continues:

We navigated with Gee and used H for bombing. The Canberra was flown round the Gee-H circle. There were two lines on the 12-inch cathode ray tube, one of which was the tracker. The bomb aimer directed the aircraft onto the required track, briefed the pilot on the direction of the transmitter and final heading, then helped him maintain track by reporting distance off-track as 'too near' (to transmitter) or 'too far' (from transmitter) plus distance off – '25 yards, 50 yards, 75 yards' or even more. At the same time the navigator controlled the timing device (the 'Mouse') which calculated bomb release, calling 'bomb doors open' at the appropriate time. Provided the bomb release switches had been put on and the bomb doors opened, the system released the bombs automatically. This was far more accurate than visual bombing, especially from 40,000 ft. Canberra visual bombing was inaccurate compared with that achieved with the Doppler-fed bombsight in the Valiant. In the Canberra, the run-in to the target required constant correction: in the Valiant, once the target had been located in the bomb-sight, corrections were rarely required. I was qualified in both Canberra navigation roles and to this day I remember my 40 Squadron Canberra – WJ727. If you were lucky enough to get an English Electric-built aircraft, you guarded that with your life. An Avro-made aircraft was second and those made by Handley Page and Shorts were third equal. I did fly other Canberras – you had to when your aircraft went into hangar for servicing – but 80 per cent of my flying was on WJ727.

For our war role we carried six 1,000-lb bombs on Avro triple carriers. There was no target study – higher authority was never specific on targets: we worked to deliver 1,000-lb bombs as accurately as we could from 40,000 ft, though we practised much lower down. During exercises we attacked on a broad front. On one exercise in 1954, the simulated drop line ran diagonally up the east coast from Manston in Kent (51.20N) to Leuchars in Fife (56.22N). Along that line, there was a Canberra every mile. After the 'attack', you could switch your navigation lights back on.

For lone rangers we had Gee and Rebecca but no radio compass. We flew lone rangers as far as Aden via Idris in Libya and Khartoum in Sudan. You could get a true bearing from Idris out to 100 miles but that was that. So you deliberately aimed to port till you saw the Nile and flew down to Khartoum from there. It was a bit hit-and-miss but it worked. Between Khartoum and Aden, you got plenty of true bearings courtesy of International Aeradio stations. I think they were paid for each true bearing they transmitted and when they heard an RAF jet coming through, they knew they would get their money.

I did slightly over two years on 40 Squadron before joining the first Valiant bomber course. With its amiable aerodynamics and docile flying characteristics, the Canberra was a well-liked aircraft. I was the plotter on the 49 Squadron Valiant that dropped the first real British hydrogen bomb south-east of Christmas Island in the Pacific on 8 November 1958. The thermonuclear bomb exploded with a force of 1.8 MT around 8,000 ft. Back up at 45,000 ft, we just waited for the shock wave which came some two-and-a-half minutes after weapon release, it was definitely noticeable, but a non-event compared with rolling a Canberra! ▨

GEORGE WORRALL completed his navigator training in Winnipeg during 1952-53.

I had my first flights in a Canberra when I was temporarily assigned as a 'safety observer' with 15 Squadron at Coningsby. On 11 December 1953, HQ Bomber Command stated that two navigators were to be carried on all details involving the release of practice or live bombs, the second being there 'solely for monitoring purposes'. The workload involved, together with a series of incidents concerning practice bombs falling outside the designated danger areas, led to a pilot and two navigator crews – one nominally the plotter and the other the bomb aimer who worked Gee – becoming the norm.

Fitted with wing-tip drop tanks, the range of the Canberra B2 was just sufficient to reach the Soviet satellite countries of the Warsaw Pact. At the time, the aircraft was the mainstay of the RAF bomber force, with its trained crews aimed at discouraging any ambitions the Soviets may have in threatening the integrity of either us or our allies. Most mass exercises were designed to reflect this, but normal training was dedicated to improving crew skills. For navigators, this meant navigation and bombing exercises by day and night using all means at our disposal: radio aids, visual, astro-navigation and of course, mental dead reckoning. For me and many others, the most remarkable feature of the Canberra was its service ceiling. Cruise climb profiles might see us getting just above 48,000 ft but only above 45,000 ft did its performance begin to decline sharply. We regularly operated above 40,000 ft and a Select crew was cleared to visually bomb a practice target from 45,000 ft.

JOHN ROBERTS joined the RAF in 1952 as a National Serviceman.

I signed up for four years and went to aircrew. During training they said I would make a useless pilot but a good navigator. On 25 November 1952 I went to No. 3 Air Navigation School at Bishops Court in Northern Ireland. We weren't quite the first entry to go through but we were very close. I remember that they hadn't got round to providing any heating in the hut. We did ten months training, finishing on 23 September 1953. With the ending of the Korean War there was a surplus of aircrew so I was sent to kill time at Kirton in North Lincolnshire, where I ended up teaching maths. Then in April 1954 I went to do advanced navigator training at Swinderby. Then I was off to Lindholme for the bombing course before joining 21 Squadron at Scampton on 20 September 1954.

Each Canberra bomber had a three-man crew. I became number three in the crew – designated as the bomb aimer – with Sgt Tom Johnstone as pilot. It was all Gee-H bombing in those days and I gave the Gee position to Dave the nav plotter to put on his chart. We only dropped 25-lb practice bombs.

We were still in the WW2 bombing age back then. All exercises were simulated thousand-bomber raids, carried out by day and night. I recall Tom saying on one exercise that he counted no fewer than 76 other Canberras, staggered by both height and time, in the sky around him. Another squadron would be ten miles to port.

We had four Canberra squadrons at Scampton and all four of us would lift off to meet up over the North Sea. For a mass raid we would take off at one-minute intervals but we would land with three-minute separation. Being crewed with a sergeant pilot, we were always at the back of the queue. We were given a landing time at base but we often had to trombone out as far as the Isle of Man before being allowed back onto final approach. The average Canberra B2 trip lasted between three and three-and-a-half hours. I recall a Best Lights Competition where we would fly up the east coast to see which settlement had the best lights.

Gee-H accuracy over the UK, where all the ground stations were orientated, wasn't bad. I recall that one target was a smelter in Sheffield. But over Germany, by which time the beams had fanned themselves out, accuracy was degraded. Normally we descended to 20,000 ft to practise visual bombing over ranges such as Wainfleet, Chesil Bank and Luce Bay in Scotland.

Where you flew on lone rangers was determined by your classification status. Crew categories were Combat, Combat Star and Select. We were Select and we could go where we liked, provided we got back to base on time. I remember flying to Habbaniya in Iraq, and we came back via Gibraltar.

After 21 Squadron I went to be a nav radar on Valiants where we had designated targets – we had nothing like that in the early Canberra days. We did no target study and electronic warfare didn't feature. I left 21 Squadron in October 1955. We were more highly regulated on the V Force. You could borrow a Canberra and go somewhere like Newquay for the weekend provided you flew to a master diversion airfield that would let you fly back on Sunday evening. We just had to be airborne for at least two hours.

The aircraft was totally viceless but there were two problems with every Canberra. First, in very cold conditions, the engines tended to flame out. Pilots were instructed not to change throttle settings in the climb, but you could re-light after descending to 15,000 ft. Second, there was trim runaway. I remember one fatal asymmetric accident – taking the right action on the approach was critical. If one tip tank stopped feeding, you could only trim out the imbalance so far. You had to land with one aileron held full over by sheer brute force. ■

The first Canberra 'runaway' tailplane occurred on 26 July 1953 and subsequently there were 50 reports of serious actuator faults, 14 of them resulting from runaway tail trim. In one 231 OCU B2 incident on 26 September 1955, three of the four crew members survived after the tailplane actuator moved to the fully nose-up position and the aircraft became uncontrollable. By rolling it into a steep turn the instructor 'regained partial control until the two navigators had ejected and the student pilot had escaped through the entrance hatch. He then made a safe ejection

WH924 and WH922 of 61 Squadron with WH741 of 109 Squadron between them out of Hemswell in 1955. (Peter Green Collection)

himself, but was slightly injured during the descent when his parachute became tangled with the ejection seat. The student navigator's body was found still strapped into his seat; the remaining two crew members landed without injury.'

A runaway tailplane actuator would cause the aircraft to go into an irreversible steep climb or dive and following seven incidents on B2s, five of which were fatal, all Canberras with single-speed actuators were grounded. The fault was eventually traced to mechanical 'sticking-on' of the single pole trim switch which caused the actuator to run out to full travel after the pilot had released the switch. The 'fix' was to progressively retrofit all marks of Canberra with a new dipole duplicate trim switch, improved wiring integrity and revised actuator stops to reduce overall travel.

John Brownlow recalls that 'there were really two problems. Apart from the cabling, there was the actuator itself, which could simply "run away" of its own accord. As originally installed, the actuator was a very fast-acting device and one remedial measure was simply to slow it down. Other modifications were introduced too – you may recall that it became necessary to select and hold "trim" before you could actually change the incidence on the tailplane, which meant that the circuit was only live when you wanted it to be and could not, therefore, operate inadvertently. Similarly, if you let go of the "trim" button, the tailplane actuator was electrically isolated and thus instantly deactivated.'

JOHN ROBERTS believes:

It is now hard for people to equate with service life in the mid-fifties. The first thing was, that discounting the 'older ones' – (approximately six out of a squadron totalling 36 aircrew), few of us had a car – but one was quite a car, a Bentley! This meant we were forced to remain on the station throughout the week and only visited Lincoln at weekends.

Added to this, on our squadron, only about six members were married – I am sure this was the same for the other three squadrons on the station. This meant that there were about 120 young officers in the mess. When I say young, between the ages of 19-23, and many of us were away from home for the first time. Essentially the recruitment of aircrew was from school leavers and I do not remember anyone who had been to university. I had left school at 16 and had therefore worked for two years before being called-up. As you can imagine mess life was lively, with someone always celebrating a birthday or just making an excuse for a party. I had to fly on the evening of my 21st birthday – but I don't think I was missed when I saw my bar bill.

Junior officers were allowed to spend a maximum of £7 ten shillings a month on mess bill drinks – an interview with the squadron commander resulted if this was exceeded. Monthly pay was about £70.

The working day was 0800-1700. The usual briefing consisted of the met report, the flying schedule for the day and other general information. If you weren't flying you had very little to do for the rest of the day. In consequence a considerable amount of time was spent talking/reading or playing cards. You could play sports e.g. squash/badminton as that would only involve two to four people. Although we were given other responsibilities they generally didn't occupy much time. For example I was responsible for the NAAFI equipment inventory.

I did get one assignment that was not quite the normal. Following a week in Ely hospital I was grounded only to be told I was defending officer at a court martial. Panic – I lost the case and recommended the accused should be 'dismissed the service'. The judge advocate told me I had done a good job but that I had been asking for a harsher sentence than the one given – a period in jail. Later I once again acted as defending officer, again I lost and then as prosecuting officer, when I won! When I asked why I was given these jobs, the answer had a certain amount of logic 'you are the only officer with experience'. When I queried about the first occasion, answer 'your records show you had done it before'. I suppose John Roberts was quite a common name.

I have analysed my logbook and I only flew 585 hours on Canberras in just under two years — approximately 25 hours per month — I would assume this was more or less the same for other aircrew. As few trips lasted three hours it meant you only flew two/three times a week. I think Group/Command planning department tried to keep us busy as over the two years I have listed eleven exercises in my logbook. Most of them, using second war tactics, took place over the UK/Continent. One exercise Red Trident lasted a week with the US 6th Fleet in the Mediterranean and we were flying out of Nicosia. Akrotiri hadn't been built in those days. One 'max effort' exercise I do remember. As I flew with a sergeant pilot we normally took off last, but on this occasion we were first, an unusual situation. On returning to Scampton it was fog bound so we were diverted. The diversion airfield had limited space so an unused runway was employed. The trouble was we were first and parked at the end of the runway and everyone else was behind us. So when we came to leave we were the last to take off!

The only time I dropped 'real bombs' was in 1955 on exercise Arab Twitcher in Aden. 8 Squadron, flying Hunters at that time, normally tried to keep the local population of Arab tribesmen in order. Someone thought it would be a good idea if we joined in. The procedure was 8 Squadron went out in the morning and dropped leaflets to say we would be back later to shoot/drop bombs on them. As all sorties were visual, and we didn't know the local terrain, we followed a Hunter which dropped a flare and we bombed on that. Needless to say we didn't get any feedback as to how successful (most likely not) we had been. I expect the local tribesmen had a fright when bombs exploded the wrong side of them. This had happened when we dropped practice bombs at Mafraq, Jordan. The local Arabs used to gather on the range once they heard aircraft to collect the scrap metal – because of the accuracy of the fighters they congregated close to the target. They wouldn't have equated us at 20,000 ft with bombs. The range crew thought it amusing when the Arabs scattered as our bombs fell outside of them.

B2 WH914 of 100 Squadron bombing up at Wittering in October 1955.
(Peter Green Collection)

The highlight for most crews was a lone ranger. The programme for one we did to Habbanyia in February 1956 was as follows:

Day 1: Waddington – Idris	Flying time: 3 hours and 30 minutes
Idris – Abu Sueir	2 hours and 25 minutes
Day 2: Abu Sueir – Bahrain	Flying time: 3 hours and 5 minutes
Day 3: Day off	
Day 4: Bahrain – Habbanyia	Flying time: 1 hour and 45 minutes
Habbanyia – Abu Sueir	2 hours and 10 minutes
Abu Sueir – Idris	3 hours and 20 minutes

We had left Bahrain at 0535 and got to Idris at 1700. You will note the difference in time between the two legs Idris – Abu Sueir and return. This was due to the jet stream that was not really understood in those days and was usually only discovered when encountered. Your first thought was that the navigation was inaccurate.

Day 5: Idris – Gibraltar	Flying time: 3 hours and 10 minutes
Gibraltar – Waddington	3 hours and 30 minutes

The real reason I detail this is to show the freedom a crew had to plan and carry out a lone ranger. The only thing expected was that you would return to base on schedule.

May I add that Gibraltar was a favourite last call as you could get duty-free cigarettes out of bond. 20,000 was the usual amount brought back – we all smoked in those days and 'friends' would ask for a packet of cigarettes which meant 200 not 20! We all knew the risk – if caught we were expected to resign. However, timing our arrival at Waddington for high tide at Grimsby generally meant the customs officers were too busy and would not visit. One crew did get caught but declared everything, much to the surprise of the customs officer, and paid the duty. Honours even.

I look back fondly on the Canberra. We had the best time of all because we had much more freedom. There weren't many senior officers around and almost everyone had wartime experience. Informality was the norm.

The Canberra was generally described by those involved as 'no bother at all'. It was manoeuvrable enough for a formation aerobatic team to be formed in 1956 with four aircraft, but the limitations of the navigation and bombing equipment confined B2 Canberras to tactical battlefield-support in Europe. Fast, high-altitude Canberras would have survived much better than the Blenheims and Battles of 1940 but those at the top of the RAF were under no illusions about the efficacy of the strike effect. Back in September 1951, VCAS wrote to ACAS (OR) to say, 'My own feelings are that Gee-H has surprised us by the accuracy which can be achieved, now that crews know how to use the set; but that the serviceability is bad and will never be good...we must consider seriously how quickly we can replace it by better equipment.' Such limitations of the Canberra force were bought into particularly sharp focus when it was sent out to take part in the Suez campaign.

CHAPTER 5
CANBERRA DEVELOPMENTS

418 Canberra B2s were delivered in all, with 410 going to the RAF. BOB FAIRCLOUGH was ideally qualified to describe post-Canberra B2 developments and variants.

CANBERRA PR MARK 3

The two-man PR3 was derived from the B2 as a specialised photo-reconnaissance aircraft, to specification PR31/46. The fuselage was lengthened by 14 inches to accommodate an additional bay, forward of the bomb bay, to house seven cameras. Flares could be dropped from the rear half of the bomb bay and there was a tank in the front containing sufficient fuel to extend the aircraft's range by almost 1,000 miles. It had the same RA3 engines as the B2, and, apart from the increased range, performance was very similar. The prototype, VX181, made its first flight from Samlesbury in the hands of Peter Hillwood on 19 March 1951. Thirty-six were delivered to the RAF.

B2 WH733 of 21 Squadron with bomb doors opened in 1953. WH733 was later converted into a U10 pilotless drone for use in guided weapons development. (Peter Green Collection)

CANBERRA T MARK 4

Since the Canberra would fly twice as fast and twice as high as the Lincoln, the type which it was to replace, the need for a dual-control trainer had been recognised from the outset. The front fuselage was modified to seat the instructor pilot alongside the trainee. The bomb-aiming station was deleted, along with its glazed nose, and the single navigator was seated behind the pilot. Bee Beamont flew the first T4, WN467, from Samlesbury on 12 June 1952. Sixty-six T4s were built as such and another sixteen were added by recycling B2s. Seventy-five were built including nine for export.

Canberra PR3 WE140 of 540 Squadron at Heathrow airport. The PR3 fuselage was stretched by 14 inches to accommodate an additional fuel tank, plus a camera and flare bay.

CANBERRA B MARK 5

When the B2 entered production it was still regarded as an interim standard, with the radar bombing and navigation system to be added at a later date to create what would become the definitive Canberra bomber – the B5. In the event the radar system was still not available when the prototype was built, and the B5, which had actually been ordered as a target marker to specification B22/48, did not enter production. However, it did have several features that were to be introduced into later Canberras, the most significant being integral fuel tanks in the leading edges of the outer-wing panels. These tanks contained 900 gallons of extra fuel, which conferred a substantial increase in range, and, to compensate for the additional weight, the B5 had Avon RA7 engines, providing 7,500 lbs of thrust. The sole example, VX185, was flown for the first time from Samlesbury by Johnny Squier on 6 July 1951.

CANBERRA B MARK 6

The increased fuel capacity and up-rated engines of the B5 were applied to the basic bomber to create the B6, conferring a range advantage of some 800 miles compared to the B2. Since VX185 was considered to have proved most of the innovations, there was no B6 prototype, as such, and the first production aircraft, WJ754, flew from Samlesbury on 26 January 1954. Thereafter the B6 became the main production version, although it was built only by English Electric and Shorts. One hundred and six were built including 12 for export.

CANBERRA B(I) MARK 6

The 'I' in B(I)6 stood for 'interdictor', the Mk 6 being known as the 'interim interdictor'. The role involved low-level attacks, mostly at night, typically against transport targets.

The B(I)6 was basically a B6, with some changes to the weapons fit. The most significant of these was the fitting of a gun pack, containing four 20-mm cannon, in the rear of the bomb bay. To compensate for the loss of internal capacity, a pylon, capable of carrying a 1,000-lb bomb, was provided under each outer wing. Again, there was no prototype and the first of 22 production aircraft, WT307, flew for the first time on 31 March 1955. All aircraft were built for the RAF.

CANBERRA PR MARK 7

The PR7 was essentially a PR3 incorporating the upgrades that had been applied to the B6 – Avon RA7 engines and integral wing tanks which extended the range by a further 750 miles. The first example, WH773, took off for the first time from Samlesbury on 16 August 1953. Seventy-one were built.

TOP: Canberra B6s and crews of 139 Squadron at Hemswell, 3 August 1955. The Blue Shadow aerial is on the forward fuselage and the fin flash is red and white. (Peter Green Collection)
MIDDLE: B(I)6 cockpit. (Peter Green Collection)
BELOW: PR7 WT519 of 31 Sqn at Gütersloh, 1960. The 'Goldstar' badge was based on the Star of India because 31 Sqn claimed to be the first military unit to fly in India. (Peter Green Collection)

CANBERRA B(I) MARK 8

The B(I)8 was the definitive interdictor. It was basically a B6, featuring the gun pack and underwing bomb pylons of the B(I)6, but with a completely redesigned crew compartment. The pilot's ejection seat was still offset to port, but he now sat higher and under a fighter-type canopy which provided much better visibility. While this canopy could be jettisoned in an emergency, it did not open and access was still via the crew entry hatch on the right-hand side of the front fuselage. The navigator was no longer provided with an ejection seat, his options being confined to a seat fixed to the bulkhead (which he was supposed to use for take-off and landing) or a swivelling seat at his work station, which was now in front of and below the pilot, or he could lie in the nose when map-reading or for visual bomb aiming. In terms of navigation equipment, armament and performance the B(I)8 was much the same as the B6/B(I)6. Since the new nose was a major departure, a prototype was required and this was created by rebuilding the only B5, VX185, which made its first flight as a B(I)8 when Bee Beamont took off from Samlesbury on 23 July 1954. The first production aircraft, WT326, flew on 8 June 1955 and the RAF received 55 aircraft, which served exclusively with squadrons based in Germany. A further 17 were for export.

CANBERRA PR MARK 9

The PR9 was the last British new-build Canberra variant. The basic design work was done by English Electric at Warton. Detail design and modification of the prototype was delegated to its subsidiary company, D. Napier & Son at Luton, but 23 production models were eventually built by Shorts at Belfast. The Mk 9 was intended for high-altitude photo-reconnaissance at altitudes up to 60,000 ft or even higher. In order to reach these higher altitudes, the wing area was increased by extending the wing chord inboard of the engine nacelles, and by increasing the span by 5 ft 5 inches through the addition of new squared-off wing tips. A substantial increase in power was provided by installing Avon RA24s of 11,250-lb thrust. Cameras were carried in bays fore and aft of the bomb bay, which carried flares and an extra fuel tank, as in the PR7. The prototype was a modified PR7, WH793, which made its first flight with the new wings and engines, but retaining the standard PR7 nose, in the hands of Mike Randrup from Luton on 8 July 1955. The first production aircraft featured a B(I)8-style nose but its limitations were clearly demonstrated when this aircraft was lost in an accident; the pilot survived by using his ejection seat while the navigator died because he did not have one. As a result, the nose was completely redesigned. The pilot's ejection seat was still offset to port under a fighter-type canopy but this one was hinged at the rear to provide access via an external ladder. The crew entry door was taken out and the navigator was now provided with an ejection seat in a separate compartment in the extreme nose which was hinged and could be swung to starboard to permit entry. Incorporation of this modification delayed production and it was 1960 before the first PR9s were delivered to 58 Squadron, although, having served for 46 years, the last of them would not be withdrawn until 2006.

CANBERRA U MARK 10

The U10 was the first Canberra variant to be produced by converting earlier models that had been withdrawn from service. The U10 was a pilotless target drone for use in guided weapons development. About 25 were converted from B2s, the first being WJ624. Deliveries began in late 1958, most aircraft being used at the Woomera weapons range in Australia.

CANBERRA T MARK 11

Designed and re-manufactured from redundant B2s by Boulton Paul, the T11 had an AI 17 radar in the nose, protected by a distinctive conical radome, and was intended to provide airborne experience for prospective radar operators destined for all-weather fighters. The first of eight T11s, WJ610, first flew as such on 29 March 1958.

CANBERRA B(I) MARK 12

The B(I)12 was built against an RNZAF order for 11 B(I)8s, differences from the RAF version being confined to some minor equipment changes.

CANBERRA T MARK 13

To support its B(I)12s, the RNZAF ordered two T13s, which were similar to the T4.

CANBERRA D MARK 14

The six D14s (initially designated as U14s) were converted from U10s for the Royal Navy for use as pilotless target drones in ship-to-air missile trials; the first one, WH921, was delivered in May 1961.

CANBERRA B MARK 15

The B15 was a conversion of the B6 for operation in the low-level tactical strike role. In terms of armament and avionics, the 39 aircraft produced differed little from the B(I)6 except that they were armed with underwing rocket pods, instead of a gun pack, and thus retained the full use of the bomb bay. From 1962 B15s were further adapted to carry the Nord AS30 air-to-ground missile which involved an additional pylon being mounted outboard of the existing one.

CANBERRA E MARK 15

After being withdrawn from front-line service, several B15s were refurbished and modified to become E15s for radar calibration duties with 98 Squadron, and then 100 Squadron. The first E15, WH972, was delivered in August 1970.

CANBERRA B MARK 16

The 19 B16s were converted from B6s and were similar to the B15s except that the equipment fit included a Blue Shadow sideways-looking radar on the starboard side, which meant that one of the rear crew ejection seats had to be removed, the second navigator being obliged, as in the B(I)8, to use a portable chest parachute following his escape via the entry door.

CANBERRA T MARK 17

The T17 was a B2, extensively modified to permit it to create a hostile electronic counter measures (ECM) environment in which to provide realistic training for all branches of the armed forces. This involved the aircraft being equipped with a number of aerials installed beneath a bulbous nose radome and a variety of other unsightly excrescences, which did nothing to enhance the Canberra's graceful lines. To power the jamming equipment, much of which was carried in a crate mounted in the bomb bay, the T17 had a bleed-air turbine-powered generator installed in each wing just outboard of the engine. The development aircraft, WH863, began testing at Warton in late 1964. The first of 24 'production' conversions, all of which would serve with the jointly RAF/RN-manned 360 Squadron, was WJ977 which first flew in September 1965.

CANBERRA TT MARK 18

The TT18 was a target tug created by modifying retired B2s to carry a Rushton winch (made by Flight Refuelling Ltd) under each wing from which a variety of targets could be towed up to 50,000 ft behind the aircraft. Beginning with WJ632 in March 1966, 22 TT18s were eventually produced. Operated by both the RAF and the RN, the Mk 18 remained in service until 1997.

CANBERRA T MARK 19

With the run-down of the Javelin force, the requirement for an AI 17 trainer had lapsed by 1966, rendering the T11 redundant. The radars were, therefore, removed and replaced with ballast weights. The seven aircraft involved (the first was WH903 which appeared in June 1966) were redesignated as T19s and soldiered on as targets for interception exercises.

CANBERRA MARK 20

Forty-eight Canberras were built under licence for the RAAF in Australia as the Mk 20. The first 27 were similar to the B2, the remainder being equivalent to the B6, but all were designated as Mk 20s.

CANBERRA MARK 21

To support its Canberra bombers, the RAAF converted two B2 pattern aircraft that had been supplied by the UK plus five of its locally manufactured Mk 20s into dual-controlled Mk 21s, equivalent to the RAF's T4s.

CANBERRA T MARK 22

The T22, the final Canberra variant to be produced for the British armed forces, was a PR7 conversion fitted with a Buccaneer's Blue Parrot radar in the nose. The first T22, WT510, appeared in June 1973 and was followed by six others, all of which served with the FRADU to train the battle management staffs of HM ships to engage hostile aircraft.

CANBERRA PRODUCTION SUMMARY

Totals: 925 – 782 for the RAF; 143 for export

Built in Australia: 48

Built in USA: 403

Grand Total: 1,376

Air Chief Marshal SIR MIKE KNIGHT flew around 2,500 hours on various marks of Canberra.

I never got my hands on either of the two that never entered service: the original B1 and the B5. Nor did I fly any of the marks sold to various foreign nations – with the exception of the RAAF's Mks 20 and 21 and the RNZAF's B(I)12 and T13. The one I did fail to make was the T19 (RN update of the T11 airborne AI trainer) but it wasn't all that different from the T11. I was ready to fly it up at Marshalls' where I was doing some in-service modification work for the old Ministry of Aviation, but the aircraft went crook at the wrong time.

To compensate for those failings, I did scramble into the air in such relative rarities as the U10/D14 unmanned targets (luckily with a set of conventional flying controls in case of a computery 'pigs') and to 70,000 ft in a USAF RB-57F – though that was cheating, as I was in the back!

It was all a very long time ago – and it would never have happened had I heeded the medics' advice that I was far too long in the leg ever to fly a Canberra. I still have the kneecaps to prove it.

WHAT MIGHT HAVE BEEN

Having realised the mature Mks 6, 7 and 8, the EE drawing office continued to exploit the basic design to produce increasingly sophisticated potential derivatives of the Canberra. One example was the P12 all-weather fighter project of 1956. Based on the B(I)8 airframe but with the RA24 Avons of the PR9, it had additional fuel in the forward bomb bay and the options of a (possibly Scorpion) rocket motor or the standard gun pack in the rear. Primary armament was to have been a pair of semi-active homing Red Dean missiles with target illumination provided by an AI18 radar in the nose. In the late 1950s this would appear to have been a more than adequate bomber destroyer (albeit lacking an ejection seat for the navigator).

The P28 low-level strike/attack project of 1958 was the ultimate expression of the B(I)8 concept. Wingspan was significantly reduced and additional fuel was carried in 500-gallon tip tanks. The 1965 variation on the theme would have had a 57-foot wingspan, Spey engines, the avionics from the recently-cancelled TSR2 and the crew compartment of the PR9 (with ejection seats for both crew members). In the early days, some thought was even given to adapting the airframe as a transport seating up to 34 passengers.

CHAPTER 6
LONG-DISTANCE FLIGHTS

World altitude record holder Walter Frame Gibb in his Canberra cockpit. Born near Port Talbot, Gibb joined the aero-engine division of the Bristol Aeroplane Company as an apprentice in 1937 before joining the RAF in May 1940. In March 1945 he was credited with shooting down five enemy aircraft during long-range night intruder sorties over Germany and France. He became Bristol's chief test pilot in 1955. A burly, imposing man, Gibb was modest about his many achievements. When asked in later life what had given him the greatest pleasure, it was not reaching 65,876 ft but working as an apprentice on the Pegasus engine that powered the Wellesley aircraft that created a world long-distance record in November 1938.

The Canberra held some 19 distance records but the altitude ones were equally impressive. Walter Gibb was twice decorated for gallantry as a night-fighter pilot before becoming a test pilot with the Bristol Aeroplane Company where he test flew both the Brabazon and the Britannia airliners. On 4 May 1953, Gibb and his observer, F. M. Piper, took off from Filton, near Bristol, in B2 WD952 powered by two Bristol Olympus engines. Climbing to the west, the Canberra reached an altitude of 63,668 ft, more than 4,000 ft higher than the previous record. This flight attracted worldwide attention and Duncan Sandys, the Minister for Supply, sent a telegram of congratulation in which he said: 'To reach these truly Olympian heights is a triumph for the pilots, designers, research staff and workpeople of the Bristol Aeroplane Company and English Electric Company.'

Flying in the same Canberra, fitted this time with more powerful Olympus engines, Gibb attempted to break his record on 29 August 1955. Again taking off from Filton, he climbed over the Bristol Channel towards Ireland, levelling off at 50,000 ft to burn off fuel to lighten the aircraft before continuing his ascent. Gibb turned east and finally reached a new record altitude of 65,876 ft (nearly 12.5 miles high) over Taunton. Gibb, who was flying solo this time, observed: 'The last 500 ft took an awfully long time. It was the most difficult flying I have ever experienced.'

The highest climbing Canberra of all was WK163 which, on 28 August 1957, at the hands of test pilot Mike Randrup and observer Walter Shirley, took off from Luton to test a prototype Napier Double Scorpion rocket engine. The Scorpion was brought in at 44,000 ft and this additional boost enabled the Canberra to reach a new world altitude record of 70,310 ft. WK163 is now being returned to flight by the Vulcan to the Sky Trust.

TERRY HAYWARD joined the RAF in 1955 and, as a navigator, flew Canberras (with 12 and 213 Squadrons) and Vulcans. DAVID BROUGHTON spent 31 years in the RAF and he flew 23 Aries flights – of which 21 reached the North Geographic Pole. Both are leading lights of the Royal Institute of Navigation and these are their recollections.

Before talking about the Canberra Aries flights in the North Polar Region and other long-distance flights, it is useful to outline what is so difficult about flying to the North Pole. To state the obvious, it's a long way, not just as an absolute distance but also from the practical viewpoint of the availability of bases from which aircraft can operate. And then there are the inhospitable weather conditions and the means of forecasting them. There is a paucity of easily identifiable features and, until recently, few accurate maps by which to navigate and the trusty magnetic compass becomes increasingly less trusty the further north you travel. In 1945 the RAF sent Aries I, a modified Lancaster, on a series of experimental and exploratory flights, to locate the magnetic pole accurately and to develop methods of navigating in polar regions. These flights were continued by two Lincolns, Aries II and III flown by crews from the RAF Flying College at Manby.

In the spring of 1953 the college took delivery of Aries IV, a Canberra B2, WH699, which was fitted with a 650-gallon auxiliary fuel tank in the bomb bay. This aircraft had already made one remarkable record flight when two English Electric test pilots flew from London to New York and back in a single day. For several years navigator pupils on the specialist navigation course at Manby had carried out high-latitude flights as part of their syllabus in piston-engine aircraft. In February 1954 Aries IV, flown by Wg Cdr Stanbury, flew to Churchill on Hudsons Bay to carry out an Arctic proving flight from there. A few months later Air Cdre Gus Walker, then commandant of the Flying College, instigated a series of experimental flights using a base in northern Norway as a jumping off point for Arctic flights. These flights led to the first attempt by an RAF jet to reach the North Pole. Not the first jet, unfortunately, because the Americans had already achieved this with a B-52 in the previous year.

The successful Canberra flight took place during the night of 14/15 October when Aries IV, flown by Wg Cdr Andrew Humphrey and navigated by Sqn Ldr Dougie Bower and Flt Lt F. R. Wood, took off from Bardufoss at 69° North in Norway, overflew the Geographic North Pole and, after a flight of six hours and 43 minutes landed at

Bodø. For administrative reasons the flight had to be carried out in mid-October, at which time the relative positions of the sun and moon were not favourable for good fixing, so a night flight was planned. The relative shortness of the night further complicated planning.

Astro was to be the primary navigation aid using the periscopic sextant to determine both position lines and heading checks. The standard gyro-magnetic compass was put into gyro above 78°N, with half-hourly heading and position-line checks and an hourly cycle of full fixes. Fuel was so critical that the aircraft was towed to the runway prior to take-off and the sortie flown in the most efficient cruise climb possible. The pole was overflown at 2313Z on 14 October 1954, although with outside air temperature down to -65°C, life became extremely cold for crew and equipment; the radio-compass and Rebecca packed up altogether, the VHF almost so and the sextant mounting became extremely stiff. They took off at just after 2100, cruise climbed to around 45,000 ft over the pole and eventually reached over 50,000 ft on the return flight. Adverse weather conditions prevented a return to Bardufoss and the aircraft was diverted to Bodø where it landed at 0400 on 15 October. The flight had covered some 2,620 nms.

A round trip to 90° North was only possible from Bardufoss, where the airfield lies in a narrow valley flanked by 4,000-ft mountains, so good visibility and cloud base were essential. Fortunately, because of the less stringent weather limitations at Bodø, the fuel reserves required were exactly the same as for Bardufoss so it was possible to take off from Bardufoss, fly over the pole and return to Bodø. This arrangement left no margin to cover the loss of an engine or cabin pressure, but, beyond the single-engine point of no return, it would still be possible to divert to Thule in north-west Greenland. Nearly half of the total available fuel was carried in auxiliary tanks and, because there was no guarantee that these would drain completely, and because no forecast weather information was available for north of Spitsbergen, it was necessary to cater for in-flight revision of the radius of action.

The aircraft's navigation fit was rudimentary by modern standards, consisting of a Mk 2 periscopic sextant; a back-up hand-held Mk 9 sextant (which would have been hung on a suspension bracket under the canopy next to the pilot's seat); a radio compass; an air mileage indicator (the use of the API [air position indicator] was impracticable when gyro-steering unless the gyro wander rate was both small and regular); and Rebecca distance-measuring equipment. The standard gyromagnetic compass unit was used for gyro steering. The radio compass and Rebecca were employed solely for the terminal homing and let down. This was an important aspect of the flight and portable Eureka beacons were erected at the two airfields. A well-tried and satisfactory high-latitude navigation technique already existed for piston-engined aircraft and it was both practical and desirable to apply it to the Canberra flights with the minimum of modification. Grid navigation was used throughout the flight but gyro steering was not used until 75° North. Once at height the only fixing aid available was astro.

In the Canberra, the relationship between all-up weight (AUW) and relative pressure was critical and could be a controlling parameter during cruise. After a normal climb the aircraft was stabilised at initial cruising altitude and astro fixing commenced shortly afterwards. Astro was also used for heading checks. The plan was to produce two position lines on the half hour as intermediate progress checks and a full four position line box fix on the hour but, for much of the flight, fixes were actually obtained every half hour. On the northbound trip the stars selected were either substantially ahead of the aircraft or on the beam. This was so that the pilot only had to concentrate on flying an accurate speed or heading so that he was not obliged to concentrate on both simultaneously. Acceleration errors were thus kept to a minimum.

On the return flight this procedure was not possible because a suitable selection of stars was not available. Thus it became necessary to take shots on relative bearings of around 45° and 315°, which made the pilot's task correspondingly more demanding because both heading and speed had to be held accurately (and there was no autopilot). During this and subsequent flights the behaviour of the steering gyro was more erratic than that previously experienced in piston-engined aircraft. Throughout the flight, troubles were experienced with radio aids and this was subsequently shown to be due to the temperature in the radio bay falling below the design limits of the equipment; additional heating and insulation was installed prior to later flights and this solved the problem. The results of the flight were judged to be sufficiently encouraging to warrant going ahead with the plan to run a series of similar flights for the benefit of Flying College students attending the specialist navigation course (aka 'the Spec N'). All of the navigators concerned had previous high-latitude experience, having taken part in polar flights in Hastings aircraft earlier in the year, and they had all flown on long-range exercises in the Canberra in medium latitudes. Practice flights to Jan Mayen Island shortly before leaving for Norway, enabled the navigators to become familiar with the new techniques. The training flights proper took place during the period 13-17 December and used Bodø as their base.

WH699 had already flown its way into the record books on 17 December 1953, to celebrate the 50th anniversary of the Wright Brothers' first

Wg Cdr M. Lyne (centre), Sqn Ldr D. Bower (right) and Sqn Ldr R. Seymour (left) after they flew in Aries IV from Bardufoss, over the North Pole to Ladd AFB in Fairbanks, Alaska on 23 June 1955. (Aries archive)

powered flight. It was flown by Wg Cdr C. G. Petty, Sqn Ldr T. McGarry and Sqn Ldr M. Craig, the 5,168 nm from London to Cape Town being covered in 12 hours, 21 minutes and 3.8 seconds. This new record was about twice as fast as that achieved by Aries II nearly seven years before. The return journey established another record time of 13 hours, 15 minutes, 25.2 seconds. The crew on this occasion was Wg Cdr Humphrey, Sqn Ldr Bower and Sqn Ldr R. F. B. Powell. On 23 June 1955 Aries IV, crewed by Wg Cdr M. Lyne, Sqn Ldr Bower and Sqn Ldr R. Seymour flew from Bardufoss, over the North Pole to Ladd AFB in Fairbanks, Alaska, a distance of 2,776 nm in six hours and 30 minutes. From there Aries IV was flown on to Ottawa and on the night of 27/28 June 1955, this time piloted by Wg Cdr Ivor Broom, but with the same navigation team of Bower and Seymour, it broke the Ottawa to London record by flying the 2,864 nm in six hours, 42 minutes and 12 seconds – an average speed of 431 kts. This was the swan song for WH699 as Aries IV, although it soldiered on at the RAF Flying College until it was written off in a crash at Strubby on 28 November 1959.

Aries IV's replacement – Aries V – was Canberra PR7, WT528, with extra fuel tanks which enabled it to carry 4,065 gallons. WT528 had already been used for long-distance flights. It had broken the London to New York and New York to London records on 23 August 1955 in seven hours, 29 minutes, 56.7 seconds and six hours, 16 minutes and 59.5 seconds respectively. In doing so it also achieved the first two-way crossing of the Atlantic in a single day. A total distance of 5,947 nm in 14 hours, 21 minutes and 45 seconds, including a 35-minute refuelling turn round at Floyd Bennett Field. The silver-painted aircraft with its 'Arctic red' fin, tailplane, wing tips and fuel tanks soon added to its laurels when it was flown over the North Pole from Haneda airport, Tokyo to West Malling in Kent on 25 May 1957, a distance of 5,110 nm in 17 hours, 42 minutes and 2.4 seconds. In the spring of 1958 it was flown on a round-the-world trip, visiting Rhodesia, South Africa, Australia and New Zealand.

The flight returned to the UK on 14 May and this proved to be the final flourish both for Aries V and for the whole Aries programme. By this time, larger jet aircraft were becoming available for testing navigation equipment and there were other agencies better equipped to carry out trials on new techniques. Aries V was sold to BAC at Warton in 1962, whereupon it was modified to PR57 standard for the Indian air force.

Having received its shiny new Canberras, the RAF was very keen to show them off to the world. On 18 April 1952, C-in-C Bomber Command Sir Hugh Lloyd flew to the United States in a Canberra, returning on 9 May. On 28 September he went in another Canberra to Nairobi in nine hours and 55 minutes. But the most impressive 1952 foray overseas was mounted by four B2s of the newly-reformed 12 Squadron, which left Binbrook on 20 October for a 24,000-mile goodwill tour of South America led by AOC No. 1 Group, Dermot Boyle. Each Exercise Round Trip Canberra had a three-man crew and on the outward flight AVM Boyle set up an unofficial record on 23 October of four hours and 27 minutes for the South Atlantic crossing from Dakar to Recife. Subsequently, *Flight's* American correspondent reported that it had been very good for British prestige in Latin America. He also made the point that in some of the smaller Central American states, the aircraft were described as being American, the assumption being that only the US made jets. He added that it was not considered necessary to send out any spare Avon engines for the Canberras, and nor did they need any, but it was a pity that this fact was not publicised.

JOHN BROWNLOW took part on Exercise Round Trip:

> During mid-1952 a goodwill tour of South America was being conceived. The original idea was to celebrate, on behalf of the UK, the change of presidency in Chile, but once other South American and Caribbean governments learned that the first British jet bomber was visiting their continent, demands for visits escalated. I was lucky enough to go along as Dermot Boyle's navigator and ADC. The planned route was as follows: Binbrook – Gibraltar – Dakar – Recife – Rio de Janeiro – Montevideo – Buenos Aires – Santiago – Lima – Bogota – Caracas – Belize – Mexico City – Havana – Kingston – Ciudad Trujillo – Port of Spain – Belém – Recife – Dakar – Gibraltar – Binbrook.
>
> We set off on 20 October and arrived back at St Eval in Cornwall on 5 December, having been diverted because of bad weather at Binbrook. Navigation, and the relatively short range of the B2s for the South Atlantic crossings, were initially regarded as major problems. However, the B2's range was extended by fitting a single 300-gallon auxiliary tank in the bomb bay. This was in addition to the normal tip tanks which were in general use by then. Navigation was helped by the addition of a Marconi radio compass in each aircraft, and a Marconi HF radio in the aircraft flown by OC 12 Squadron, Sqn Ldr Les Press. I had the benefit of a Hughes periscopic sextant in WD987 which was flown by Dermot Boyle with the reserve pilot, Sgt John Simms, also on board.

B2s WD987, WD983 and WD996 of 12 Squadron with Hastings transports at Binbrook in October 1952 prior to Exercise Round Trip to South America. The B2 closest to the camera was flown by AVM Dermot Boyle with John Brownlow as the navigator. (Peter Green Collection)

A Marconi employee, Mr Shelton, was given a temporary commission as a pilot officer, and flew with Les Press to operate the HF set, maintain long-distance communication, obtain bearings and service the radio compasses if required. WD987 had previously been used for a record flight from London to Nairobi, captained by Wg Cdr Pat Connelly who had taken over from Hamish Mahaddie as Binbrook's wing commander flying. Since we had no idea what the winds would be at cruising altitude, our chief anxiety was the strength of any jet streams that we might encounter. In those days, jet streams were little understood, of course, and no information on them existed for the South Atlantic or South America. For about 600 nm during the crossing we would be without external navigation aids. The strategy was, therefore, for each crew to navigate independently to the start of the 600-mile gap, around 1¼ hour's flying.

We all started off using a common flight plan, based on an assumed wind, and we took off with no more than a minute or two between aircraft. On reaching the start of the gap, each crew was to check its fuel state and, if excessive consumption was evident and it was concluded that they could not complete the flight against a 100-knot jet stream, they were to return to Dakar. To everyone's relief, as each Canberra reached the checkpoint, the crews reported that they were continuing. In fact, once we were out of VHF range the Hughes periscopic sextant was useful for plotting single position lines using the sun, and these gave what proved to be quite accurate track checks. This was confirmed when we were eventually able to pick up a non-directional beacon (NDB) situated on an island north-east of Recife which indicated that we were pretty well on track and on ETA. I can't recall whether we ever got an HF bearing. The east-west crossing was made in an unofficial record time of four hours and 27 minutes on 23 October (and west-to-east in four hours). We all arrived in the circuit at Recife at about the same time, and taxied in together. This was the first jet crossing of the South Atlantic in both directions.

There were few operational problems during the tour, the main ones being due to the weather. On arrival at Rio de Janeiro, for instance, it was so bad that we had to let down to low level over the sea using the radio compass and the Santos Dumont NDB, and then pick our way visually through coastal hills to Santos Dumont airfield at Rio. The next problem involved a very strong jet stream flowing north to south, roughly parallel with the Andes, which we came across en route from Santiago to Lima, and which had not, of course, been forecast. The approach to Lima was also a little fraught, because of poor visibility. We had to make a visual approach to an unfamiliar airfield, the only assistance being the local NDB and a map. An engine handling problem that cropped up occasionally was caused by the two-position swirl vanes on the earlier Mk 101 Avon engines. When taking off in a strong crosswind the swirl vane blades would stall on initial engine acceleration unless the aircraft was first positioned into wind on the runway and then held on the brakes until the vanes opened. The aircraft then had to be edged round onto the runway heading before take-off power could be applied.

However, throughout the tour, the serviceability of the Canberras was excellent. And, as usual, the RAF ground crew, all members of 12 Squadron, were superb. We were supported on the trip by two Hastings, one of which was captained by Jock Kennedy. There is no doubt that the South American tour was a great success, and it resulted in many export orders for the Canberra to South America, notably to Argentina, Peru, Ecuador, Chile and Venezuela.

But most long-distance Canberra flights were less newsworthy if equally dramatic. RUSS RUMBOL enjoyed two significant careers of about equal length, but:

It is odd that I think more about the first, as an RAF navigator, than the second as a college lecturer. I went from lecturer one to deputy head of the science department in 15 years at the same college. The RAF equivalent would be going from pilot officer to wing commander at the same station – I certainly never did that.

Also, my squadron tours were on Lincolns and Valiants. I think I did pretty well but my 'best' effort was on Canberras, which I flew much more rarely.

The memorable flight was in 1965. We, two pilots and two navigators, were to fly in a Canberra from Manby to Akrotiri, Cyprus and then to Tehran, Iran. A word about geography and recent political history will help here. A navigational chart is not necessary – you can follow it with a school atlas. It was very much in the Cold War and Armenia and Azerbaijan were part of the Soviet Union. Iraq was also 'unfriendly' but in Iran, in pre-Ayatollah days, we were most welcome. Still, there was a fairly narrow channel to get through.

We were competent and experienced navigators but we did note that nearly all the route had gone over to voice omnidirectional range (VOR). Our aircraft did not have this facility and we would have to rely on our radio compass with the very few NDBs that were still on the route. Never mind, we had Green Satin (Doppler radar) and there was nearly always the sight of ground in those parts. We weren't a bit worried.

Roy Evans, my co-navigator, and I were amused to see Bill Lamont, the captain, running around trying to find the VHF frequencies of Tabriz radar, a ground defence unit in Iran. What did he want those for?

Roy navigated the first leg to Cyprus. The Green Satin wasn't working but he had no real difficulty. We put the Green Satin u/s and it was fixed at Akrotiri.

Next morning, I got a double shock at met briefing. The forecast winds at our planned altitude were northerly at the very unusual speed of 140 knots. You have to believe the forecasters – that's what they're there for. Further bad news was that there would be total cloud cover over the whole route. Not much now to navigate with – lucky we had Green Satin.

As we took off, the Green Satin aerial swung to one side and stayed there. I hoped the one NDB on route – at Diyarbakir – was working. The first leg to just inside Turkey took an age. Our ground speed, using dead reckoning (DR) with the forecast winds, was unusually slow. We couldn't see the ground of course.

After turning east, I managed to raise Diyarbakir on my radio compass and the bearing it gave, just west of north, seemed right. My plan was to take three bearings as we passed close to and north of Diyarbakir and have what we call a running fix, a positive position at last.

To my surprise and consternation, the bearings changed very slowly. There could be two explanations. Either the equipment was faulty (very unlikely) or we had turned considerably north of Diyarbakir, the winds being much lighter than forecast.

The Soviet Union was not very far away and we could have been flying straight towards part of it. This was not long after the U2 Gary Power incident and the Communists would shoot us down or escort us to land at a Russian base. I had no real position but something had to be done quickly. The Canberra wasn't a slow aircraft. I was not the captain but it was clearly a navigation decision, not the pilot's. I altered course 60° starboard, stayed there for a while, using pure intuitive judgement, and then returned to the original heading.

I knew it was crude in the extreme but the Russian danger should have passed. If I was wrong, we'd be over Iraq, not a good prospect either. There was some tension in the Canberra. No doubt I was blamed for these unusual tactics. Bill Lamont remembered that we had the Tabriz radar frequencies. He called them up. They gave us a fix exactly on track. I hadn't expected that! After my crude navigation, I'd have been satisfied to be somewhere near it. But caution was still vital. We knew that some operators (especially overseas) could be incompetent, lazy or indifferent and could put us on our planned track just to keep us quiet. I asked Bill to try again after a couple of minutes. Once again, the fix made sense. I thought I deserved that bit of luck. Everything went smoothly then and we were soon in Tehran control.

If I'd expected congratulations after landing, I certainly didn't get them. There seemed to be a general impression that I'd over-reacted. Bill Furnell, the co-pilot, left me in no doubt. Even my friend and co-navigator, Roy Evans, said I'd been wrong. He understood the appalling problems I'd had but he said, 'The thing to do in those circumstances is to proceed on flight plan and, on ETA, start screaming for help.' 'Not so, Roy. If I'd done that on DR with those forecast winds, we wouldn't be here now.'

He was a more experienced, and probably better, navigator than me but his flying was nearly all in Transport Command. He wouldn't have met forecast winds anything like those and I doubt if he'd been as near to the Soviet Union. Although we carried no weapons, the Canberra was a bomber. A Russian controller, seeing a NATO bomber, unauthorised and unexpected, penetrating Soviet airspace, would have been within his rights to bring it down. I had no doubts that, with other navigators in that position, an aircraft and crew might have been lost. I'm still waiting for the AFC! ■

CHAPTER 7
INTO GERMANY

On 29 March 1954 it was announced that four Canberra B2 squadrons would form within 2nd Tactical Air Force (2TAF). The first squadron to arrive was 149 Squadron which took its ten B2s from Cottesmore to Ahlhorn on 24 August 1954. They moved on to Gütersloh on 17 September to be followed by a newly re-formed 102 Squadron on 20 October, 103 Squadron on 30 November and 104 Squadron on 15 March 1955.

DENNIS SAWDEN reported to FTS for pilot training in April 1953.

I had already served in the RAF for over two years. I had been called up for National Service on 9 January 1951 and, during a week at RAF Padgate for kitting etc., we were addressed by two RAF flying instructors and told that if any of us had any interest in applying for NS pilot training, we should note that the length of the training had just been increased and therefore vacancies for pilot training were very limited: even so, there was a good chance that our two years' service would end before we had qualified so we were discouraged from applying for pilot training. This all came as a complete surprise and those of us interested just had to accept that we would have to do something else. At that stage, I had no interest in staying in the RAF after my two-year conscription period.

Next, I spent six weeks at recruit training school at RAF Melksham in Wiltshire. Here I was put forward for commissioning and, because I had been in the army cadets at school, I was posted to the RAF Regiment Depot at Catterick. I completed a physically demanding and arduous course, concentrating on weapon training – and generally training to be 'a soldier in RAF blue': I was as fit as a fiddle when the course ended. Next, my nine-week OCTU course at RAF Spitalgate near Grantham led to me being commissioned as a pilot officer in the RAF Regiment on 19 July 1951. This was followed by six weeks under canvas at RAF Watchet in Somerset, as a supernumerary member of staff at the RAF Regiment Light Ack-Ack Gunnery School. Here I spent many happy summer days, observing and assisting on the 40-mm Bofors live-firing range, out over the sea, the drogue target being towed by Hawker Tempest aircraft from RAF Chivenor.

I was posted to British Air Forces of Occupation (BAFO) in Germany, to 54 (Rifle) Squadron RAF Regiment, as the flight commander of over 35 airman gunners, based at RAF Luneburg, near Hamburg, arriving in October 1951. Early in 1952, the whole squadron was moved to RAF Gatow, Berlin, to conduct armed patrols of the airfield at night, to prevent German civilians stealing the lead insulation on the airfield lighting installations. After three months my squadron returned to RAF Luneburg and shortly afterwards we moved permanently to join the RAF Regiment Wing at the newly-opened large NATO airfield at Wildenrath close to the Dutch border. Here the station commander was the famous former Battle of Britain pilot Group Captain J. E. 'Johnnie' Johnson, who required each of the three Vampire ground-attack squadrons to pair off with one of the three Regiment squadrons – in my squadron's case with 71 (Eagle) Squadron. This led me to spend a lot of time with their pilots and flying with them in Vampire T11s – or with other pilots in the station's de Havilland Tiger Moth biplane. As a result, I knew I wanted to apply to train as a pilot. Just before my two-year National Service ended, I was successful in my application to transfer to aircrew.

I was sent to 9 FTS at Wellesbourne Mountford near Stratford-upon-Avon in Warwickshire for my BFTS course on de Havilland Chipmunks. I was the only previously-commissioned officer on the course of 33 trainee pilots (otherwise all acting pilot officers) when we started flying in May 1953. I completed 70 hours day and night flying on this fine little aircraft by early August 1953, but by then several of my course colleagues had fallen by the wayside. Staying on at Wellesbourne, I progressed to the AFTS stage on the North American Harvard 2B. To whet our appetites for what was to come, on 13 January 1954, we were each given an exhilarating 20 minutes 'famil' ride in the rear seat of a Gloster Meteor Mark 7 trainer. I was one of just 11 of the 33 trainees left on the course to be awarded our wings on 31 March 1954.

I was posted to 211 AFS at RAF Worksop near Retford in Nottinghamshire for my advanced jet flying training on Meteor Mks 7 and 8, and I started flying on 27 April 1954. In addition to the challenge of converting to fly jet and much faster aircraft for the first time, I also had to learn how to handle two engines. Most sorties lasted just 40 minutes, but I remember them being action-packed sessions, when one had to work hard to cover the wide range of aspects in the syllabus. Great emphasis was placed on single-engined flying, high-altitude flying and amazing aerobatics in such a high performance aircraft, with a maximum airspeed of 515 knots – quite a contrast to the Harvard. It was not unusual to be asked when flying with the CFI, Wg Cdr J. B. Cowerd, to go straight into a roll-off-the-top, from take-off, often when there was 8/8 cloud cover, so one zoomed upwards hopefully and usually found oneself in bright sunshine as one rolled the aircraft out into level flight. Also, it was not unusual when overshooting from a normal twin-engined practice approach to have the high-pressure cock on one of the two engines pulled up by the instructor, closing down that engine, so one had to quickly gain control of the aircraft and fly on one engine. Single-engined flying, and re-lighting, became a regular feature of the course. But to my intense relief, after 41 hours dual and 40 hours solo flying by day and night, I completed the course on 15 September 1954.

I was informed that I would next be posted to RAF Leeming, to the night-fighter OCU in October: this surprised me somewhat, as I had never seen myself as a fighter pilot. Then, in October, my posting to Leeming was cancelled, and I was told that instead I would be going to the Canberra OCU in late November, but that, first, I must attend a two-week 'Gee-H' radar blind-bombing course. I was delighted at the prospect of flying Canberras. I was posted to the Bomber Command Bombing School (BCBS) at RAF Lindholme for a two-week course. After a few days of instruction on the ground, meeting newly-trained navigators on the course with us who would be operating the bombing radar in the aircraft, and learning the principles of G-H and visual bombing, as well as seeing the equipment for ourselves, we were all given airborne instruction in the Vickers Varsity, a twin-engined training aircraft, with dual controls and a tricycle undercarriage. We pilots were to fly as second pilot, in the right-hand seat, and our captains were all very experienced staff pilots, most with wartime experience, several of them Polish. Our navigator colleagues on the course were down at the back of the Varsity, taking it in turns to give bomb-aimer's instructions to the pilot. Sorties lasted between two and three hours and pilots and navigators on the course took it in turns to either give or follow bomb-aiming instructions. I did a total of 11 hours flying there, the last sortie being on 8 November 1954. This was a very different world to the Flying Training Command atmosphere I had been used to. I recall particularly being programmed to fly one Varsity sortie with a Polish Master Pilot Gustowski, whom I had never met until then. I was sitting in the crew room, awaiting my sortie, when this short, burly figure came in and called my name; when I replied, his pre-flight briefing consisted solely of: 'Kom – vee fly'!

OCU

I arrived at 231 OCU at Bassingbourn in mid-November 1954 to join 53 Bomber Course. We embarked on an intensive few weeks in the ground school, being taught and examined on all the aircraft systems in the Canberra which by now had been in service for just over two years, so one felt privileged to be getting to know one's way round and let loose on such a modern aircraft. The OCU was very busy training aircrews for both bomber and photographic reconnaissance squadrons throughout the RAF. There were two officer messes and accommodation was so short that, for the first few weeks, newcomers slept in four-berth civilian caravans parked around No. 2 mess which, in mid-winter, was not much fun! During the ground school phase of the course, we were encouraged to crew up as soon as possible and I was soon approached by two navigators, who had obviously already teamed up and were looking for their pilot. John Eggleston came from Sussex and had served in the Royal Navy during the war as a petty officer in Signals; he wore the Atlantic Star in his war medals and became my nav plotter. Norman Blanchard was a direct entrant who had worked in the drawing office of a steel works at Scunthorpe before entering the RAF: he became my nav radar/bomb aimer.

On 22 December 1954, I flew my first sortie in the Canberra T4, a famil session of one hour and 45 minutes, with a staff QFI and a staff nav. A week later on 29 December 1954, I flew another T4 trip, a one hour and 55 minutes session on asymmetric flying, with John Eggleston as navigator. Two more trips in a T4 on 4 and 10 January 1955 led to a dual check in a T4 on 1 February. Soon afterwards, I flew as passenger (sitting on the rumble seat) of a B2 bomber version with a QFI and staff nav, plus John Eggleston, for a 40-minute demo: I was then sent for my first solo, with John Eggleston as my nav, for 55 minutes. On 2 February 1955, with my crew of John Eggleston and Norman Blanchard, we flew a short cross-country, our first trip together as a crew. Further sorties in the B2 followed, on G-H tracking and screening for visual bombing, plus several cross-countries, so we soon built up useful hours. On passing my instrument rating test, we progressed to medium-level bombing, dropping 25-lb practice bombs on Otmoor and other ranges and we also undertook many simulated blind bombing (SBB) runs at various radar plotting locations, one being on Southend Pier. In early March, we completed the night-flying phase of the course, which included more live visual bombing and SBB trips. Cross-countries covered a lot more ground than we had been used to: one I recall was Base – Land's End – John O'Groats – Base. On fine days, the view from the cruising altitude of over 40,000 ft was really impressive, to say the least, and we soon got used to these extreme and previously unused altitudes. We completed the OCU course with a night visual bombing sortie, dropping ten practice bombs on the Wainfleet range in The Wash.

Like many crews on our course, we were told that we were being posted to 104 Squadron, which had been reformed at RAF Gütersloh, a former Luftwaffe base near Bielefeld in Germany, to serve on one of four Canberra B2 squadrons forming the new 551 Wing, the Bomber Command element of 2TAF. After embarkation leave, we all reported to Liverpool Street station one evening, to catch one of three military boat trains to Harwich, for the overnight crossing to the Hook of Holland. Much of the next day was spent in a slow-moving military train which reached Gütersloh in the late afternoon.

Sqn Ldr Shuster's (OC 103 Squadron) B2 at Gütersloh. WD999 sports the 551 Wing badge on the nose. (Peter Green Collection)

Canberra B2 WH713 of 149 Squadron undergoing maintenance at Gütersloh in July 1956.
The fin crest was a horse shoe and a flash of lightning interfaced. (Peter Green Collection)

104 SQUADRON

At Gütersloh in April 1955, the CO was Sqn Ldr Edward Stephenson, who had flown Lancasters with 12 Squadron at Wickenby at the end of the war and since then had become an experienced QFI. Initially, he had just one flight commander, Flt Lt Norman Greenhow. All crews were brand new, straight from the OCU, so it must have been quite a challenge in terms of supervision and management, but the squadron soon settled down and played its part in the overall effort of 551 Wing which consisted of 102, 103, 104 and 149 Squadrons – each equipped with ten Canberra B2s.

All our early flying on 104 concentrated on G-H and visual bombing practice, dropping 25-lb practice bombs by day and night on ranges at Nordhorn and Sandbanks in northern Germany, or in the UK. Full-load bomb-load take-offs featured once a month, with six x 1,000-lb sand-filled bombs. Most of the airframes we had were brand new and we had our crew names painted beside the entrance door: my crew's airframe was WJ628 and we took great pride in it. We flew the B2 version with wing-tip tanks fitted; this gave us a total fuel load of 1,800 gallons and so sortie lengths gradually settled down at an average of three hours. Every so often, we were required to fly limited-aids cross-countries, using no radar but relying on radio bearings to navigate: these could last for nearly four hours, but were tedious in the extreme, just sitting at extreme altitude, always over 40,000 ft and up to 48,000 ft (our limit), where the cockpit heating was often found wanting – and frost could occasionally be seen forming inside. Squadron exercises led us into participation in major exercises, like Bomber Command 'Bombex' or 2TAF Command exercises. All the time, new crews, initially graded as 'non-combat', were working to achieve good bombing accuracy, leading to an acceptable category of 'Combat', which as a crew we achieved on 5 August 1955. Higher categorisations were Combat Star and Select, but, within a few months, time was to run out on us and we didn't progress further on these.

On exercises, radio silence was strictly applied, so start up and taxiing were done with Aldis lamp signals from the runway caravan for take-off. With each of the four squadrons contributing perhaps eight of their ten aircraft on strength, this meant a string of 30 or more take-offs at one-minute intervals, with each aircraft climbing to extreme altitude, to follow an identical route. The Canberra unstuck soon after 100 kts was reached and was then soon into the climb at 330 kts. This was maintained until the Machmeter showed .72 Mach, at which speed the rest of the climb was completed, usually levelling off at 45,000 ft or just above, depending on the altitude separation decided. Time to this height (with tip tanks fitted, and just one or two 25-lb practice bombs on board) was 18 minutes. We cruised at .74 Mach and this gave a groundspeed of about 420 kts. Visibility at high altitude was of course excellent and one could see for miles around, by day and night. One never saw the aircraft ahead or behind, but one was conscious of the need for accurate time-keeping and navigation, as the route usually included at least one or two SBB runs on a radar calibration 'target' on the ground, either in the UK or Germany. Radio silence continued throughout, except of course at the SBB or G-H bombing range, where we called at the initial IP and 'bomb gone': the range replied with 'bomb observed', but we had to wait until debriefing on the ground to hear our accuracy. It was not unusual to drop a single practice bomb using G-H on a range in either Germany or the UK, from altitudes of 45,000 ft and above, and amazingly good bombing accuracy was achieved: 'direct hits' were not unusual.

One memorable night, on 23 September 1955, we took off just after dusk in one of these streams at one-minute intervals, on Exercise Beware. We climbed up through 20,000 ft of 8/8 cloud cover and emerged into what was still partial daylight, above all the cloud, continuing the climb to our transit altitude above 40,000 ft, on a route over Land's End and Glasgow, before returning to base over the North Sea. We dropped our single practice bomb on Luce Bay range in south-west Scotland through complete cloud cover and landed at three-minute intervals after three hours and 35 minutes in the air. But as we were walking back from dispersal to the squadron hangar, after midnight, with the last few Canberras in the stream still landing, suddenly we heard a Canberra on its final approach open up the engines to full power: shortly afterwards it crashed and a column of flames leapt into the air. Knowing it must be one of the 104 Squadron crews, we later discovered that it was Plt Off 'Jonah' Jones, who had flown a tour on Manchesters in Bomber Command during the war. Apparently his pilot's canopy had suddenly misted up completely (a known fault in the early days, through descending from high-altitude temperatures). Suddenly blinded and unable to see the runway ahead, Jonah attempted to overshoot and go round again: however, the early Avon engines could surge when the throttles were opened too suddenly – and, with one engine stalled, this caused his aircraft to turn over and crash. All three crew members were killed, so, soon afterwards, we were introduced to pall bearer duties at the Commonwealth War Graves Cemetery near Hanover.

Very occasionally, the follow-my-leader route took us to a pre-arranged point, such as the Brest peninsula – and then at the appointed second, the whole stream turned through perhaps 90 degrees, onto the same heading, to produce a vast line-abreast approach usually to the south or east coast of the UK . In this way in the early stages, we tried to swamp the day-fighter resources and for a while we only saw night-fighter (NF) Meteors staggering up to altitudes well below us, unable to get near us. Then at a second appointed time en route, the whole line-abreast formation turned onto a given heading, which, in theory, should have put us all in extended line-astern again – but it never happened that way. Each crew would have been given a time to report at the entry point for the standard let-down procedure, designed to bring 30 or more Canberras back on the ground, but landing at three-minute intervals, rather than the one-minute intervals which had applied when they took off: this was to avoid turbulence from jet-wash. There was great jostling for position at or near the vital 'entry point' (usually at about 20,000 ft) and one had to have a good look out, in case another Canberra zoomed in from nowhere and made the radio call first, to take your entry time. This meant an extended trombone of time-filling, until one's new entry point time was achieved. Once into the standard let-down, all was straight forward, as a strict order for landing had been established and this led into a ground-controlled approach (GCA) or precision approach radar (PAR) as they were later called. This let-down procedure could take up a significant amount of time, at the end of the sortie.

Air Staff instructions did not permit Canberra pilots to 'join battle' with intercepting fighters at extreme altitude, by taking evasive action. This was because, as explained earlier, the Canberra's early Avon engines were susceptible to surge if the throttles were handled harshly at height, for instance when taking evasive action. But a number of brave souls did engage with Hunters and Javelins, once they started to reach our altitudes (in 1956), and inevitably these Canberra pilots experienced either single or double-engine flame-outs. The problem was that the procedure to relight the Canberra's Avon engine required descending to 20,000 ft before the re-light button could be used, so it was easy to be found out. However, I never heard of a Canberra pilot being unable to relight his engine(s) at this lower altitude.

Squadron flying continued through the winter months of 1955, with further radar or visual bombing – and more exercises, including the Bomber Command Bombex on a Thursday night. For a while, in the very cold weather, we encountered problems in the starter cartridge housing. This could result in the whole assembly exploding, sending hot metal shrapnel flying in all directions and damaging adjacent aircraft in dispersal. However, this was soon solved with a local modification and different grease in the assembly. My average monthly flying hours were about 25-30, including two or three night sorties in a month. But in March 1956, an 'hour's race' developed between the four squadrons on the wing at Gütersloh and I totalled 49 hours and 35 minutes by midnight on 31 March 1956. It was at about this time that I was invited to apply for a permanent commission, which I was obviously pleased with, as I had discovered that the RAF way of life suited me well. I was interviewed by the station commander and later by our AOC, AVM S. R. Ubee, at 2 Group HQ, Sundern, across the other side of Gütersloh town. In due course, my permanent commission was confirmed.

But the next morning (and it was 1 April 1956), the station tannoy made an unusual announcement that all aircrew were to assemble in the wing briefing room. Here we were given the shattering news that all Canberras throughout the RAF had been grounded – because of tailplane actuator failures. The motor driving and controlling the movement of the whole tailplane had been found to be faulty, causing the tailplane to run away, outside its normal traverse, resulting in the aircraft bunting or going into a steep climb. (We had had no cases of this at Gütersloh.) There was no forecast of the duration of the grounding, so we had no aircraft to fly, thus about 120 members of aircrew were seemingly out of a job. We dispersed to our squadrons and over the next few days a new pattern of life evolved. Places were found on courses in Germany and the UK, a golf course was built by 'volunteer aircrew' on the far side of the airfield and, generally, aircrew were permitted to undertake anything reasonable that they could come up with. In my own case, I had by this stage established myself as a member of the station and command competition rifle and .38 pistol teams and it was known that my range conducting officer qualifications (from my two years in the RAF Regiment) were still valid. With the unit's regiment officer away on a long course in the UK, I found myself conducting all range practices of station personnel for their annual qualification shoot over the next few months – thus I was able to practise ad lib for shooting matches in Germany and at Bisley.

The tailplane actuators on the Canberra T4 trainers on each of the four squadrons were the first to be modified, and I flew our T4 twice in May 1956 to keep current. We then had more shattering news – the wing was to be disbanded, because of a change in NATO policy. We were all interviewed by personnel staff from Command HQ and asked whether we would like to return to the UK, or stay in Germany (on another unit) or stay at Gütersloh. I chose the last: my plotter, John Eggleston, chose to return to the UK, as he had become engaged to a nursing officer in the QAs (Army Nursing Service). Norman Blanchard had married during our first year in Germany and his wife had come out to join him, so he elected to stay at Gütersloh too. The B2's tailplane actuators had been modified by July and I flew a B2 twice later in that month. The wing officially disbanded on 31 July 1956.

CHAPTER 8
PHOTOGRAPHIC MEMORIES

The Canberra PR3 entered service in 1953. Although capable of reaching above 50,000 ft, long-range navigation was a problem pending availability of the first Green Satin Doppler radar navigation system after 1954-55. As it happened, the 14-inch extension to the PR3 fuselage coupled with redistributed mass resulted in excessive vibration which delayed the PR3 into operational service. It was not until December 1952 that 540(PR) Squadron, hitherto equipped with Mosquito Mk 34As, received the first production PR3, WE135, at Benson.

DENNIS WANKLYN joined the RAF in 1941 as a Halton apprentice.

I was ground crew on 58 and 540 Squadrons until I started navigator training. My first flying tour was on PR Mosquitoes in 1952 on 81 Squadron at Seletar in Singapore. After a long tour at Seletar I returned to the UK to convert to the Canberra PR3 before joining 69 Squadron at Laarbruch. Then to Malta – still on PR3s – where the squadron was renumbered 39 Squadron. From there I was posted directly to 17 Squadron at Wildenrath, this time on PR7s. After short breaks on the ground I went to Brüggen on 80 Squadron. From there I went on a ground tour at Wyton and then to the school of photography at Cosford. From then on I was involved with several photography-related ground appointments until I retired. Overall, I was in PR the whole of my service career.

One highlight of my life in the service was around 1954 when we took a couple of Mosquitoes to Negombo, Ceylon. They played a part in the film *Purple Plain* starring Gregory Peck. We took the nose cone off and substituted a new nose with broom handles inserted to simulate forward-firing guns. Happy days!

I amassed over 4,000 flying hours in total, of which around 1,000 were on Mosquitoes and the rest on Canberras. I completed the Bassingbourn OCU in early 1956. Initially, I couldn't believe the speed at which we charged across the chart on Canberras. From 240 kts on the Mosquito we were flying 420 kts average operating speeds. It wasn't so much comical as mystifying. I hung onto my Mosquito charts but they were no good. It just took time for me to become convinced.

Notwithstanding all the years I spent in the Canberra empire, we had nothing like the accidents we had on Mosquitoes. I flew in several Mosquitoes that were written off (I actually broke my neck in one Mosquito prang) and after another, when the undercarriage folded on landing, my pilot and I carried the station MO off from the scene on a stretcher (running out to the crash site, he'd fallen into a drainage ditch and broken his leg!). But I recall barely a single incident on Canberras.

My pilot was Colin Sharp at Laarbruch and Malta. We flew both high- and low-level photography though the RAF Germany squadrons specialised in low-level PR. We did high-level photographic surveys of North Africa from Malta, combined with rangers to and from Marham. We just trained to take photographs – we had no specific war role. ◼

Lewis 'Bob' Hodges (left) and Bob Currie (right)

The introduction of the Canberra PR3 into RAF service was followed by development of the Canberra PR7 with Avon RA7 engines, wing lead-ing-edge fuel tanks and Maxaret anti-skid brakes. As if to proclaim its capability the first PR7, WH773, was entered for the England-New Zea-land Air Race in October 1953. In the words of one PR navigator, 'it was set up for Wg Cdr Lewis "Bob" Hodges from HQ Bomber Command to win the race'. However, although WH773 covered the 5,416 miles between London and Colombo, Ceylon, in 10 hours, 25 minutes and 21 seconds (at an average speed of 519.5 mph), and it flew non-stop from Colombo to Perth (omitting the Cocos Islands), WH773 then went u/s with generator and filler-cap trouble and so Hodges and his navigator, Sqn Ldr R. Currie, came fourth. The race was won by Flt Lts Roland 'Monty' Burton and Don Gannon, flying PR3 WE139. WE139 spent just 90 minutes on the ground as RAF personnel, who had been pre-positioned at each of the four refuelling stops, serviced the aircraft.

At the time SQN LDR BOB CURRIE was senior navigator for the RAF Canberra crews. Referring to Bob's logbook, his son IAN noted that:

WH773 was collected by Wg Cdr Hodges and my father from the English Electric factory at Samlesbury on 11 September 1953 and taken to Wyton, after a few shake down and familiarisation sorties. Hodges, my father and 773 arrived at London Airport on 3 October 1953 for the build up to the air race. WH773 was to be Canberra number one of five (others being RAF PR3s and RAAF B2s).

Hodges, my father and 773, set off on the air race at 1735 hrs on 8 October 1953 heading for their first fuel stop at Shaiba, and then on to Negombo. They set an official speed record for the London to Colombo leg of 10 hours and 25 minutes (836.004 kmh/520 mph/452 kts).

They then pressed on to Perth and were well in the lead, but sadly a double generator failure cost them precious time. They eventually reached Christchurch New Zealand in the early hours of 10 October 1953 and were placed fourth, though they had the fastest flying time of 22 hours and 22 minutes from London to Christchurch. The winning Canberra PR3 – WE139 – is in the RAF Museum at Hendon. My father's last connection with WH773 was on 27 October 1953 when they flew it from Pearce to Changi, thereafter he switched to a PR3 for the final legs back home. ■

A year earlier, RAF Bomber Command experienced high-level jet operations when a special duties flight was formed at Sculthorpe in Norfolk with three North American RB-45C Tornados. The offer to loan them had been made by General Hoyt S. Vandenberg, Chief of Staff, USAF, in early 1951 and the flights made in them on 17-18 April and 12-13 December 1952 were the fastest and longest high-level sorties flown by the RAF in jet aircraft up to that time. The three captains included Sqn Ldr John Crampton, the second Canberra CO of 101 Squadron and the sorties were flown at 32,000-42,000 ft with the aim of obtaining radar photographs of potential V Force targets in western Russia. One route ran through Germany to cover targets in the Baltic states, another to the south of that towards Moscow and the third further south to take in Ukrainian industrial complexes. The flights were deemed to have been successful although weather and engine troubles delayed their return to Sculthorpe. Later flights were less productive and on 16 December 1952, C-in-C Bomber Command wrote to the commander, 7th Air Division to say: 'I am only sorry that the operation ended as it did – without the answers.'

For many years there has been a story that the RAF flew a Canberra B2 complete with large, oblique camera deep into Soviet territory around 1953-54 to photograph the Kapustin Yar ballistic missile test site before landing in Iran. There is circumstantial evidence that the RAF did indeed fly Canberras over Warsaw Pact territory around this time, and in November 1952 permission was sought from the Norwegian government to operate out of Bodø air base over north-west Russia using 'the new two-engine British jets'. PR3 squadron ORBs make no mention of any such missions but these record books were only cleared to secret so that isn't conclusive. Chris Pocock, the foremost authority on U-2 operations and associated spy flights, has documentary evidence that Kapustin Yar was not photographed from the air until September 1957 and anyway, the idea that the RAF and the USAF collaborated to squeeze a 100-inch focal length camera into the aft fuselage of a standard RAF Canberra B2 is fanciful in the extreme. Why not use a PR3 for starters?

On 26 March 1953, 540(PR) Squadron with its black PR3s moved from Benson to Wyton near Huntingdon, together with 58(PR) Squadron with Mosquito PR35s and 82(PR) Squadron with Lancaster PR1s which started converting to the Canberra PR3 the following December. These three PR squadrons comprised the UK Photographic Reconnaissance Unit (PRU) which formed part of Bomber Command.

KEN EDMONDS was stuck in a pre-OCU supernumerary job at Wyton in 1952 after completing navigator school.

I was then detached to 40 Squadron to act as a safety observer such that when I went to do a refresher course on Varsities at Swinderby, I came out on top and was offered my pick of postings. I chose PR Canberras and was sent to Bassingbourn, but after a couple of weeks I was moved forward two courses to join a pilot whose navigator had been chopped. This pilot was Vic McNabney GM who had done a tour on PR Meteors and he was an absolute ace. We joined 82 Squadron and we were the first PR crew to make 'Select' at Wyton. ▪

The first squadron to equip fully with the Canberra PR7 was 542 Squadron which re-formed at Wyton on 15 May 1954. 82 Squadron initially operated PR3s from November 1953 as did 58 Squadron a month later. 540 Squadron undertook the PR7 intensive flying trials, known as 'Seven Up', in June 1954, with 82 Squadron next to get the PR7 from October 1954. Ken continues:

We flew a crew of two on PR and it was a dream job for a 20-year old. We did a lot of high-altitude photography with our horizon-to-horizon fan of six F52 36-inch cameras plus an F49 for survey work. We flew Ordnance Survey lines at 16,666 ft or 8,333 ft to give the appropriate scale for the OS people but a lot of the time we would cruise around the Mediterranean photographing North Africa. With no upper airways, I would put my straight edge on the map and fly direct from Wyton to Luqa and then perhaps east as far as Habbaniya near Baghdad. To reach Habbaniya from the Canal Zone, we flew to Aqaba till we saw the pipeline, turned right and flew until we saw a patch of green which was the irrigation around Habbaniya. We did no target study and we had no specific war role. We trained in case something came along – I don't remember training for anything in particular.

We would photograph visually from the nose. As I remember, none of the PR3s or 7s were fitted with the T2 bombsight. The fore-and-aft yellow banana sight was common to all the PR Canberras at Wyton and the New Zealand Air Race PR3 in the RAF Museum is still fitted with a banana sight. If you hold one finger up about nine inches in front of your eyes, you see double – the navigator simply directed the pilot to follow the desired track between the two images. It could not have been less sophisticated, but it worked. One day, we were briefed to fly at 40,000 ft west up the Thames Estuary to beyond Heathrow on behalf of British Rail or the Greater London Council. It was such a gin clear day that I could see my house in south London. We took an incredible set of prints and I'm sure that one of them was used as the opening shot of *Eastenders* before the Dome was built. ▪

Across in Germany, Laarbruch near the Dutch border housed 34 Recce Wing which was principally composed of three Canberra PR squadrons. 69(PR) Squadron re-formed in October 1953 with Canberra PR3s before moving to Laarbruch on 13 December 1954. It was joined by 31(PR) Squadron which re-formed on 1 March 1955 with PR7s, and the wing was completed by the re-formation of 80(PR) Squadron with PR7s the following August. Each Canberra squadron had a mobile field processing unit attached to it.

On 1 June 1956, 17(PR) Squadron re-formed with PR7s at Wahn, moving to Wildenrath on 3 April 1957. The 'high-level' PR Canberras were complimented by the 'low-level' Tac-R Swifts and Meteor FR9s based at Gütersloh. However, this was a largely artificial divide. High-level PR was frequently impracticable over the cloudy skies of Europe and in the words of an *Aeroplane* magazine evaluation of 2ATAF on 8 June 1956, 'when it is necessary to assess the area of damage caused by atomic weapons against enemy targets, low-level coverage or even visual reconnaissance may be resorted to by PR aircraft in bad visibility'.

GORDON DYER joined the RAF in December 1952 and was posted to RCAF Winnipeg for navigator training. Following a supernumerary post at HQ Bomber Command, he joined the Canberra PR7 OCU at Bassingbourn in April 1955. Posted to RAF Wyton in August 1955 he served initially on 82 Squadron and then 58 Squadron.

August Bank Holiday weekend in 1956 at Wyton had a dramatic twist. There was a general recall of 82 Squadron with orders to report for briefing at 0800 hours on Saturday 7 August. Four crews, including mine, were to be detached to Cyprus the next day. Our role would be to monitor activity at Egyptian airfields, particularly for the build-up of Soviet aircraft. This was a highly secret move and we were forbidden to tell anyone where we were going or what we would be doing. On Sunday morning we were seen off at the dispersal by AVM Sir Kenneth 'Bing' Cross, C-in-C of Bomber Command. To have this happen meant that our mission was regarded with some significance. We were to reinforce the Canberra PR7s of the newly-formed 13 Squadron based at RAF Akrotiri. We operated at a very high level – up to 50,000 ft, using 48-inch focal length cameras. This gave a scale of 1:10,000 on the photographic prints enabling the RE interpreters to differentiate between types of vehicles and aircraft. Our aircraft were equipped with a so-called shufti-scope. This fitted into the sextant mount and allowed a view behind the aircraft to look out for fighters. The shufti-scope was operated by a third crew member sitting on the rumble seat. As part of crew rotation policy I returned to Wyton on 7 October after two months. Though the Suez operation didn't start for another month I had played some part in the gathering of pre-operation intelligence.

I was only home for three months before I was off on a three-month-long detachment, this time to RAF Changi, Singapore. The task was the survey of Malaysia and North Borneo. The detachment was small, just two aircraft and three crews. During 80 hours of flying, I did 16 survey sorties of Malaysia covering some 6,000 square miles, including hydrographic survey of a section of Borneo coastline. Some sorties had a dual purpose of trying to trace communist insurgents who were proving troublesome. While there the unit received a request from the RAF station commander Kai Tak, Hong Kong, to take some photos of Mount Kinabalu in North Borneo. He was leader of the RAF Far East mountain climbing team and they hoped to climb the 13,000-ft mountain. He asked for sideways oblique photography to enable them to find a good route up the mountain. The short trip to RAF Labuan, which was maintained to support the Gurkhas involved in the then confrontation with Indonesia, was memorable for several reasons. It really was an outpost and our visit by Canberra was the first. ATC asked if we could do a bit of a show on arrival. Ted Kortens, my pilot, did a great job and he really beat up the airfield

Ted Kortens and Gordon Dyer outside PR7 before take-off for Kinabalu (notice the oblique camera ports). The orange sheet was to keep the aircraft cockpit cool – there were no cold air blowers. (Gordon Dyer)

doing several fast runs at 450 kts very low over the tower. Ted really took to 'beating-up' and turned over a native dug-out canoe when we left next day to photograph Mount Kinabalu. As we approached the mountain I saw that it had a near vertical face, and so I decided that I would do camera runs every 1,000 ft along the face of the mountain. I calculated the stand-off distance from the mountain face to ensure that each strip of photography would provide overlapping coverage, and we duly flew the runs. The prints when developed back at Changi were good and when they were laid down they provided a complete mosaic of the mountain face.

This success earned me a trip to Hong Kong to deliver them to the station commander who was very pleased with them. The flight to Hong Kong was via the then RAF facilities at Labuan and the Philippines, and then via Saigon on the return leg. Hong Kong was an amazing place to visit in those days – shopping, eating and night life. I did the typical tourist things – bought a dinner service, then crossed by ferry from Kowloon to Hong Kong island to see the funicular railway, visit Aberdeen fishing village and chose the fish to eat from a tank. Then it was time for a drink in the harbour bars. Somehow I got separated from the rest of my group and when I went back to the pier to catch the ferry I discovered that I had missed the last sailing. As we were leaving early next morning I had no option but to take the only other way back to Kowloon, by sampan. It was one of the scariest rides I have ever had. As I sat in the sampan with the inscrutable Chinaman rowing across the black water I was on edge thinking, 'Has he got a knife?'...'Will I ever make it to the other side?'

TONY BURT did his first navigator tour on Sunderlands before being posted to PR Canberras in November 1955. Around this time the 231 OCU PR element of 11 Canberras and 11 Meteors was detached to Merryfield in Somerset to spread the workload.

My first flight at Merryfield was in PR3 WE143 with Flt Lt (later Air Chf Mshl) John Gingell on 13 March 1956. I was crewed up with my pilot Phil Taylor though I didn't fly with Phil until a T4 refresher exercise on 7 May. Why the refresher? Our PR course should have run for twelve weeks to parallel 'the long bomber course', with a new intake every month. The problem was the tailplane actuator runaway snag which bedevilled the Canberra for a long time. The effect on my OCU course was that we had a lot of gardening leave which generally took the form of us disappearing off to visit such exotic locations as Lyme Regis, Seaton and Beer.

We flew our first PR3 conversion sortie with Flt Lt Hardless (on the Rumbold seat) on 24 July in WE171. On 14 August we progressed from pinpoints to feature line overlaps in PR3 WE172. Our first 'Opex' (navigation and photography), and longest trip of the course, was on 28 August in PR3 WE150 – 4.40 hours. We progressed to small-area cover photography in PR3 WF923 on 29 August (we were in our stride then!). Our final handling test was with Flt Lt Hardless on 30 August. Then we went on leave pending our departure for Germany. Phil and I were posted to 31 Squadron where we converted to PR7s at Laarbruch – we had the banana sight but I found it got in the way. I tended to eyeball everything – I was never a black box man.

My first flight on 31 Squadron was with the then flight commander, Flt Lt L. A. Ferguson, on 29 September 1956. We flew Canberra PR7 WT509 from Wildenrath to Laarbruch, the squadron having operated from Wildenrath for a short period. 31 Squadron was one of four PR Canberra squadrons with 2nd Allied Tactical Air Force based in Germany on the so-called 'clutch' stations. The squadrons were required to provide photographic reconnaissance along the NATO front 'from Norway to the Mediterranean, depending on operational requirements'.

I see from the 31 Squadron ORB that the tailplane actuator problem had grounded 31 Squadron's PR7s for a week in November 1955. The ORB also recorded, in February 1956, that a

Tony Burt (left) and his pilot Phil Taylor. (Tony Burt)

tailplane actuator modification was now being incorporated and an airframe limitation of 250 knots IAS imposed. I'm intrigued to see that I was sensitive to the problem for some time. On 29 November 1957 I flew with the flight commander (now Sqn Ldr L. A. Ferguson) in WH773 for an air test of the 'tail actuator'. This was followed on 9 December (again with Tony Ferguson) for an air test in WT523 – an air test of 'tailplane actuator and throttle synchronisation'. I think I kept a crafty eye on air tests thereafter – where tailplane actuators might be involved.

In December 1956 my logbook gives an idea of how far we fanned out over northern Europe in our PR training sorties. On the 5th, 14th and 31st I was airborne with different pilots on low-level UK cross-countries. On the 6th and 17th of December I was airborne on high-level cross-counties over France. And on the 15th and on the 17th I was airborne for low-level cross-countries over the British zone of Germany. 17 December must have been very busy for me – the French trip was three hours and 25 minutes and the second sortie was airborne just under two hours after we landed back. Why so frenetic I have no idea.

On 18 December 1956 I took part in the Sassoon Trophy competition for the first time, having arrived on the squadron that September and starting flying in October. This was one of the competitions for PR squadrons. I was not flying with my regular pilot but with Fg Off Pete Thomas. We had a good day after getting airborne at 0955 in Canberra PR7 WJ816 for three hours and 20 minutes. The squadron F540 ORB gave the results in March 1957. 'Sassoon Trophy. 541 Squadron now at Wunstorf won. 31 Squadron in second with average score of 177 out of 200. Fg Off P. H. Thomas and Flt Lt A. T. Burt are to be congratulated upon flying the best sortie of the Command, with a total of 192 and a half points out of 200.' I recall that the targets were respectively a pinpoint, a feature line overlap and a small area cover. 31 Squadron had taken over 541's hangar at Laarbruch.

Don't forget the ground crew, who made all Canberra flying possible. PR7 WT534 with 17 Squadron ground personnel, possibly at RAF Wahn in late 1956. (Glyn Lockett)

PR7s of 31 Squadron in formation.

I competed for the Sassoon Trophy again in November 1957 with my own pilot, Phil Taylor. We were airborne on 5/7/9/11/12/13/14 and 15 November. But the competition was plagued with bad weather and our every sortie was logged either DNCO or DPCO – duty not or partially carried out. Interestingly, on 9/11/12 and 13 November I recorded the same route, 'Jever – Norwich – Manston – Base' and sortie times varied between one hour and 50 minutes to three hours and 15 minutes. The weather was pretty poor some days as we tried to cover the target.

My final Sassoon was in February-March 1958 with Phil. This time there was a lengthy practice period of visual and photographic reconnaissance in the period 20 February to 5 March, with dress rehearsal on 9 March – in the British zone (of Germany) low-flying areas 1 and 6 – and the actual competition on 10 March in British zone low-flying areas 1 and 2. Our practice sortie on 26 February in WT515 was in British zone low-flying areas 5 and 1 and we were airborne for two hours and 55 minutes. On competition day we were airborne 40 minutes. That was my last sortie with 31 Squadron and I never heard the results of the competition.

Formation flying was a rare event on the squadron and I have only four log entries referring to such occasions. On 22 February 1957 I was airborne with Pete Thomas in Canberra PR7 WT515 and logged, 'Formation for air test of 531'. This is interesting because on the day before I had been airborne in WT531 (with pilot Fg Off Eric Davies) for an air test. Why we needed to keep an eye on WT531 on 22 February I can only speculate – so won't! A second formation occasion was on 15 August 1958 when Phil Taylor and I brought WT523 back to Laarbruch from Wildenrath, where we had been detached overnight. My logbook entry reads, 'Wildenrath-Laarbruch and formation'. Three squadron aircraft had been at Wildenrath for 'High Straight', which preceded the 1958 Royal Flush PR squadrons' competition that followed in September. A third formation entry came on 30 October 1958 when Phil and I were airborne in WT523 and I logged 'formation flying plus QGH, GCAs and BABS (blind approach beacon system)'. No information on other squadron aircraft. Perhaps the most likely source of the accompanying formation photograph is 20 November 1956. I was airborne that day with Fg Off Rayner in WT510 for two hours and I logged 'formation fly-past SHAPE HQ Versailles'. Another clue to the date is that the aircraft are uncamouflaged – as they were to be later, reflecting the low-level role of RAF Germany squadrons.

The next exercise that comes to light in my logbook is Exercise Amled on which I flew my first two sorties on 29 March 1957. The purpose of the exercise was to test the Danish air defences and I flew ten Amleds between March 1957 and July 1958. The 31 Squadron ORB noted in January 1957 that Exercise Amled introduced 'intruder sorties in Denmark to exercise them'. The longest Amled sortie (three hours and 15 minutes) was with Fg Off R. E. T. (Dick) Taylor in WT514 on 27 June 1957 – but that trip included local training on return to base. My sortie with Fg Off Sparrow in WT518 on 1 November 1957 was better logged. We were airborne at 1355 and I recorded 'Low level Denmark. BZ low-flying areas and link routes'. I flew two Amled sorties on 28 February 1958 in WT510 with Flt Lt 'Red' Dunningham, but no sortie details. But on 27 March 1958 I flew two Amled sorties with Flt Lt Bromley. We took off in WT519 at 0835 to find target 'F. Dog 304' – and took off again at 1355 in WH773 to find Amled target 'F. Dog 315'. My final Amled sortie was with Phil Taylor in WT515 on 31 July 1958 when we were airborne at 0935 to find a target logged as 'Rail Junction target 6'.

One of my recurring log entries between April 1957 and October 1958 is 'BZ photos 1377'. On 3 and 5 April 1957 I flew two such sorties, and a clue to their purpose comes in my log entry for 11 April 1957 when I logged '1377 Pinpoint Norvenich airfield'. That day I flew a 50-minute sortie in WT519 with Eric Davies. By 4 October 1957 I was getting more focused and logged 'Task 1377' but the sortie was 'DNCO bad weather'. On 10 February 1958 Phil Taylor and I flew WT523 on 'Task 1377 and F95 photo' in a sortie of three hours and 5 minutes. Clarity comes in my sortie of 17 April 1958 with Wg Cdr Kennedy in WH773. Our duty I logged as 'Task 1377 photography of BZ airfield approaches'. Task 1377 formed part of our duty on 13 May 1958 when Phil and I were airborne for three hours and 25 minutes in WT523. Revelation comes in our trip of 7 October 1958 when we flew WH773 on 'Task 1377. BZ airfields 10,000 ft and F95'. And I also logged 'aircraft recalled'. Why? Hard to believe now but we were airborne that day at 1000 and landed at 1120 – only to be airborne again at 1130 to fly Exercise Battle Call. Clearly we taxied in and were handed our target information for 'Primary target Spangdahlem'. This implies that Battle Call was a no-notice exercise.

CHAPTER 9
THE SUEZ CAMPAIGN

In 1956, 13 Squadron became the first Canberra unit in the Mediterranean area, having previously operated Meteor PR10s at Abu Sueir in the Suez Canal Zone. When the British agreed to evacuate the Canal Zone, 13 Squadron moved to Akrotiri in Cyprus where it received its first two Canberras in May 1956.

While 13 Squadron was adapting to its new PR Canberras, President Nasser started making waves in Egypt. He wanted the finance and specialist help to construct an enormous dam on the upper Nile while taking weaponry from the USSR including MiG fighters and Il-28 bombers. Failing to get western support for his Aswan project, Nasser announced on 26 July 1956 that he would nationalise the Suez Canal to use the dues that came from world trade.

George Worrall was on 18 Squadron in July when 'we were designated for Operation Alacrity (a wing of 24 aircraft available to reinforce the Middle East Air Force at 96 hours' notice) and to be trained for shallow dive-bombing in readiness for short-notice deployment

Getting ready for Suez – B6 WH960 of 12 Squadron bombing up at Hal Far, Malta, October 1956. The standard Canberra internal 6,000-lb bomb load comprised two 'triplets' of 1,000-lb bombs. (Peter Green Collection)

overseas. The technique called on the nav/bomb-aimer from his prone position to guide the pilot as he winged over to turn into the target. Once lined up and in a shallow dive, the pilot could then release the bomb load himself. Though we did not know it, we were being earmarked and prepared for the Suez campaign.'

The Anglo-French element was codenamed Operation Musketeer. Five Valiant bomber squadrons participated in Musketeer together with 11 Canberra bomber squadrons – 9, 12, 101 and 109 (all with B6s) based on Malta and 10, 15, 18, 27, 44, 61 and 139 (all with B2s apart from 139 Squadron which operated 12 B6s in the target marker role) from Cyprus. In all, 91 Canberras were assigned to the operation in addition to seven PR7s.

With so many aircraft crammed on Cyprus, fear of a Pearl Harbor attack dictated that the priority was to eliminate the Egyptian air force, if possible on the ground. An NBS-equipped Valiant was to lead each attack and drop a red proximity marker on the selected target. Canberras operating out of Cyprus would then fly in at low level using the light from the proximity markers to identify the actual target and drop green target markers to act as the aiming point for the bomber force. The lead Canberra would direct the main force to drop visually on the green marker. This was not the most accurate way of depositing gravity bombs from around 40,000 ft but outside the range of any Gee-H station, there was no other option.

Phase 1 was to start on 31 October 1956 but knowledge comes before power and from 1 August, 13 Squadron at Akrotiri was augmented by a 58 Squadron detachment from Wyton. By September the 58 Squadron detachment, commanded by Flt Lt Bernie Hunter, consisted of four Canberra PR7s (WH775, WH779, WH801 and WT540) in anticipation of the covert Suez operation. RAF Middle East Command was assured by the UK Chiefs of Staff Committee that the 'chances of detection are very small. Indeed, apart from some misfortune due to engine failure or a fortuitous interception, the risk of interception can be discounted.' Nonetheless, it made sense to be prepared and preliminary aerial reconnaissance started on 20 October when a 58 Squadron Canberra PR7 flew along the Egyptian coast at a height of 30,000 ft. The mission, which had been specially authorised by the Air Ministry, provoked no apparent Egyptian reaction. Anthony Eden later wrote in his memoirs: 'For some time we had been keeping occasional and informal watch on the Canal and Egyptian troop movements. We had done this by means of Canberras flying high and often a little way out to sea. There had never been any attempted interference with these flights and we believed them to be unperceived.' In reality, the EAF was fully aware of them, but had clear instructions from President Nasser not to interfere or provoke the British. 13/58 Squadron's Canberras were not yet permitted to fly over the Egyptian mainland but Anglo-French intelligence staffs were given high-altitude pictures of the Canal Zone taken from USAF Lockheed U-2s operating out of Turkey.

On 28 October, the day before the Israelis invaded, the first 13/58 Squadron sortie captained by Flt Lt G. J. Clark in WJ821 began photographing the Suez Canal Zone. The PR7 was photographing EAF airfields and military movements but the RAF Middle

East Air Force's sole Canberra PR squadron lacked its own film processing and inter-pretation equipment. Films had to be sent to Episkopi to be processed and then brought back to Akrotiri, adding from three to four hours to the analysis timescale.

The following day at 1150, still before Israeli paratroopers began dropping near the Mitla Pass in Sinai, Canberra PR7 WT540 flown by Flt Lt John Field and Fg Off D. J. Lever left Akrotiri. It landed back safely at 1600 despite being fired upon by 'ineffectual AAA'. In Prime Minister Eden's words, 'late on the evening of the 29th I had a talk with the Minister of Defence and the Chief of Air Staff. I told them how important it was for us to have information upon which we could depend for certain, as early as possible the next day. A dawn reconnaissance was ordered by four Canberras flying at a great height, 30-40,000 feet. They would locate and, if possible, photograph the opposing forces. The Canberras carried out their instructions.' Thus it was on 30 October that four Canberra PR7s flew along the Suez Canal at 35,000 ft. Two PR7s were intercepted and attacked during these early morning sorties. One crew, consisting of Fg Off Jim Campbell and Fg Off R. J. Toseland (flying WH801), saw cannon shells from a MiG-15 flash past both sides of their cockpit. The Canberra was hit in its port elevator but managed to escape. The second aircraft (WT540), flown by Flt Lt Hunter with Fg Off Urquhart-Pullen as his navigator, was also intercepted and fired on, but not hit.

The crews of 13 Squadron, most of whom had been attached from 58 Squadron, had carried out previous trials with a shufti-scope, fitted in the mounting unit used by the periscopic sextant for astro-navigation. This enabled the navigator to watch the rear of the Canberra for contrails of attacking aircraft.

As BERNIE HUNTER recalled:

One of the problems of flying the PR Canberra on operations was that the pilot was involved very much in flying the aircraft as a steady platform for photography. The navigator was 100 per cent involved in taking the photographs and making sure the cameras were pointing at the piece of ground or territory that he wanted to take. So we had, as crew members, complained that the PR Canberra was not a good aircraft when it came to looking after your own tail.

Due to the MiG interceptions, HQ decided it would be safer to fly operational sorties in future with a lookout occupying the navigator's normal position, a third crew member with a periscope mounted aft of the aircraft. He was supposed to be there doing nothing but protecting the tail from attack. The periscope was very much tem-porary equipment. I think all our aircraft were so fitted, but I think it ran foul of AHQ Levant. HQ Mediterranean was directing the operational set-up through a team of people they had brought out from London. There was a little cell formed, particularly on the recce side, and these people were making the operational decisions regarding the squadron. AHQ Levant was in fact omitted from the operational chain. Therefore,

AHQ Levant was not involved with the operational control of the squadron during the fracas and the lookout man and a rear-seat periscope, call it what you will, were not there with its authority. AHQ Levant felt it should have been informed. ▓

The opening attack was to be made on Cairo West by Valiants and Canberras from Malta, together with Canberras from Cyprus, to prevent Il-28s from getting airborne. Four Canberra B6s of 139 Squadron lifted off from Nicosia at 1715 hrs.

PAUL MALLORIE was OC 139 Squadron at the time.

Events leading up to the Suez affair for 139 Squadron began in October 1955, some ten-and-a-half months before the event. In that month, the Canberra B6 was cleared for the first time to drop 4½-inch parachute flares. The aircraft was already cleared to drop 250-lb target indicators, and the role of the squadron at Suez was to be target marking – providing the aiming point for main force Canberra and Valiant crews and, in the event, indicating the dropping zone for parachute forces near Port Said.

In December 1955, the squadron was a main force Canberra unit. In the face of the current threat at that time we were trained for high-level bombing using G-H as a navigating and aiming system. Unlike the rest of the Canberra force, except for 109 Squadron, we had no visual bombing capability; the bomb aimer's position had been taken out and replaced by a sideways-looking radar called Blue Shadow, which gave the navigator a print-out of radar returns at 90° to the right of the aircraft up to a distance, I think, of about 60 miles, depending on the height. We had no operational directives on the use of this equipment, but presumed that all would be revealed when necessary, and we used the equipment partly because we had ground crew who were trained to service it and partly because it was quite fun to use.

139 Squadron had inherited, from its wartime Mosquito forebears, a low-level, shallow-dive target-marking role. That had regressed over the years since the war to occasional visits to the range at Wainfleet by day, and occasionally by night. At night it was well lit and we dropped details of practice bombs from the theoretical 30° dive. In practice we found that the steeper you went, the better the results and we had no bombsights and were just fortunate there were no casualties. The navigation problem was one of distinguishing between the lights of the range, and those of The Prussian Queen, which was a nearby pub which had unwisely invested in a set of floodlights.

In the first months of 1956, the main task for the squadron was to improve its G-H results and to qualify crews at increasing altitude. In March 1956, a detachment was flown to Libya to devise a low-level target-illumination and marking technique. On our own initiative we tried out low-level Blue Shadow navigation as a means of reaching targets and, as I recall, we had no operational or intelligence staff guidance and were left entirely to our own devices. Fortunately, we had a supernumerary squadron leader,

Canberra B2s of 61 Squadron en route from Cyprus to Egypt during the Suez campaign. The pilot of WH907, which sports black and yellow 'Suez stripes', was Fg Off M. Freeston. The black semicircle in the foreground is the DV window in the cockpit of the pilot taking the photograph. (Peter Green Collection)

Terry Kearns, who had wartime-marking experience. But years had passed since the end of the war, and I don't think it was realised how operationally naïve we were. For the short trial we had, we were more concerned with the technical problems of lighting a target in sufficient time to lay down markers, than with problems of our own vulnerability. Our trials were curtailed (they unfortunately interrupted the Easter weekend) but we did develop a procedure for a technique involving two illuminating and two marking aircraft, and that technique was modified in August when mixed loads of flares and target indicators were approved and four aircraft in the marking team then each carried eight flares and two target indicators. Navigation was a problem, and it was decided by higher authority to add a third crew member to assist with low-level navigation – essentially map-reading – and to improve our flexibility the bombsight was reinstalled and some training was done in visual bombing at medium altitude. The third crew member had to sit on the jump seat alongside the pilot, wearing one of those harnesses and, somewhere down in the rubbish, there was a parachute that he was supposed to clip on.

In the meantime, life on the squadron continued. In April we took part in a massed fly-past for the benefit of Messrs Bulganin and Khrushchev, and in July a similar exercise on the occasion of Her Majesty the Queen's visit to Marham. In August, there was a full-scale exercise when we acted as markers for the main force, hence the complaints that we were disturbing the ducks. We were assisted by a single marker, dropped from high altitude by a Valiant using its 'highly sophisticated equipment', but found that the lack of this equipment made this more of a distraction than an assistance. About this time, we provided training for 18 Squadron, which was then under Sqn Ldr Alan Chamberlain, which converted to the marker role for the Suez operation. In October, as the political tension was building up, half of the squadron and all of its ground crew were in Malta on exercises which included taking off with full bomb loads and fuel, as training as a main force squadron. At the end of this detachment we were on our way home when we were ordered to Cyprus. At Cyprus, we were finally brought up to full strength with 12 aircraft and 14 three-man crews, compared to the nine aircraft and a dozen two-man crews that we had been a year before. In Cyprus, during the 12 days before operations began, the last aircrew members joined the squadron and the ground crew was brought up from our normal 60 to 145. So we had a 75 per cent increase in aircrew and 140 per cent increase in ground crew. We then had aircrews that had been drafted in from five squadrons and a supporting ground crew hurriedly assembled from four different stations.

As squadron commander, I was concerned about the lack of training for the newly-formed aircrews and the unknown capability of many of the ground crew. On 29 or 30 October we received our first intelligence briefing. I would like to emphasise that we had no briefing or consideration of defences when we were developing the marking technique which was about to be put to the test. Intelligence material, certainly at our level, was surprisingly sparse; we had very dim, rather foggy, pictures of airfields. The initial operations were planned, and then delayed one day. The following night, as the lead aircraft (and for that particular target it was Flt Lt John Slater) was about to leave dispersal there was a hammering on his aircraft door, which was opened and he was informed that his target had been changed. He was told then to attack Almaza, rather than Cairo West. It was just fortunate that Almaza was marked on his map, as the main force was already en route from Malta to Cyprus. Curiously, the markers would take off from Cyprus after the main force had gone, partly because we were flying low level and we didn't have to climb up and form up; hence the motto, 'I must hurry and catch up with them, for I am their leader!'

On that occasion, the revised target was attacked successfully and, fortunately, air-to-air communications worked well – and there was no opposition. The squadron operated between 31 October and 5 November. A number of airfields were marked for night attack, and on one occasion, the second attack on Luxor, at last light. On that occasion the marker aircraft carried a mixed load of target indicators and 1,000-lb bombs which were proximity fused. I'm sure that Boscombe knew nothing about that. Having dive-bombed with target indicators (TI) in the last light, we were supposed then to see the raid through and add our contribution of straight and level attacks with the thousand pounders. By that time, the gyros were completely toppled, the navigators confused and the bombsights useless. So we made dive-bombing attacks on the parked 'Beagle' aircraft (i.e. Il-28s) which were there, with high explosives. There had been some over-provision of marker capability so the squadron provided crews and aircraft from time to time to augment the main force. The last squadron operation was marking the Suez dropping zone near Port Said on 5 November. Thereafter we flew on local training at low intensity until we returned to base on 23 December, just in time for Christmas. During this period one aircraft, which had collected a bullet hole during the operation, was to be flown home by a ferry crew. Shortly after taking off it returned to Nicosia on one engine and crashed on landing; regrettably there were no survivors.

My experience on 139 Squadron was far from typical. Most squadrons maintained their personnel and performed, more or less, in the role for which they had been trained, apart from 18 Squadron which retained its personnel but learnt the new technique of marking in a fairly short time. At the time I was, and in retrospect I remain, astonished at the rather casual way we were left to develop the marking system which was suitable for Canberra aircraft but without any high-level guidance which I can recall, apart from clearance to drop armaments. I remain surprised at the way in which the squadron was able to absorb, without serious difficulty, new crew members and ground crew to within a few days of flying operational sorties. Indeed the development of the technique and the reorganisation of the squadron appeared to me then as slightly haphazard. Yet there must have been sound long-range contingency planning to clear the aircraft to drop flares in the first place ten-and-a half months before Suez, and to ship the flares and markers needed for the trial experiments in North Africa nine months before the event.

A note on morale. Morale rose with the pace of work and the opportunity which came to exercise initiative. It then fell with the uncertainty and apparent pointlessness of the long delay between the end of operations and the return home. To a few, certainly, and perhaps to many more within the squadron, the Suez affair appeared at the time as being politically questionable, but this was not generally discussed, not often mentioned in the normal way, as we had the deeply ingrained tradition that we were part of an apolitical service. It was assumed that there were intelligent and national considerations of which we were not aware. The sight of the Soviet military aircraft and the other equipment which was to be seen in Egypt once the operation began seemed to confirm that view. That, then, was the Suez operation from this squadron commander's point of view.

CLIVE ELTON was one of Paul Mallorie's junior pilots.

I joined the RAF in October 1953 on the short service commission and went through flying training on the piston Provost and Vampire. I elected to go to Canberras rather than Hunters but there was a big hold up at Bassingbourn so I went to fly Hastings at Dishforth. Then it was back to Feltwell and thence to Worksop to fly the Meteor. I did the pilots' bombing course on the Varsity at Lindholme, where I sat in the right-hand seat learning the patter. Then to Bassingbourn just as the tail trim runaway was impacting. I finally finished the OCU in the spring of 1956 whereupon I joined 139 Squadron at Binbrook on 29 May 1956.

At that time 139 Squadron was the only marker squadron in Bomber Command. Training involved visual bombing with the observer in the nose using the standard bomb-sight, Gee-H bombing controlled by the navigator plotter and shallow dive-bombing which was very much the pilot's responsibility (and delight!). We did shallow dive-bombing similar to that in World War II – it was very low-tech with no navigational aids to assist us at all.

We used a number of different bombing ranges around the country such as Donna Nook, Jurby, Wainfleet and Chesil Bank. My crew became operational just in time for a detachment to Luqa on 22 September 1956. Returning to Binbrook on 18 October, I was about to set out for home when at 1900 we were recalled to the squadron to be informed that as an Alacrity squadron we were to depart the next morning for Nicosia. Although very junior, (or perhaps for that very reason) I was to be first away at 0700 on 19 October.

There was a shambolic air about much of the Suez campaign. DEREK HOPKINS was a pilot on IX Squadron tasked with bombing Abu Sueir airfield from Malta on 31 October.

At Hal Far we were issued with an escape kit, which comprised a silk map of North Africa, a length of wire that allegedly could cut through prison bars, six gold sovereigns, a .38 revolver and 12 rounds. I later found out that my gun was u/s and would only have been useful for throwing at potential captors.

The trip to Abu Sueir was five hours and 15 minutes return, with four thousand-pounders. To have a chance of getting home we had to conserve fuel so we cruise-climbed all the way there and back, up to 55,000 ft, which gave us temporary rheumatism in all joints. Our bomb-aiming computer only operated up to 25,000 ft, and we were to drop from 44,000 ft, above anything the Egyptian Meteors could reach. So, we had to go back to WW2 techniques of extremely careful and accurate straight-and-level flying while Sam Slatter, the bomb aimer, used the sighting head and the written table of settings provided.

It was a great tribute to Sam, and to our training, that we had a direct hit, two bombs either side of the marker flare, and we had good results again two nights later, bombing the Huckstep Barracks in Cairo.

B6s at Hal Far, Malta in October 1956. Eight aircraft from 101 Squadron are in the front row and the second row is predominantly 12 Squadron. (Peter Green Collection)

As John Slater said to waiting journalists after the initial Almaza raid, 'we were in fact 30 seconds late after a 25-minute flight. With other Canberras we flew high over the target. There was no fighter resistance but there was some light flak up to 8,000 ft. The airfield we attacked was beautifully lit up. There were many planes on it.' Slater's crew were known as Marker 1 and with his bomb aimer, Fg Off Geoffrey Harrop, they were expected to drop their eight 4½-inch flares at 8,000 ft, then break to port and orbit at 4,000 ft. Marker 2, Flt Lt N. M. North's crew in WT369, followed suit before orbiting at 5,000 ft. Two follow-on 139 Squadron aircraft carried just 12 flares each. Once the target was illuminated and identified, the marker crews went into a shallow dive to place their target indicators: Slater and North's aircraft carried two TIs each. In the words of Flt Sgt Mike Heather, the Marker 2 navigator on WT369, 'the Egyptian gunners seemed to shoot at the flares rather than us, so marking the target was easy, although by the time we finished all the lights had been turned out'. The other two marker aircraft, WJ768 and WJ778, released their flares over the target that had been identified, whereupon seven Canberras from 10, 15, 44 and 139 Squadrons dropped 41 1,000-lb bombs. On landing back at Nicosia, the crews reported that the marker was on the aiming point and that their bombs had straddled hangars, runway and hardstandings. Unfortunately, they were on the wrong airfield because the force had bombed Cairo International by mistake. Although the proximity of Almaza to Cairo International was a contributory factor, in the words of Air Cdre David Lee who was then secretary to the Chiefs of Staff Committee, 'the mistake would never have been made by experienced crews had the normal time for flight planning been available to them'. It was an inauspicious beginning.

CLIVE ELTON's first two operational sorties were to Luxor where the Egyptians had moved their aircraft believing that they were out of RAF range.

A night raid on 1 November was highly successful from the marking point of view. The team consisted of four aircraft namely Marker 1 (who was also the bomber leader, in this case Sqn Ldr Terry Kearns), Marker 2, Flare 1 and Flare 2. We were very fortunate in having Terry Kearns, with his masses of WW2 experience, leading us young guys and we departed from Nicosia at, I think, two-minute intervals (it may have been one minute) with a similar spacing for time on target. Marker 1 and 2 each had six flares and two 500-lb target indicators but with target marking, you first had to find the target. Marker 1 would fly in at 8,000 ft from a known point – in this case, a bend in the Nile – with flare release after a timed run. The two marker aircraft then dived through the flares to drop their TIs as near as possible to the centre of the airfield. Red and green were the two colours used – I never knew whether the colour chosen had any particular significance. As very much the junior boy, I was Flare 2. Flare aircraft just had 12 parachute flares which we were to drop either on time or if the target was already illuminated, to back up those already floating down. A 30-40° dive was steep enough with the nav shouting out every 100 ft in the descent. You had to release at 1,200 ft and you dropped when the target appeared just above the cockpit coaming. Marker 1 had to stick around until he reached his fuel limits but I just headed back to Nicosia.

Although the marking was accurate, the main force proved ineffective from 30,000 ft with most of their bombs falling in the desert so it was decided to repeat the raid in daylight the next day. CLIVE ELTON again:

In daylight you kept the target just to the left of the nose and at the right moment you dived and rolled from 4,000 ft. When dropping a 25-lb practice bomb over a UK range, we were accurate to within 25 yards. For the daylight Luxor raid, the marker aircraft carried a mixed load of TIs and 1,000-lb bombs. We (nominally the two flare aircraft) had six 1,000-lb bombs which we dropped from 10,000 ft using the visual bombing technique. The main force bombed from high level again.

We knew our target in the morning because the BBC announced which places Egyptians should stay away from. On 3 November I teamed up with John Slater and we flew at low level over sea and sand, by day, to mark and bomb Almaza Camp. We each had two 500-lb TIs and three 1,000-lb bombs. This included some dive-bombing during which the Egyptians had the impertinence to shoot at us with what I presume was light ack-ack. It did produce puffs of black smoke nearby, but not too near.

The last 139 Squadron operation marked the Suez dropping zone near Port Said on 5 November. CLIVE ELTON concludes:

That was it for me, just as we were all getting into the swing of it. However, we stayed on in Nicosia until departing back to Binbrook on 22 December.

Once the shooting started, the Allies were keen to verify reports that Russian MiGs were being delivered to secret airstrips in the Syrian desert. There was a regular Canberra PR 'milk run' over Latakia, Aleppo, Homs, to within 5 km of Damascus and then a turn westward over Beirut back towards Cyprus. The PR7s generally followed the same flight path to photograph Syrian, Iraqi and Lebanese airfields and shortly after 0800, the Syrian frontier post at Abu Kamal on the River Euphrates reported a British Canberra was operating at extreme range from Cyprus. Lt Hafiz al-Asad, the future president of Syria, was sent in pursuit but he was only able to open fire from a distance before the Canberra escaped towards Cyprus.

At the time, the Syrian air force had one squadron of Meteor F8s, mainly based at al-Mezze airfield south-west of Damascus. The PR7 crew pursued by al-Asad had found their targets covered with cloud and on their return they reported being 'chased by Meteors in unidentified markings'. Despite having lost the precious element of surprise, Air HQ in Cyprus insisted that a second Canberra immediately be sent to get the required photographs of Syrian airfields and the oil pipeline. Bernie Hunter decided to fly this sortie with Roy Urquhart-Pullen as his navigator in WH799. The third member of the crew was Sam Small, another Canberra pilot, who had come out to reinforce the squadron during the Suez crisis and who provided another pair of eyes up front.

In BERNIE HUNTER's words:

We went off (at 1230) to photograph Riyaq (in Lebanon), Aleppo (Nairab air base), and Al-Rashid (near Baghdad in Iraq). Navigation was extremely good, under cloud cover, then towards 12,000 ft, then down to 10,000 ft slowly in order to get overlaps. We were heading towards Damascus, when to our horror – blue sky! Normally a pilot's dream, but under operating conditions we were, to say the least, in a very unenviable position. My first reaction was to climb on full power to get back into cloud cover, as it would have been absolutely fatal if we tried to go over Damascus airfield at that height and speed. At about the same time Sam Small warned of a pair of Meteors coming in from port or starboard, I can't remember which. I had to turn into their attack. I think it was port, I can't remember. So there were three factors in this particular problem, none of which was helpful to the others as no matter where the Meteors were coming from, I had to turn towards them. It went on like this for a few minutes, which seemed like several hours, and during the first attack almost certainly we did not get hit; then Sam said almost immediately after the first attack, with us still climbing, another pair (probably the same pair) were coming in, so we turned again. I turned hard towards them and that's when the starboard engine was hit.

I had been calling Roy, who was in the prone position to take photographs, to come back to the Rumbold seat. He got the message, I think, but did not come back. Eventually, it got to the stage where I was rapidly losing control of the situation, one engine out, still burning. I told Sam to get out, to eject, and from the rear navigation position he ejected quite safely. We were still under attack and I started the desperate business of trying to get hold of Roy. I never did contact Roy on the R/T and, as far as I know, he must have gone back to the rear navigation position to try to eject. Since the ejection seat had gone, I assume he tried to bale out. I am not sure, but I think I heard a big thud on the aircraft, which could have been Roy's body hitting the tail plane. I suspect it was. I then ejected and it seemed only seconds before I hit the ground and broke my left ankle. The sequence of events was very quick so I couldn't possibly estimate how low I was, but can remember thinking at the time: if I don't get out now I won't get out at all.

I didn't know whether I got out over Lebanon or not [the Canberra crashed in the Bekaa Valley in Lebanon]; my mind was revolving round the fact that if I'm in Syria they're not going to be very friendly. But Lebanon was largely a Christian country although Arabs lived there. A crowd got together almost immediately they saw the parachute. We were not armed since I failed to see much use for a pistol with six bullets, and that became our saviour in fact, as I was surrounded by people, mainly young kids and old men who automatically assumed I was an Israeli as I was wearing normal flight kit – overalls. The crowd grew very quickly; they got sticks and started to hit me – I received a number of injuries on my hands as I tried to protect my face, but soon, thank the Lord, I heard somebody speaking English and shouting at the youngsters to keep away. It turned out he was a Christian teacher at the local school. I said to him, tell these people I am not an Israeli, I am RAF. He eventually got his way and simmered things down. To this day I'd like to thank him; without his help, I might not be here. I was handed over to the military at the border post and interrogated by a Syrian. I convinced him I was doing weather recce over the Lebanon and had got lost. That was all that happened for some little time, until I saw Sam brought in. 'Weather recce, got lost', was all I was able to say. Heat of situation removed.

The two survivors were taken to a hospital in Beirut from where, after a visit by the British deputy air attaché in Lebanon, both were spirited away in a small boat to Cyprus. As Bernie feared, Roy Urquhart-Pullen was killed when the Canberra crashed. This would mark the last time that an RAF crew in an RAF aircraft was shot down in air-to-air combat.

CHAPTER 10
NUCLEAR TRIALS

The first British operational nuclear weapon was Blue Danube with a yield of around 10 kilotons (kt). A working party on the operational use of atomic weapons chaired by the MoD's chief scientist assessed that Blue Danubes would not be powerful enough to destroy the UK's primary targets in the USSR 'such as airfields or ports with a single bomb…The possession of a bomb in the 5-10 mt range offers this possibility and would go a long way towards overcoming the need for improved terminal accuracy.' On 16 June 1954, the British government decided 'to initiate a programme for the production of hydrogen bombs'.

A Bomber Command memorandum issued on 12 May 1956 stated that live nuclear tests overseas would begin with Operation Mosaic involving ground-detonated bursts at Monte Bello off Western Australia. This would be followed by Operation Buffalo, an air drop of an atomic weapon at Maralinga, South Australia and then Operation Grapple air drops over the Pacific Ocean. The principal bomber forces involved in these trials were to be: 76 Squadron Canberra B6s to support Mosaic, Buffalo and Grapple; 100 Squadron Canberra PR7s to support Grapple only, and 49 Squadron to supply two Valiant B1s for Buffalo and eight for Grapple. After Grapple, the UK expected to have enough information to produce

B6s of 76 Squadron at Weston Zoyland in October 1956 on the eve of their departure for the Montebello atomic test in Australia. 76 Squadron was the special air sampling unit. (Peter Green Collection)

a free-fall H-bomb for the V Force, a megaton warhead for the Blue Steel stand-off missile and a warhead for the Blue Streak ballistic missile.

The first Mosaic nuclear tests used a Canberra B2 (WH738) with a modified starboard wing-tip tank to trap nuclear particles. What was known as Operation Hotbox provided valuable experience about aircrew safety and aircraft contamination, and 1323 Flight was then established at Wyton with six B2s as a dedicated nuclear sampling unit. In February 1954 it deployed four B2s to RAAF Laverton to sample tests conducted by the US at Bikini Atoll. During what was known as Operation Dogstar, WH738 went missing over the Pacific with the loss of three crew.

On 1 November 1955, 1323 Flight was re-designated 542 Squadron and moved to Weston Zoyland near Bridgwater, Somerset, to prepare for the next series of Mosaic tests in Australia. 76 Squadron had re-formed at Wittering with Canberra B2s in December 1953 and it too moved to Weston Zoyland on 15 November 1955 to become a specialist air-sampling unit. 76 Squadron started converting to B6s in December 1955 and by the following May there was a 76 Squadron detachment at Edinburgh Field near Adelaide. On 11 October 1956, Sqn Ldr Ted Flavell's crew in Valiant WZ366 dropped a Blue Danube 'within 110 yards of the aiming point' while 76 Squadron measured the yield of the atmospheric nuclear detonation.

A survey in 1955 selected Captain Cook's Christmas Island as the best base for the Grapple tests and by April 1957, this piece of coral (the highest point of which was only 25 ft above sea level) boasted two runways, hardstandings and accommodation for a Task Group of 1,300 men. The Bomber Command element of the Task Group were to be responsible for the air drops, cloud sampling, high-level meteorological reconnaissance and cloud tracking, plus high-level PR of each burst. Canberras were also to rush cloud samples back to the UK. It was a firm requirement to obtain post-detonation samples from 'as great a height as is possible' and 'it is hoped to obtain the samples in the Canberra B6 in the band 50,000 to 53,000 ft'. At the other extreme, the Canberras' mission was to reconnoitre ground zero from a height of 2,000 ft within 15 minutes of detonation 'to assist with the immediate assessment of correct weapon functioning'.

The first live drop of a British thermonuclear weapon was made by Valiant XD818 on 15 May 1957, captained by Wg Cdr Ken Hubbard. Ground zero for the burst was 400 miles south of Christmas Island near Malden Island at 45,000 ft. As he approached release, Hubbard put XD818 into a slight dive and immediately after release he rolled into a turn to port, through 130° at a constant measurement on the accelerometer of 1.7 g at 0.76 m. When Hubbard finally rolled out, and as the weapon detonated at 8,000 ft, the slant range between XD818 and the air burst was 8.65 nm. As the nuclear cloud mushroomed up the pilot of the 100 Squadron Canberra photographing from a safe distance was heard to remark over the R/T, 'If you do that again, you'll have to marry me!'

Besides XD818 there were seven other aircraft airborne in the test area – a 'Grandstand' Valiant (to give crews experience of flash and blast from a thermonuclear weapon), five 76

Squadron air sampler Canberra B6s and a reconnaissance/meteorological Canberra PR7 of 100 Squadron. In the first B6 the Sample Controller (Air), Air Cdre D. A. Wilson, assessed the heights and dimensions of the nuclear cloud and made the final decision, based on radiation-measuring instruments, that it was safe for sampling aircraft to penetrate the cloud. Secondly, a radio link and target recce B6 was halfway between Christmas and Malden Islands in case of ground communications failure to and from the Joint Operations Centre. Once the Valiant was on the bombing run, this B6 orbited 76 miles from the target and just after release, it began a maximum-rate descent towards Malden Island, levelling at 2,000 ft. It then continued towards the target to see whether the bomb had in fact exploded at the correct altitude by looking for abnormal sea waves and fires on Malden Island, and by taking radiation measurements. Then there was the primary sampler which took off in time to arrive in the target area 30 minutes after the burst. Receiving the cloud's position from the airborne controller, it aimed to penetrate about an hour after bomb burst. The crew took particulate and gaseous samples until the cumulative dose rate reached 6 roentgens, and this B6 carried limited fuel so that the aircraft could reach as high as possible. A secondary sampler followed the same profile 30 minutes later and the fifth B6 acted as reserve sampler in case the primary or secondary went u/s or later samples were needed – it was only used on the first Grapple. OC 100 Squadron, Sqn Ldr Douggie Hammatt, with Flt Lt D. Andrew as navigator, were responsible in their PR7 for weather reconnaissance and post-burst photography.

The first Grapple trial was a disappointment in that the 10,000-lb two-stage weapon exploded with a force of 300 kt rather than the predicted yield of about 1 mt. 58 Squadron also lost a Canberra PR7 during the final approach in inclement weather at RCAF Goose Bay, Labrador, on 16 May 1957 when Plt Off John Loomes and Fg Off T. R. 'Monty' Montgomery sustained fatal injuries. The PR7 had apparently arrived over the Goose at 48,000 ft after a four-hour and 22-minute flight from Namao, near Edmonton, Alberta. The crew, doubtless under pressure to get the precious samples back to the UK as quickly as possible, had had no proper sleep in the previous 26 hours and no proper meal for the previous 18 hours, and they made their airfield approach in very adverse weather conditions.

For 100 Squadron navigator **JOHN CLUBB**:

> 8 November 1957 was, I suppose, one of the high points of my life so far, when, at precisely 1747 GMT, the equivalent of several million tons of high explosives went off about 25 miles away from where we were orbiting. This was Grapple X, the fourth air-dropped H-bomb in the series of tests flown from Christmas Island, and we were flying at 43,000 ft in a Canberra PR7 in a predetermined orbit waiting to photograph the development of the nuclear fireball.
>
> Grapple X followed on from Grapples in May and June of the same year. I had been on these operations too, but the visual impact for me was unspectacular because the three bombs of that series had been dropped off Malden Island – 400 miles south of

Christmas Island. My part with my pilot, Frank Stokes, had been to obtain high-level wind and weather information post-burst and to photograph the – by this time – much decayed nuclear cloud, so we had missed the really spectacular part. Grapple X was very much more personal and impressive.

For me the story began late in 1956 at RAF Wyton when 82 Squadron disbanded and overnight its crews and Canberra PR7 aircraft became 100 Squadron Reconnaissance Detachment. All crews were volunteers for the operation and the aircraft were extensively modified with navigation equipment (Doppler Green Satin, ground position indicator and the Marconi radio compass) to help us to navigate over long stretches of water and over the United States where we had to be able to fly airways using radio compass reporting points. Long-range high-frequency voice radio equipment (HFRT) was also fitted to allow us to pass position reports and – our main role during the tests – weather information to the forecasters. We also had a side-facing camera for cloud (normal and nuclear) photography.

Most of our flying from Wyton during the winter of 1956 and the spring of '57 was to test our new equipment and to practise navigating over long sea legs, windfinding and use of HFRT. In those days, flights across the Atlantic by operational aircraft were rare and few of us on the squadron had had this experience in any aircraft – let alone a jet. Consequently, it was with not a little trepidation that I donned my immersion suit (another first) on 24 April 1957 for the first leg from Wyton to Aldergrove, Northern Ireland, to top up with fuel, then to Goose Bay in Labrador. Incidentally, after that first leg, we never wore the immersion suits again. It was too uncomfortable – and we didn't have much confidence in their lifesaving qualities.

From Goose we flew to Travis AFB in California via Namao (Edmonton, Canada), then the Pacific crossing to Hickam AFB, Honolulu – 2,100 miles against the wind – which often turned into a 100 mph-plus jet stream, about which little was known in those days. For Grapple X we had a fairly dramatic flight, arriving at Hickam short of fuel and virtually out of oxygen to a very relieved welcome from the met staff. They weren't half as relieved as we were after a flight lasting six hours and 40 minutes – over an hour more than our flight plan time based on forecast winds.

The flight from Honolulu to Christmas Island was nice and short. The radio beacon at Christmas Island was pretty weak, as was VHF radio reception, so navigation had to be accurate. On first sight from the air I was impressed with the size of the island – around 26 miles long and about 10 miles across at its widest. A typical tropical lagoon and white beaches galore – very much as I had expected, except no grass skirts. Hot, very hot, but not too humid. A fair number of coconut palms but not much else seemed to grow there. The whiteness of the coral was impressive, and we soon learned that it reflected the sunlight most effectively – and could cause serious sunburn to the unwary. During a two-month stay, most of us soon became acclimatised, but even late in the detachment there were some cases of severe sunburn for people who stayed out too long in the sunlight.

We slept, worked, ate and drank in tents and, despite frequent showers during the initial operation I don't recall getting uncomfortably wet. Also, although there were occasions when the runway was unusable after a tropical downpour, it cleared quickly and we were diverted only once for that reason.

The day after we arrived we were off on a five-hour weather sortie which entailed cruise climbing to 45,000 ft and starting a 12-minute windfinding cycle, reporting the wind, temperature and visual assessment of cloud cover to Joint Operations Centre at Christmas Island. Often we would use the few tiny islands in the area as turning points and, when visibility allowed, we took vertical photographs of the islands of Malden, Jarvis, Starbuck, Palmyra, Fanning etc. to prove that we'd managed to be on track at least part of the time. What a difference a satellite position indicator would have made. Generally, the work-up flights went well, with a few snags caused by the Doppler equipment's inability to lock on when the surface wind speed was insufficient to roughen up the sea.

Intervals between sorties were filled with the almost daily operational briefings. So frequent and so detailed that, by the time the day of the first drop came, each crew had a clear idea of what the others' roles were, what time they would take off and where they would be at any given time. We knew that 'sniff boss' and 'sniffs' 1, 2 and 3 were the Canberra B6s which would fly through the cloud and obtain samples which courier Canberra PR7s from our squadron or 58 Squadron would ferry back to the UK within 24 hours of the drop. We knew that the 'search' and 'lookout' call signs belonged to the Shackletons which were searching the danger area for ships unaware that history was about to be made (they found one during Grapple X) also obtaining weather information at low level and taking post-burst photographs. We also knew that the search and rescue Whirlwind helicopters and the Transport Command Hastings and Dakotas – and the DDT-spraying Austers – would also be performing their important support roles before, during and after the tests. And, of course, we knew off by heart our weather tasks in the days and hours before and after the drop and photo during the minutes following the explosion.

On the day of the first drop – 15 May 1957, my 28th birthday – everyone not directly connected with the operation was moved as far as possible from the airfield end of the island in case the Valiant carrying the bomb crashed on take-off. All 3,000 or so people on the island had to be accounted for before the Valiant could start its take-off run. Once it was safely airborne we resumed our normal activities, but kept ourselves aware of events 400 miles to the south, just in case the 'chain reaction' predicted by some of the tabloid newspapers did materialise and the world did the opposite! The progress of the operation around Malden Island was relayed to Christmas Island and broadcast over the island's PA system.

That the end of the world didn't happen was just one more reason for a fairly good party that night. Spare time – what little there was between rehearsals and live drops – was spent fishing, sunbathing (the lagoon wasn't really deep enough, nor safe for swimming) by day. In the evenings, Watneys and Tennents ruled, although there was very little, if any, overindulgence – at least until the final drop was over.

The Task Force commander – AVM W. E. Oulton – established a tradition whereby, at weekends or stand-downs, he and the senior officials of the three services and the senior scientists would tour the messes and join in the festivities. I believe this had a huge effect on morale – even though morale was generally good anyway. The opportunity to talk informally with the very top brass about this very special operation was unique for most of us and our guests always gave a good account of themselves. I will always remember a conversation a small group of us had with Dr William (later Sir William) Cook – the scientific director – one Saturday evening. We were asking him how he could be sure that the explosion just off the end of Christmas Island the following week wouldn't damage the camp or those of us on the island. After a complex scientific explanation of over pressures, air density, dissipation of forces etc. he said, 'Anyway, I'll be a lot nearer the burst than you people will,' – and walked away, hands behind his back with all his fingers crossed!

Finally, on 8 November 1957, Brian Taylor and I were called from our evacuation positions where we were expecting shortly to feel the heat of the flash on our backs, to take over as last-minute substitutes for 'Photo 1' – Sqn Ldr Monaghan and Flt Lt John Pomford – whose oxygen was running out much too quickly as they prepared to take up their orbit for the Valiant bomb run. We were airborne pretty quickly and just managed to climb to our operating height in time for a last-minute drift and ground-speed check for the Valiant bomb aimer before taking up our orbit for post-burst photography. The tension as the Valiant started its live bomb run was like nothing I had felt before. To prevent flash blindness we faced away from ground zero just before the bomb left the Valiant, then closed our eyes and covered them with our hands as the bomb was falling and burst time approached. Despite these precautions and the fact that my small window was fully covered by a curtain, it was impossible not to see the flash of the explosion 25 miles away as a brilliant white light (some people saw the bones of their hands as if x-rayed). After 20 or so more seconds the operations controller gave the order that we could open our eyes and look towards the explosion.

I must say that when I saw the red and black fireball rising above its black stalk (before the characteristic white stalk and mushroom cloud developed) my first thought was that someone must have miscalculated and we would soon be heading north to Hawaii as the island would not be available for landing. My second thought, as I saw the dark concentric rings of blast waves coming up towards us, was that we wouldn't be flying at all after they had hit us. Then the training took over and we had to concentrate on taking the photographs as the fireball developed. As it happened, the

Shackleton and Valiants on the pan at Christmas Island.

scientists hadn't miscalculated, Christmas Island was undamaged. The blast waves just gave us a gentle nudge and we took some very good photographs. Six days later we were on our way back home.

The weather played a part in several difficult situations experienced by 100 Squadron and 58 Squadron aircraft. A double flame-out caused by a combination of extremely cold temperatures and turbulence at height, another similar 'nearly' when we found ourselves still in turbulence and cloud at 52,000 ft with an outside temperature of minus 85 degrees. We suffered a split undercarriage hydraulic jack, possibly due to the extreme cold at height, but fortunately we had got our wheels down and landed at Canton Island before all the fluid drained away. Another of our Canberras was less fortunate and landed wheels-up at Christmas Island.

Sqn Ldr Douggie Hammatt, our detachment commander on Grapple, had a hair-raising ride when an unforecast jet stream, failure of navigation equipment and underpowered ground radio at Christmas Island combined to leave them 'temporarily unsure of their position'. Thanks to good luck and good airmanship, they eventually landed at Christmas Island with almost dry tanks. A similar incident almost led to the loss of two VIPs, William Cook and Dennis Wilson, flying from Christmas Island to Honolulu by courtesy of 76 Squadron. Their Canberra B6 landed with dry tanks – on a disused dirt airstrip on the island of Maui. It says a lot for the training and flexibility of the crews involved that none of these 'near-misses' turned into anything worse.

Many years later I still feel a sense of pride in being part of such an important event which had been conducted 'on a shoe string' in such a professional manner. From the top to the bottom, everyone involved knew what he was supposed to do, did it and did it successfully.

The Recce Detachment of 100 Squadron was disbanded on its return to Wyton in August 1957, with crews and aircraft being handed over to 58 Squadron which remained involved until the last Grapple test on 11 September 1958.

In early 1957 **PETER LANGDON** was posted as flight commander to 100 Squadron.

My immediate predecessor had been promoted and was therefore unavailable to the squadron who were in the midst of working up to go to Christmas Island for the H-bomb trials. On 26 April we departed for Christmas Island. As briefed we landed at Aldergrove to fill the fuel tanks to the brim. Once we arrived at the re-fuelling point it was discovered that one of the twin front tyres had been punctured. It was almost immediately discovered that the tailwheel of the Shackleton was identical with the Canberra's nose wheel. That was fixed and we put on our immersion suits for the Atlantic crossing and away we went taking only a total of five hours and 45 minutes from Wyton via Aldergrove to Goose Bay, Newfoundland. The all-rubber immersion suit was a very tight fit around the wrists and ankles but otherwise was comfortable and re-assuring with the Atlantic ahead of us. Both the navigator, Peter Batchelor, and I were very glad to have had the experience of flying across this stretch of water.

The next morning we started engines before we left the hangar and flew from Goose Bay to Namao, Alberta. It was just as cold there, even when we were taken into the hangar in an air-conditioned bus, and even with the hangar doors closed. I was very excited to be in Canada. The following day all the pre-flight checks and drills were completed and the engines started before we left the hangar. This was wildly different

from the UK practices where the aircraft always had to be well away from the hangar before the engines were started. Now for the first time I came across a Canadian voice giving flight clearance instructions on the radio. At the beginning neither the navigator nor I had the foggiest idea what the controller was saying or seemingly which language he was using. He appeared to talk at lightning speed. After asking for several repeats we managed to understand what they wanted us to do as we left the airfield. One of the difficulties was understanding the continual use of the word 'slash' but we began to appreciate their procedures before the exercise was over. We had a spectacular flight across Canada in almost perfect conditions.

The Grapple Y explosion as photographed from a PR Canberra on the morning of 28 April 1958. With a yield of 3 MT, this H-bomb was the largest British nuclear test ever conducted.

We were met at Travis AFB in California by an RAF squadron leader who had been positioned there to assist and control the many RAF aircraft using the base en route to Christmas Island. After a day off we're on our way across the Pacific to Honolulu. That was a six-hour flight with nothing but sea below us until we got to Honolulu, although on the way we were scheduled to pass directly over *Ocean Station November.* The navigator was as good as his word and we did pass over the ship, and I remember that she looked exceedingly lonely moored out there in the middle of the Pacific. A few days later when we were doing another flight from Christmas Island to Honolulu we were very interested to overhear the crew of a US B-57 Canberra lining themselves up to bale out over the ship. They had mishandled their fuel load to such an extent that once over the ship they'd insufficient fuel to safely get to either Travis or Honolulu. Before we left the area we knew that both crew members had been safely rescued from the sea.

Honolulu and Pearl Harbor, to be there really meant something to me. There are two airfields abutting one another, all aircraft land on the civil airstrip and then military aircraft taxi to the military strip. I don't believe that I'd ever had to taxi so far before. There was nothing special to report as far as I remember. I do recall going for a short walk along the beach, which was right outside the mess door, and being entertained by an Hawaiian band who appeared as if by accident, or magic, from behind bushes and gradually joined up into a 15-piece orchestra to entertain visitors, before wandering around with the collection boxes.

And so on to Christmas Island – just a very small island in a vast ocean. It was good to be amongst our squadron people and I was told by one of my friends that 'if when you get to the mess then you see a lot of people that you think shouldn't be there, you're quite right but they're from the Atomic Weapons Research Establishment (AWRE)'. We were given a two-man tent amongst dozens of other tents, told to ensure that we had no land crabs within the tent and that there was a 'barge board' right around the tent. The wretched land crabs were everywhere, as were hermit crabs which had invaded empty shells which they immediately adopted as their home. They were probably a little larger than a very large snail and were present in thousands, particularly at night. They were a scarlet colour and whenever one was squashed it smelt to high heaven. Any vehicle movement at night caused a massacre, which didn't seem to affect their numbers at all. When lying in bed after things had quietened down for the night one would hear occasional thumps against the barge boards as the crabs bumped into them. Only occasionally did one penetrate to the inside.

THE TASK

Our task on the operation was to fly meteorological reconnaissance flights on a daily basis so that the forecasters could draw up accurate charts. The average length of each sortie was four hours and 30 minutes and there was at least one flight a day. A few days before the first bomb was exploded we had a full dress rehearsal. This involved me flying from the island to Hickam Field, Honolulu to position a reserve aircraft in the event of the courier aircraft becoming unserviceable en route on one of the first two legs. The courier would carry air samples from the target area to the UK in the shortest possible time, with crew changes occurring at strategic points. I was to have with me an armourer equipped with appropriate tools to transfer the 'load' to the reserve aircraft in the event that the first aircraft required replacing. On the day of the first detonation everything went off according to plan. We left the island and climbed en route through a large cumulonimbus cloud. Three-quarters of the way through a very bumpy cloud one of our engines stopped. Continuing towards Hickam I reported the problem to the controller on the island, who offered to control our return. I decided to continue ahead for a period, and reduce height so that we could attempt to re-light the failed engine at the appropriate time. The crew are fairly busy on such occasions, and sitting beside me watching everything with interest was the corporal armourer who was being positioned to swap the samples if necessary. After a while we came out of the cloud into a typical equatorial day with a brilliant blue sky and not a cloud in sight. Re-lighting the engine provided no problem and we climbed back to our operating altitude. After a short interval 'Syph' – that being his known name throughout the squadron – enquired as to what was going to happen next. When told nothing we hope until after we land he said, 'That was quite exciting, can't we have something else?' We should have thrown him out then!

We arrived at Hickam safely as did the other aircraft, which was quickly 'turned around' for its flight to Travis AFB California. We all watched its departure. No one was happier than 'Syph' as he came up to me and said, 'Thank heaven he got away sir, I forgot the tools I was supposed to have brought with me'. We returned to Christmas Island the next day.

On the last day of the month we were part of the deployment for the second big bang – another extraordinary experience. When 'it' went off we were at height in a 180-degree turn – I am wearing an eye shield over one eye and have my hand over the other eye. At the appropriate moment the Task Force commander broadcasts that we can now open our eyes and look at the result. Our next task is to position the aircraft so that our fixed cameras can record the developments. All of this requires quite a bit of concentration, and suddenly when neither of us were expecting anything it feels as if some external force has given the aircraft a terrific kick, twice. This was, of course, the shockwave from the explosion. It all added to the excitement. We spent five hours on this flight.

The detachment continued until the middle of June when we had an uneventful flight back to the UK, arriving on 24 June 1957.

PR7 navigator GORDON DYER regarded his month on Christmas Island in November 1957 as an incredible experience:

Aged 23, I navigated a 58 Squadron Canberra PR7 halfway round the world and was then involved in supporting British H-bomb tests on a Pacific atoll. The outbound journey to Travis AFB, San Francisco was straightforward. However, there was uncertainty in the upper wind forecast for the next leg to Hickam AFB, Hawaii. Radiosonde information was available from only three places: Hickam, Travis, and *Ocean Station November* positioned halfway along the 2,100 nm route. For safety in crossing the Pacific, two Canberras flew in formation with me as lead navigator. The flight plan time was five hours and 35 minutes. This was safely within range as the aircraft had tip tanks. We settled down for a routine flight, initially starting at 33,000 ft with engines set for maximum range at 7,200 rpm and an airspeed of 0.72 Mach. Initially, all was well. Our Doppler showed the winds were much as forecast with 60 kts headwind. On time/track at the weather ship we had a cheerful conversation with its radio operator. We passed critical point and the point of no return. Shortly afterwards, the other aircraft requested our Doppler ground speed. I glanced down. It only indicated 290 kts i.e. the head-wind had suddenly increased to 130 kts. The other aircraft confirmed 290 kts. We were clearly in the core of a jet stream. A check on the fuel graph on the implication of our reduced speed did not provide good news: it seemed that we could run out of fuel before Hickam. We discussed various options for action, including increasing altitude to see if we could get out of the core of the jet stream but this required rpm increase, and thus increase in fuel consumption. It would take us into colder air and reduce airspeed. The best thing seemed to leave engines settings and rely on reduced all-up weight to improve fuel economy. I had to ensure that we did not drift off-track.

Fortunately the sun was abeam and offered a good track check, so I took several sun-shots as we flew on. ATC reaction to our predicament was immediate. Hickam scrambled an air-sea rescue Constellation which set off towards us. It was not long before we heard the voice of the Constellation's captain, who assured us that he would get us out of the sea if it was necessary. I was slightly alarmed when I saw that my pilot, Alpin 'Mac' MacGregor, was reading 'Sea Survival Notes for Aircrew'. Later, Hickam's radio beacon confirmed we were right on track and we were cleared for a straight-in approach and landing. We dropped like stones towards the runway. On final approach we overheard a conversation between a BOAC Clipper which called the tower for take-off clearance on the parallel runway. The controller's response has stuck in my mind. He said, 'Negative, negative, I have two transoceanic jets on fuel minima'. Fuel minima it was too, for tank checks afterwards indicated only 120 gallons remained, less than that required for an overshoot. We were lucky lads that day. Our flight time was six hours and 40 minutes, over an hour more than pre-flight planning had suggested.

Our PR7 Canberras had three roles: to provide weather recce, to photograph the explosion and to return a sample of nuclear cloud material back to the UK. Weather recce was crucial. The key parameter was wind direction. A northerly upper-wind was essential for a drop so that any fall-out would drift towards Antarctica and not Japan. Photography of the cloud was for historical record. The courier function required that the sample, collected by crews of 76 Squadron, was returned to Aldermaston within 24 hours after the explosion.

Weather recce involved flying, as high as possible, a 400 nm sided square route around the island, and radioing wind and cloud data every six minutes. By the time we landed the forecasters had already drawn up a complete upper-air wind chart from our data. Night sorties were timed for a 0200 local take-off, which on a runway base of crushed coral lit only by glims, was quite exciting. Because of the high tropopause in the equatorial Pacific, the typical outside air temperatures at our operating height of 50,000 ft was extremely low – around minus 80°C. This extreme temperature was problematic for the Canberra's Avons and as we discovered could cause engine flame-out in a normal rate turn. This happened around 0300 on 2 November when turning at the north-west corner of our route; both engines flamed out. It was very scary as we drifted down towards the ocean in complete darkness. Fortunately, the batteries continued to provide power and when Mac used engine restart procedure at 19,000 ft, both engines relit.

Our task on D-day 7 November was as courier escort; we flew as reserve alongside another PR7 that carried the cloud sample to Hickam. The flight was straightforward except that the effect of intense rain, limited servicing and spares back-up began to show on our aircraft. The radio compass, a main navigation aid, was showing signs of un-serviceability. The main courier aircraft was fit to go on, and another crew that was pre-positioned flew it on the next leg. We remaining two crews had instructions to stay at Hickam waiting for the next drop and then be the courier team for that sample to fly to Travis. This was six days later. As we were flying eastwards it would be mostly at night, but flying in formation would help to minimise any risks arising from unserviceabilities. The westerly jet stream that we had experienced on the way out had gone; a 30 kt easterly wind was forecast. The route to Travis was complicated by an ADIZ along the west coast. An aircraft entering US airspace had to follow a prescribed route, which was only assigned to the crew at pre-flight briefing. It was not a case of a straight line but dog-legs down various corridors of airspace.

The first part of the flight went well; we were tucked in close to the lead aircraft. Darkness fell after two hours and we were in clear skies. Suddenly, our aircraft turned port and began losing height. I called out to Mac to ask what was happening. He gave a muffled apology and said that he had had a touch of vertigo and got stars mixed up with the instrument panel. We regained height and course but too late, we had lost touch with the other aircraft. If I had been a bit laissez-faire with navigation to then, I really had to work hard as we were on our own. The task would have been easy had all avionics been working properly but the radio compass was definitely unworkable. There was also complete cloud cover below. So with a minimum of external information I gave Mac instructions to fly the ADIZ route entirely on dead-reckoning. We had good radio contact with Travis but when we called up for radar homing and descent, we got the very disturbing news we were not visible on radar. Without a radio compass and with complete cloud cover we were a bit stuck. We had no option but to fly the emergency pattern hoping for detection by another radar (a triangular pattern with 1½ minutes on each leg). We descended to 21,000 ft and flew with one engine throttled back for maximum endurance. We rehearsed what we would do if we could not be traced on radar, including what we would do before ejecting. After what seemed like forever a voice came through the emergency channel saying, 'RAF Jet 503, this is Oakland Naval Air Station Radar. We have you 28 miles north-east of us, do you wish our assistance?' Of course! I plotted our position; we were almost directly overhead Travis AFB. Why they couldn't see us remains a mystery. One possibility is that when we called them initially we were directly overhead in the blank lobe of coverage. Be that it may, Oakland guided us safely down through the cloud, over the wonderful sight of San Francisco lit brilliantly at night, and onto the runway at Oakland Naval Air Station, after a six-hour flight. An incident report later and an early return to Travis next morning put us back on schedule. We arrived safely back in the UK on 20 November having flown 74 hours in 35 days. Sadly, not all the 58 Squadron crews returned safely from their involvement in Operation Grapple.

CHAPTER 11
IN GERMAN SKIES

The RAF Canberra force peaked at 34 squadrons in 1955 only for the total number to decline thereafter as V bombers began to enter service. Four bomber and one recce squadron gave up their Canberras in 1956 and ten UK-based Canberra squadrons were disbanded the following year. The Canberra light bomber force in 1956 consisted of five B6 and 19 B2 squadrons with a total unit establishment (UE) of 230 aircraft. These were equipped for visual bombing from heights of up to 43,000 ft with Gee-H. There was a chain of stations in north-west Europe extending to about 200 miles east of the Rhine, and provided seven days' warning could be obtained, plans existed to extend this coverage by positioning equipment at certain forward sites. Additional navigational aids were Rebecca – fitted to all aircraft – and the radio compass, with which a small number of Canberras were fitted for operations overseas. But like Gee-H, all these aids could be jammed. Two B6 squadrons were fitted with the Blue Shadow sideways-looking search radar.

CLIVE ELTON carried on target marking with 139 Squadron after their return from Suez.

> We had Blue Shadow which produced a roll of paper with radar traces on it. We used this to find the US Sixth Fleet on one occasion. We reported back and the main bomber force went out to 'destroy' the fleet. Low-level target-marking was antiquated by 1957 and we lost three crews in six months, but it was huge fun. Target-marking went out as nuclear weapons came in. ■

B2 WJ569 and B(I)8s of 59 Squadron at Geilenkirchen in October 1957. The fin crest was a Continental road 'danger' sign – a white triangle outlined in red and a black exclamation mark. (Peter Green Collection)

The first production B(I)8, WT326, flew at Samlesbury on 8 June 1955 and the most natural place for the interdictors to be based, up close and personal in the event of any Warsaw Pact incursion, was RAF Germany. A tactical development unit (TDU) had been formed at Ahlhorn on 23 February 1953 with four B2s fresh off the production line to prove the Canberra in the night interdictor role. To assess Canberra vulnerability, the Nordhorn range was surrounded by searchlights and LAAs belonging to the army and RAF Regiment. After the TDU's Canberras deployed to Brüggen on 24 July 1953 for airfield dispersal trials, the overall knowledge and expertise gained was fed into the final mock-up conference for the so-called 'new look' interdiction Canberra.

Former nav JOHN BROWNLOW was in at the beginning.

On completion of my tour with AVM Boyle, I started pilot training in April 1953, and 19 months later I joined 103 Squadron, one of the four Canberra B2 squadrons of 551 Wing at Gütersloh. This wing was really an extension of Bomber Command in terms of policy and concept of operations. We used G-H Mk 2 for blind bombing and the T2 bombsight for visual bombing, as we had done from the outset. The main focus was on G-H, dropping 25-lb practice bombs, usually on Nordhorn range. Strategic operational control of the wing was retained by HQ Bomber Command but day-to-day control of routine flying and administration was devolved to 2TAF via HQ 2 Group. For exercise and operational planning purposes we were integrated with the Bomber Command Canberra wings, and we used the same aircrew classification system. A most significant operational limitation of G-H was that it covered the UK and Europe only up to a line roughly Rostock–Magdeburg– Munich. As I recall there was no knowledge among the aircrews of 551 Wing about an impending change of role to tactical nuclear strike for the Germany-based Canberras.

In January 1956 I was posted with my crew to join 213 Squadron that was re-forming at Ahlhorn. Our squadron commander was Wg Cdr Harry Dodson, a qualified test pilot. We were briefed that our role would initially centre on day and night interdiction, and that training for this role would eventually lead to a tactical nuclear strike capability when our aircraft had been suitably modified. In March the first six brand new Canberra B(I)6s arrived, and we eventually built up to a strength of 16. As delivered, the aircraft were painted silver. The B(I)6 had a Boulton and Paul gun pack, containing four 20-mm Hispano Suiza cannons, in the rear of the bomb bay. Each gun was provided with 525 rounds, enough for 50 seconds firing. In addition three 1,000-lb bombs could be carried in the bomb bay, and two more on underwing pylons. We had a Mk 3N reflector gunsight above the instrument panel and a G45 gun camera in the starboard leading edge. There was also provision for a forward-facing F95 camera in the nose and we could carry 16 4½-inch flares in the bomb bay. Needless to say, the B(I)6 was a joy to fly compared with the relatively old B2s we had flown before. 213 Squadron had a mixture of experienced Canberra aircrews with different backgrounds, and new-ly-trained crews straight from the OCU at Bassingbourn.

For the first couple of years after 213's re-formation our main task was night low-level interdiction. Among our planned targets were radars, communications centres, supply depots, indeed the whole range of typical interdiction targets in Eastern Europe. Obviously we had to work up to this. A programme of intensive training was soon instituted, based on a lot of low-level cross-country map-reading by day and night, but at the time we badly needed a low-level navigation aid, later to be provided by Decca Mk 1(Air), a GPI (ground position indicator) Mk 4A and a roller map, both of the latter being driven by a Blue Silk Doppler radar, as part of the upgrade for the tactical nuclear strike role. Our role conversion included instruction in basic ground-at-tack patterns by a pilot attack instructor in a Vampire T11, followed by live firing with the Canberra gun pack on the nearby Stroehen range. To get a feel for the aircraft's response to firing the gun pack, and to practise cockpit procedures before going live on the range, we fired into the North Sea. The Canberra turned out to be a very stable gun platform and the squadron was soon achieving respectable fixed-target scores both by day and by night.

Once qualified for ground attack the squadron was tasked with 'Light Strike', which involved detachments to Valkenburg, a Dutch naval airfield near The Hague. This operation entailed simulated attacks on E-Boats in the North Sea by day and night in collaboration with a Shackleton. At night the Shackleton identified the target and dropped flares to illuminate it. The Canberra crew then acquired the target visually and attacked using the gun pack. Diving into the ball of light created by the flares, concentrating on the attack, and then pulling up into complete blackness, with one's night vision completely destroyed and thus being obliged to revert instantly to instru-ments, was one of the most disorientating situations I have ever experienced. Perhaps surprisingly, crews seemed to cope with it, but I can't help feeling that eventually there would have been a big splash.

Valkenburg was not a very suitable airfield for night operations, since it had neither approach lights nor approach path indicators, and was difficult to identify, being located very close to the large, well-lit residential areas around The Hague.

The B(I)6 of 1956 was a very different, and far more capable and flexible, aeroplane, than the original B2 of 1951. And, by this time, of course, the Canberra was beginning to take on many other roles and specialist tasks.

Speaking of which, Laarbruch near the Dutch border housed 34 Recce Wing which was principally composed of three Canberra PR squadrons. 69(PR) Squadron re-formed in October 1953 with Canberra PR3s before moving to Laarbruch on 13 December 1954. It was joined by 31(PR) Squadron which re-formed on 1 March 1955 with PR7s, and the wing was completed by the re-formation of 80(PR) Squadron with PR7s the following August. Each Canberra squadron had a mobile field processing unit attached to it. On

1 June 1956, 17(PR) Squadron re-formed with PR7s at Wahn, moving to Wildenrath on 3 April 1957. The 'high-level' PR Canberras were complemented by the 'low-level' Tac-R Swifts and Meteor FR9s based at Gütersloh. However, this was a largely artificial divide. High-level PR was frequently impracticable over the cloudy skies of Europe.

34 Wing normally engaged in high-level PR sorties from Norway to the Mediterranean. During Exercises Stronghold and Rejuvenate, Laarbruch Canberras simulated bombing runs during high-level photographic runs on targets such as Birmingham. Now that well-flown Hawker Hunters were in Fighter Command service, the Canberras seemed to be much more vulnerable though there was an element of smoke and mirrors involved.

B(I)6 of 213 Squadron at Istres in the south of France in 1961. (Peter Green Collection)

Brian 'Boz' Robinson was a young fighter pilot on 74 Squadron at Horsham St Faith and he states, 'it was never a problem to intercept a Canberra by Hunter during the annual air defence exercises – I suspect because they were told not to get too high for us!' Nonetheless, 34 Wing PR crews felt they would be safer flying right down close to the deck where ground cover would confer greater protection than performance. Moreover, in Tony Burt's words, 'it was no use photographing from 40,000 ft if the target was under a 2,000 ft cloud base. I remember that Exercise Royal Flush in 1958 had two parts – low level and high level – with Canberras doing the high-level element. But really we were entirely focused on low-level PR training on behalf of 2 TAF and 4 TAF – we kept well away from the Inner German Border and if the radar controller advised you were getting close, you turned straight away onto 270°.' By 1956, some Laarbruch pilots had developed a technique of banking their Canberras to take oblique shots at comparatively low levels.

The PR3 and PR7 had the same daylight camera fit. For night work, they carried two F89 cameras plus either a 150 capacity crate of 1.75-inch flares or a flare carrier of five 8-inch magnesium flares. In the low-level night role, the PR7 carried two F97 cameras with 5-inch lenses designed for night photography at altitudes between 400-2,000 ft. Illumination for the exposures was provided by the 1.75-inch photoflash cartridges, which were ejected automatically from a discharger at regular intervals, giving an effective exposure time of 1/50 second. Both cameras were used to photograph the same strip of ground with the flashes timed to explode at regular intervals such that the first exposure of one camera overlapped the first exposure of the other camera by 50 per cent and so on throughout the whole photographic run. The resultant image format was 5 in x 4.5 in and each camera magazine held 100 ft of film, giving 480 exposures.

CHAPTER 12
A TRIP TO BELIZE

RON MUDGE was selected as a cadet navigator in September 1952 but during aircrew grading he was persuaded to change to pilot. After training at Burnaston he was awarded his wings on Oxfords at RAF Pershore. Jet conversion followed onto Meteor Mk 3s at RAF Driffield before Ron was posted in November 1954 to Meteor PR10s on 13 Squadron in Egypt and later at Akrotiri. Returning to the UK in June 1956 he was posted to Canberra PR7s on 58 Squadron at RAF Wyton.

My own personal high moment in a fascinating two-and-a-half years on 58 Squadron was the sighting, on Friday 2 May 1958, of the silvery gleam of a Viscount aircraft flying at 16,000 ft in the Caribbean sun, approximately 160 nm east of Belize. It was a moment quite unrelated to the primary task for which we trained, i.e. the taking of aerial photographs, mainly in a vertical direction. How did Chas Lister and I come to be chasing a civil aircraft in the late afternoon a few thousand miles from Wyton?

It all started one evening, when Chas rolled up on his powerful motorcycle to say that we were no longer on standby to go to Goose Bay, but to report to Ops at 0830 the next morning with tropical kit packed.

Chas Lister with his nav bags (left), Ron Mudge (right) with their PR7 on 11 May 1958. (Ron Mudge)

We in the PR world were quite used to plans changing, but this was radical and created Operation Quick Flight – two PR7s to escort two B(I)8s of 59 Squadron to British Honduras and be there asap. Reason – HRH The Princess Margaret was due to visit the colony and the president of Guatemala had stated that members of the British royal family were not welcome, as British Honduras belonged to them. He further threatened to fly his presidential aircraft over any HRH outdoor ceremony. In the event, he didn't and we arrived back ten days later. Mission accomplished, but the 'change of plans' factor frequently occurred.

Why PR7s and B(I)8s? The latter carried a deterrent gun-pack, but little in the way of navigational aids, whilst we had the necessary navigational equipment and experience in long sea crossings. Frank Stokes, with Jimmy Hay, was to lead, plus Chas Lister and I in the second PR7. Don Attlee and George Coatsworth were the B(I)8 pilots. Throughout the night a team of RAF Wyton navigators, led by Boss Fell, had prepared a vast array of charts, maps, radio frequency plans etc. and, due to the lesser range of the B(I)8s, the route chosen was first to Lajes AFB in the Azores, then Gander, Kindley AFB (Bermuda), Montego Bay and finally Belize. For the first leg, Frank would lead Don Attlee in the first B(I)8 and Chas and I the other B(I)8.

TO BELIZE

At 14.30, the four aircraft taxied out to the take-off point, with a favourable weather forecast for the Azores. Unfortunately, Frank had to return to dispersal with a generator warning light, which called for the first change of plan – Chas and I would lead the two B(I)8s and Frank would follow. Nearing Lajes, we were told that it was raining with a cold front over the island. Problem – the B(I)8s had no radio compass and the base had no DF facilities. We tried to descend in Vic formation, but on entering cloud at 35,000 ft (which was later found to be solid to 5,000 ft), the second B(I)8 lost contact and had to climb and orbit in the clearer sky. Don Attlee was led to overhead the NDB beacon, given the outbound heading and we climbed to search for the other B(I)8. Eventually, contact was made again and we all landed safely. Flying in formation by night was considered to be impracticable and a night stop was planned. While the aircraft were being refuelled, Frank's aircraft appeared scuttling in and out of the lowering clouds and rain. First hurdle over.

New plan – take-off at 0800 the next morning. Re-fuelling OK but couldn't replenish oxygen, due to incompatibility with the hose connectors. Practical Frank and a willing USAF sergeant re-threaded a connector and at 1300 we set a heading for Gander. However, Frank couldn't start the port engine, so we were down to three aircraft again. Then, about 400 nm out of Lajes, one of the engines of the second B(I)8 aircraft flamed-out, due to the failure of a low-pressure pump. Descent was made to 30,000 ft for a successful relight and then on to Gander. The local press took an interest, but after that, we never saw the press again – in contrast to what might be expected today?

ROUTE TO BELIZE

Take-off for Bermuda was in the early evening and approaching Kindley AFB, we declared two minor emergencies – one B(I)8 was short of fuel and the other low on oxygen. In the Ops Centre, we learned that Frank's replacement aircraft had also gone unserviceable in the Azores. However, at Kindley we were met by Fred Haynes and Les Henson, who had been diverted from Goose Bay where they had been on 'Grapple' standby. Next morning, the port engine of Don Attlee's B(I)8 would not accelerate and thus Chas and I were to lead the remaining B(I)8 onward to Belize, via Montego Bay, and the others would follow. On approaching Jamaica, we were instructed to land at Montego Bay as our expected arrival clashed with that of HRH. At Kingston, we were delighted to discover ground crew from both 58 and 59 Squadrons, who had been flown to the island by a Comet of Transport Command.

The aircraft were refuelled, the gun pack on the B(I)8 armed and we were told to fly to rendezvous with the royal aircraft above Swan Island, a small island halfway to Belize. The island was equipped with a radio beacon and therefore, even if the island was hidden from view, we could be precise regarding our location.

On contacting the royal aircraft, they first told us they were five minutes ahead of schedule. Then we discovered that the ETA given was not for Swan Island, but a point 30 miles north of the island. Despite the sudden change, Chas Lister got us to the new location minus six seconds on the ETA. Then a further update – the Viscount had passed abeam Swan Island 25 miles to the north. Consequently, there was serious danger of not meeting up with the Viscount before reaching Belize. A search of the likely area was made, but without success. Fortuitously there was a solitary large cumulonimbus in the area and using this landmark and relative positions, we were able to find and take up position abeam the royal aircraft; a proud moment for both crews after a hectic 46 hours and 16 hours 40 minutes flying from leaving RAF Wyton.

On approach to Stanley Field, a further surprise awaited us – from ATC, the familiar voice of Dave Crocker. He and 'Steve' Stevens had flown in from Offutt AFB, Nebraska at two hours' notice. He had been sent to review the airfields at Montego Bay and Belize and to report on their suitability for Canberra and Comet operations. He had also carried out a number of low-level passes over the town, with such effect that some people believed that there were at least two squadrons of Canberras at Stanley airport. It was tragic when a few months later they lost their lives in a mid-air collision with a USAF aircraft near RAF Wyton.

AT BELIZE

On landing, our host – 'B' Company of the 1st Worcester Regiment – made us very welcome and did everything possible to make our stay comfortable and enjoyable. We were briefed on our task of 'showing the flag' over remote towns and villages and, on the Saturday, the first of the flights were made. On the Sunday morning, a Royal Naval survey ship, HMS *Vidal*, anchored off Belize, entertained the force but Chas and I couldn't partake of the available 'pink gins' as we had to fly later that day.

On the Monday morning, there was a fly-past with one PR7 leading the two Canberra B(I)8s, followed by the Comet, which had flown over from Kingston with the remaining two PR7s. Later in the day, Chas and I with the B(I)8 crew were taken to Government House and presented to HRH The Princess Margaret. Informal and enjoyable.

BELIZE TO THE UK

The royal aircraft left on Tuesday 4 May and Brian Crocker returned to the UK via Offutt AFB. At Montego Bay, in order to make room for those still at Belize, the Comet, PR7 and B(I)8 departed as soon as they could and had a trouble-free passage back to the UK. However, the last two Canberras continued to be dogged with minor difficulties.

After a luxury stay, albeit all too brief, at Montego Bay, we planned a very early take-off, with the aim of flying two legs per day: Montego Bay – Bermuda – Gander and then Gander – Azores – Wyton.

The flight proceeded smoothly until nearing Bermuda, when we entered the tops of turbulent frontal cloud at 41,000 ft. A let down was made by the B(I)8 from that height, but on breaking cloud at 1,200 ft, was refused a GCA owing to an emergency in progress. By means of skilful navigation, the B(I)8 located Bermuda and, after orbiting below the cloud for a considerable time, landing clearance was finally given. Meanwhile, we had let down to overhead the beacon at 20,000 ft, but were made to orbit for fifty minutes in the thick frontal cloud. It was very frustrating but one bore the difficulties in the light of the emergency. However, once we discovered that the emergency was a four-engine piston USAF aircraft with one engine running rough, we were not so accommodating.

A formation take-off and climb through the frontal cloud was not desirable, for if the B(I)8 were to lose contact with the ground and the PR7, the Americans could not provide any navigational assistance. A little later, we were told that Goose Bay, not Gander would be our transit airfield, but the weather forecast was very unfavourable.

On the Friday, the weather was still bad at Goose Bay, but with a better forecast for the Saturday, a dawn take-off was planned and

HRH Princess Margaret at Wyton where she met Ron (centre) and Chas (right) again. (Ron Mudge)

the two legs Bermuda – Goose Bay – Wyton. In the meanwhile, the crews relaxed in the warm sunshine of Bermuda. The dawn take-off was made and the aircraft flew the 1,300-mile leg in under three hours. Unfortunately, due to further problems, the final take-off had to be delayed until the Sunday. It was an uneventful trip to Wyton, with the added benefit of the PR7 being able to assist a pilot, flying a Piper from Gander to Shannon, who had severe icing problems. The PR7 became an HF radio link passing weather and ATC information between Shannon ATCC and the Piper.

So, after ten hectic days, the force of Canberras had returned to RAF Wyton. For all those involved, both on the ground and in the air there was a real sense of achievement and a potential and embarrassing diplomatic incident had been avoided. Deployment had taken place at very short notice, despite the squadron being stretched with a commitment to Operation Grapple and all had returned safely.

CHAPTER 13
FIRST TOUR RECCE –
NO CHANCE, MY BOY!

GRAHAM PITCHFORK:

Entering my third year as a flight cadet at Cranwell I noted that those navigators who did best on the course had been sent to do the one-year NBS course at Lindholme prior to joining the V Force. The thought started to give me nightmares, so what to do?

There were ten navigators in my entry and we had a brilliant course commander, Flt Lt Eric West, a Canberra bomber navigator. During a routine progress chat I alerted him to my dilemma and we also discussed what topic I should select for my assessed project paper. I had always been interested in photography and had recently read Constance Babington-Smith's book *Evidence in Camera,* which left me in no doubt about where I wanted to go after Cranwell – the photo recce (PR) world. There was one problem – a big one – the PR world did not take first-tour navs at the time.

Eric and I hatched a plot. Why not do a PR-related topic for my project. I submitted my choice, aerial survey and it was accepted. Then came a second huge slice of luck – my tutor was another outstanding instructor, Flt Lt Ken Forshaw, a Canberra man and ex-wartime Mosquito PR.

For my two-day project visit he arranged for me to go to 58 Squadron at RAF Wyton where I was looked after by a Flt Lt Ramsey Brown (more of him later). A visit to the Joint Air Reconnaissance Intelligence Centre (JARIC) to hoover up lots of aerial photographs, a crawl over a Canberra PR9 and I was hooked. Now to convince the authorities at Cranwell who continued to hold the threat of the V Force over me.

Eric West and Ken Forshaw must have worked a miracle. When the postings went up on the Senior Entry notice board, Senior Flight Cadet G. R. Pitchfork was posted to No. 101 (PR) Course at 231 OCU.

For reasons that I did not understand, I joined seven other navigators at the Bomber Command Bombing School at RAF Lindholme, the home of the NBS Course. Shock and horror was short lived thankfully since all PR navigators had to do a six-week visual bombing course. It was great fun and I met some outstanding navs, all at least ten years older than me. After some early ribbing about being ex-Cranwell and a first tourist, I learnt a great deal about life, how to drink and what to do at the Bluebell in Scunthorpe.

Arriving at Bassingbourn I was treated by the PR nav instructors with grave suspicion where the attitude was, 'if you haven't been on a PR squadron, you cannot be posted to one!' I crewed up with Terry Close, the only bachelor pilot and an ex-Cranwell Sword of Honour winner and one of the first Victor co-pilots. Our personal instructors were two great characters, Flt Lts Bob Taylor and Gus Walker. They had been a crew on 31 Squadron at Laarbruch.

After six weeks at ground school it was time to fly and spend seven trips feeling lousy down the back of a T4 whilst Terry got the hang of flying a Canberra. Finally, we progressed to the PR3 and life suddenly became a great deal more interesting. At this stage I was still being treated with great suspicion as a first tourist (the first nav I believe) and the acerbic Gus Walker kept reminding me of my status – none. Then, after what I considered to be an immaculate Gee cross-country, he failed me by one mark and I had to re-fly it. I was soon to discover that it was his way of making sure I understood my position in the PR world – rock bottom – but from then on he took me under his wing and I learnt a very great deal from him.

After some 100 hours of photographing pinpoints, line features and small area covers at high level it was time for the low-level phase and a final Opex. We passed and were now allowed to enter the then hallowed halls of the PR world. Our two instructors had been superb and, big surprise, we were posted to 31 Squadron at Laarbruch.

Arriving at Laarbruch on 2 April 1962, to more strange looks, I discovered that the boss always insisted that a new arrival should fly on his first day on the squadron. My flying kit had not arrived, neither had my pilot and the weather was filthy. No problem for the boss who had made his first acquaintance with the German countryside when he landed by parachute in early 1944. I was given the appropriate flying kit, introduced to the pilot, none other than the flight commander, the recently promoted Sqn Ldr Ramsey Brown. His navigator was a rather older gentleman who had once served in the Indian Cavalry and who pre-fixed every noun with 'wizard'. I don't recall being offered a map.

I strapped into the only ejector seat in the back and remained there for the next ninety minutes unable to see anything. I got the impression that the navigator, who refused to get off the Rumbold seat to allow me to sit there, was also having difficulty seeing out judging by his commentary to Ramsey. Understanding him was not helped by his affliction of a heavy lisp: 'We will soon cwoss a wivver over a woad….oh dear…. it's a woad over wailway, never mind.'

The sortie went on in this vein for some time as the weather worsened at which point Ramsey decided he had had enough. Despite just a few weeks' experience in Germany, he soon found his way back to Laarbruch without the aid of Whizzo the nav. I note that the flight is recorded in my logbook as, 'low-level nav demo'. Some demo, and Whizzo was the squadron nav leader.

A few days later, I was programmed to fly a check ride with the CO, Charles Dalziel. There were five targets in the British zone (BZ) culminating with a 'military installation' close to a canal south of Bremen. All went well until this final target. We set off from the IP and at the appointed time there was nothing that looked remotely like a military target. I was to learn later that this was the CO's party piece for all new navigators. When the film arrived, the CO took me through it until the fifth target ought to have appeared. He had taken some photographs and I could just about make out some old and derelict buildings. I enquired if that was the target, 'Yes, my boy,' came the reply, 'there are the remains of the camp where Herr Hitler incarcerated me for some time after I had been shot down.' He then gave me the most important piece of advice for those in the PR business: 'Always take a photograph at the elapsed time, the photo interpreter may find what he is looking for even if you don't see it.' And with that he took me off to the bar.

The squadron was equipped with the Canberra PR7, which had much greater range than the PR3s used at Bassingbourn. Half the bomb bay held a fuel tank with a photo-flash crate for night photography occupying the rear half when it was not full of aircrew luggage and spoils from trips to far-flung parts of the world.

Although the squadron was tasked primarily as a low-level tactical reconnaissance unit using the oblique F95 camera, there were also other interesting tasks. I never discovered the reason for some of the high-level photographs taken over France. Following increased tension after the erection of the Berlin Wall, a number of Inner German border recce flights were flown at medium level using an oblique-mounted F52 camera with a 48-inch lens. I recall using the airfield at Celle where a flight of 5 Squadron Javelins provided us with a fighter escort during our photo runs up and down the border.

At an early stage in transition to war, the PR squadrons would disperse four or five aircraft to bare bases taking an element of their mobile field photographic unit with them. Conditions at airstrips such as De Peel in Holland were very basic. We had no specific war role. When the hooter went, the recce squadrons would immediately launch two aircraft to cover likely enemy lines of advance. As we taxied back in, the ground crew whipped off the camera magazines which would be rushed away. We debriefed and within 20 minutes the photos would appear.

There were a number of regular features during a year including no-notice station exercises and Tacevals, national and NATO reconnaissance competitions, regular flights to NATO airfields and lone ranger flights to the Mediterranean and beyond.

During an alert exercise, there was a big advantage being on a PR squadron. Pre-planned sorties were launched immediately to carry out a line search to find the enemy's advance. Each of the three PR squadrons in Germany launched two aircraft as soon as possible – our 16 Squadron bomber chums sat in the crew room for a few hours waiting for our results. There was therefore, a great incentive to get to the squadron immediately since the first two pilots and two navigators to appear were crewed together and sent off. It became a competition to see who could arrive at the squadron first. Around Laarbruch there was a five-mile one-way ring road.

The squadrons were dispersed in each corner of the standard NATO airfield and 31 was the furthest away from the domestic site. However, by going the wrong way round the ring road, those of us in the officer's mess had the shortest route. Since all alerts happened at the dead of night, no problem. It took the married chaps ages to discover our secret.

Two aircraft were always parked overnight in a dispersal near to the hangar. The ground crew rushed to prepare them as the first pilot grabbed his kit and made for the aircraft. The nav was given a pre-planned route folder before rushing off to the aircraft that now had the engines running. Take-off was often achieved in less than thirty minutes from the alert sounding. Photographs were taken of the line search and a high-speed return flight to be met by the photographers who soon had the film magazines in the Mobile Field Photographic Unit (ours was No. 3 MFPU) and they had the film processed for interpretation within a few minutes.

The squadron had a variation of this rapid capability devised by our new boss, Wg Cdr Peter Scott, designed to impress VIPs. As the fittest nav, and one of few who could run, I was selected for this demonstration. On arrival, the VIP was met by the boss and brought to a planning table where I had a map carefully folded so that it only just crossed the River Rhine. He was invited to select a target, I drew a few lines and then sprinted to an aircraft parked by the hangar. Engines were fired up as I approached and off we roared. The VIP then toured the squadron.

I never had time to strap in, passed a heading to the pilot and at full speed we headed for the target. We took two photos, one with each F95 camera and roared back making lots of noise at very low level over the hangar to herald our return. I

31 Squadron Canberra PR7 returns to its Mobile Field Photographic Unit at Laarbruch, May 1964. (Graham Pitchfork)

31 Squadron aircrew in August 1964 with the boss, Wg Cdr Peter Scott, on the canopy and Graham Pitchfork by the engine nacelle. (Graham Pitchfork)

fixed a dayglo sticker in the nose to indicate the priority camera. We taxied up to the MFPU, where the VIP and reception committee were waiting, engines were cut, the photographers had the magazines off and I strolled to debrief our guest. A few minutes later he had a photograph of the target presented to him.

Competitions were a major annual feature for a PR squadron in Germany. The first was the RAF's Sassoon Trophy competed for by the three Canberra squadrons (17, 80 and 31) and two Hunter fighter reconnaissance squadrons (2 and 4) based at Gütersloh. We practised assiduously for both when most of the squadron crews carried out weeks of training before five and a reserve crew were selected for the competition. In our first year, Terry Close and I were included in the team. As the junior boy under the spotlight I was, quite naturally, very nervous.

Crews took off at one-hour intervals throughout the day. Each aircraft in turn was positioned on the taxiway just outside the squadron planning room some fifty yards away. The crew prepared the aircraft in advance and reached it by jumping out of the crew room window.

The umpire issued the task of three targets with an entry and exit point. After a very close assessment of the geographic features around the target, the direction of approach was decided for the port oblique. The nav selected the initial point (IP) and drew the target run as the pilot prepared a route map. The entry and exit points had only to be recognisable on the photograph but the targets had to be perfect for the photographic interpreter (PI) to prepare his post-flight report. Thirty minutes was allowed from issue of the task to engines start.

Graham Pitchfork (left) with his pilot Terry Close.
(Graham Pitchfork)

Terry Close and I were third off and had some tricky targets in the 4 ATAF region. The first, a radio mast, was cleverly positioned a few hundred yards from a radar site but the old adage of taking a photo of the exact grid reference, and not being suckered in by a more obvious 'target', worked. The second was a bridge buried in trees in the Ardennes and the last was a line search for a POL (petrol, oil, lubricants) site. Panic set in as we approached the end of the line having seen nothing. At the last minute I spotted an army fuel bowser just off the road. We took a photo in hope. On landing we discovered it was the target.

As the engines were shut down, the magazines were rushed to the MFPU for processing as we made our visual reports, which were then amplified by the arrival of the photograph negatives, which the PI studied through a stereoscope. His report had to be handed to the umpire within thirty minutes. The other four crews did the job and the squadron were declared the winners for the 1963 event.

The NATO competition, Royal Flush, was a much bigger affair with all the Central and Northern Region countries represented. In the long-range category, two of the three RAF Germany squadrons competed, one by day the other by night. The third stood down for the year and provided support to the others.

In 1964, 31 was the RAF's entry for the night phase. Three crews were selected each flying three sorties on consecutive nights. Our opponents were the USAF RB-66s flying out of Alconbury, a specialist night-reconnaissance unit with a four-man crew, including a radar operator. Our two-man day outfit was up against it. To enhance our chances, a second nav was used and his job was to monitor the Doppler and GPI and call out ground speeds and drift on the target run. He also set up the camera parameters based on the aircraft's height and ground speed.

Halfway through the night work-up my pilot Terry Close was medically grounded. Ramsey Brown's navigator was not enjoying much success at night map-reading so I replaced him. Flt Lt Jim Straughan, an ex-night fighter nav joined us down the back to monitor the kit.

The work-up was very unsociable with three long night sorties a week for eight weeks – and it was spring so some very late nights. We practised on just about every weapons range in Western Europe in order to work out routes, IPs etc.

Accurate flying was essential with the ground speed nailed at 300 knots, the height of exactly 1,000 ft above ground at the target and tracking directly over the unseen target. Ramsey Brown was a big man with huge hands but his flying was immaculate and very precise. We soon became a very effective three-man team.

At night the navigator had to operate the cameras from the nose and the photo-flash controls from his seat in the rear of the cockpit. For difficult targets this led to the need for two navigators though crews were established for one only. Flying at 1,200 ft and emitting a few million candle power every two seconds made one feel somewhat vulnerable.

Planning for the night sorties was less of a rush. Just before 2300 hours on 12 May 1964 we took off on our first sortie with three targets and we headed for the Stanford training area in Norfolk for the first, with the second on a Belgian range and the final one at the familiar Nordhorn range east of the Rhine. Jim and I shared the route nav and it was my job to get us from the IP to the target and take the photographs. The flashes went off at two-second intervals with the target, hopefully, covered by the middle of the stick. I was able to confirm we had the targets.

The second night was to three more ranges, all of which we had visited in the work-up. At the end of this night, we got the whisper that the squadron was in the lead and we were the top crew. No pressure!

On the third night we were tasked to about the only range we had never seen – it was in Denmark. The second was at Vliehors in the Frisian Islands and then to Suippes in northern France. The Danish range was the toughest one we faced. There was very little to see and I had to rely on Ramsey's accurate flying and Jim's constant monitoring of the Doppler. In the glow of the flashes I saw some tanks, which was very encouraging. We were familiar with Vliehors and all went well. Suippes was a very different matter. The range was big so the IP to target runs were long with few features recognisable at night. On an earlier training sortie we had found a small cluster of lights around a compound in the range so chose that as the IP. We arrived – no lights! A hasty decision to use a nearby river with a prominent bridge and we headed into the black. I released the flashes and there below us were three Harvard aircraft simulating missiles.

The results came out the following day. The squadron was beaten by the narrowest margin (it would not have done to beat a specialist night squadron) but the Brown, Pitchfork, Straughan team had carried off the crew award. We celebrated in fine style and it was back to discovering what flying in daylight was all about.

Competitions doubtless had some value, particularly for the photographers and photo interpreters, but the majority of squadron crews were not involved. However, Tacevals and exercises involving the whole squadron provided a great deal more realistic training that led to operational benefits and efficiency.

By the end of Royal Flush, I had been on the squadron just over two years, and having lost Terry Close permanently, the boss gave me two options. Early tourex, almost certainly to the V Force, or extend my tour and be his nav for the next twelve months. He sent me from his office to think about it. One nano-second later I knocked on his door and told him I had thought about it... 'I'll stay'. What a great decision that turned out to be.

The boss was a keen skier and as we loaded the aircraft before departure he produced a pair of skis. On the return through Cyprus, which he had decided should be over a weekend to spend time with one of his big mates, Akrotiri's OC Strike Wing, he planned to ski on Mount Troodos. Unfortunately, the skis did not fit in the flare bay so, after I had climbed into the back, he managed to slide them into the cockpit and along the nav couch in the nose.

We headed for Cyprus for the night and the first thing to appear as the ground crew opened the door were the skis followed by two wing commanders and a tired and cold flight lieutenant. There were a few strange looks. Next morning we loaded up the luggage and the skis appeared. 'But, boss, would it not be a good idea to leave them here and get them on our return?' Back came the answer, 'No, we might go u/s en route and not come back here'. So off to Bahrain on the trickiest leg for the nav using only Green Satin and a GPI. I had prepared topographical maps for the route but there was no way I could reach the nose. I soon discovered that OC Ops, a former Javelin squadron commander, was not at his best lying in the nose map-reading over the Caucasus from 40,000 feet.

The charade with the skis was even funnier in Bahrain and became hilarious on arrival at Khormaksar where the ground crew clearly thought we were crazy. So on to Nairobi and more astonished ground crew. The return had to be by the same route since over-flights of Sudan had just been withdrawn. We made Cyprus on time and the boss got his two days of skiing. It had been a heavy weekend and on the return, the aircraft went mysteriously unserviceable in Malta so it was another night in the company of two brilliant wing commanders who were probably enjoying their last squadron days after long careers.

With my tour coming to an end and no posting in sight, the boss asked me what I fancied. 'An exchange tour' was my immediate reply. Not only was he a superb boss and pilot, he was extremely well connected in very high places. He said he would look into it and the weeks passed by. Then he called me to his office. 'An exchange posting has come through for you,' he said. Immediately the sunlit beaches of California or Australia and the Rockies in Canada flashed through my mind. 'You are off to Lossiemouth in north Scotland.' Long pause then a sheepish 'thanks boss'. The Royal Navy had offered an exchange for a pilot and a navigator for their new Buccaneer.

So, a fantastic tour with some great people came to an end after three years and almost 1,000 hours of flying. Life on a PR squadron in Germany for a first-tour bachelor could hardly get any better. Lots of flying in a fascinating and very varied job, cheap booze and petrol, lots of sport and a great social life with an officer's mess full of young bachelors and some very attractive young ladies. I could not have had a better start to my RAF flying career.

A few weeks later it was off to Lossiemouth to begin the second great love affair of my life – the Buccaneer.

CHAPTER 14
SUNNY CYPRUS

The Baghdad Pact was a treaty of alliance between Turkey and Iraq with the UK acceding to the pact in March 1955. Pakistan and Persia joined subsequently but after a coup, Iraq withdrew in March 1959 and the pact was changed to the Central Treaty Organisation (CENTO). In May 1956 the UK Chiefs of Staff approved four light bomber squadrons as part of the UK commitment to the Baghdad Pact. During 1957, 32, 73, 6 and 249 Venom squadrons in the Middle East Air Force (MEAF) were re-equipped with Canberras. The deployment of 32 and 73 Squadrons was mounted from Weston Zoyland with the first two B2s of 32 Squadron reaching Nicosia on 3 March 1957. On 19 March the squadron completed its move from Nicosia to Akrotiri. 'No clearly defined operational policy exists at the moment,' said the 32 Squadron ORB, 'but a preliminary directive from AHQ Levant lays down that crews are to become familiar with ME air routes and attain a high standard of visual bombing as soon as possible. A shallow dive marker element is to be trained within the unit.' By April, 32 Squadron was equipped with eight Canberras.

73 Squadron flew its first four aircraft from Weston Zoyland to Akrotiri over 19-20 March 1957 and another four at the end of the month. The other two MEAF light bomber squadrons flew out from Coningsby in the summer and early autumn of 1957. Their arrival meant that Akrotiri now accommodated four Canberra bomber squadrons and it was expected that they would eventually carry Red Beard nuclear weapons though 'a real nuclear potential' was not envisaged before 1959.

B2s of 73 Squadron at Mauripur, Pakistan, on 6 April 1959. (Peter Green Collection)

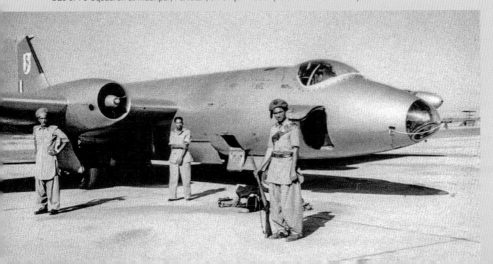

MIKE KNIGHT did four years at university before becoming a National Service pilot on 26 Squadron Hastings and Comets. On being awarded a permanent commission he went through the Canberra OCU before joining 139 Squadron at Binbrook in 1958.

We had Blue Shadow and our Canberras were known as the B6 (BS). I was a marker leader with Marker 1 and 2 plus Flare 1 and 2 leading the main bomber force. How did we target mark? We relied on decent navigators, trained in the old-fashioned way, with the assistance (when working to spec) of Blue Shadow radar. I guess there was the usual element of luck involved, combined (of course) with some superb piloting skills. Once in the target area those 'x' million candlepower flares worked surprisingly well, but the onus for final guidance of the main force rested firmly with Marker 1 and that was done visually. We would drop the flares ourselves and then dive underneath to circle the target and lay target indicators at about 3-500 ft AGL, hoping all the while to dodge the bombs. We gave instructions to the main force like 'bomb into easterly greens'. Crazy, really, but it all seemed rather good fun at the time. I recall a very sad occasion at El Adem when one of the squadron's flight commanders followed his TIs into the ground and, with ghoulish black humour the cry went out, 'bomb into the burning Canberra'. ▨

The Binbrook wing disbanded during 1959 and **MIKE KNIGHT** led four selected target-marking crews to Cyprus, where they joined 249 Squadron – the combination being colloquially known as '12349 Squadron'. In his words:

We became part of the Akrotiri Strike Wing with nuclear and conventional roles within CENTO. On 30 June 1961, my crew was sent to do a recce in Tehran prior to a Javelin detachment to the Far East. At 2am in a nightclub drinking vodka tonic – vodka in a coffee pot and tonic in a milk jug because the Shah decreed no alcohol – we received a signal via the embassy to 'return Akrotiri soonest'. We could only fly over Turkish airspace during daylight so we crossed the Turkish border as dawn broke. We were ordered to bomb up in response to a possible Iraq invasion of Kuwait. ▨

MIKE KNIGHT was given command of 32 Squadron in 1961:

On Boxing Day 1961, we were ordered to make a no-notice transit to El Adem, en route for Nairobi, where we were held for a few weeks in preparation for operations to counter one of the periodic Iraqi threats to Kuwait. We were armed with a less-than awe-inspiring load of six 1,000-lb dumb bombs and 74 x two-inch HE RPs – 37 in each of two pods. After a couple of weeks on standby, we were recalled to Cyprus. This Nairobi caper gave pause for thought – not least, because the RPs had been delivered to us with little more information than the Microcell brochure on 'carriage and release'. My PAI (pilot attack instructor) was the irrepressible 'Manx' Kelly and he took it upon himself to work the problem. We had a number of discussions – all of which pointed to the obvious conclusion that the only way to use these little beauties was to go in as low and as fast as the old Canberra could manage. At the time we were considering not just aircraft on the ground as targets but also the 'catalytic crackers' of Iraqi oilfields, which, if successful, might just get up the nose of their comparatively new leader. Whether or not such a venture was likely to be effective was hardly the point. We felt distinctly short of viable options.

We set up the first trials which, from memory, 'Manx' had calculated as a minimum 300-kt approach at precisely 67 ft AGL. In the event, experience gave us the confidence to increase the former and reduce the latter. I was designated to lead this trial and, to keep everyone sweet, I asked that a crew from each of the B15/16 squadrons be unofficially detached to the enterprise. I was delighted to welcome David Lloyd from 6 Squadron, 'Boz' Robinson from 73 Squadron and 'Curly' Hirst from 249 Squadron. Together with my own crew and that of 'Manx' Kelly I felt we had more than enough clout to get results. Galling as it was to these fine pilots, I insisted on the need for screen rides with their new leader, and these were flown on 15 July 1963 in the order Hirst/Lloyd/Robinson/Kelly, initially at 100 ft AGL. We were well aware of the propensity of the odd one of these little rockets to fly in rather eccentric manner, and there were one or two quite exciting moments. I recall that both pods discharged reasonably straight ahead, covering a vast area out to sea, though with minimal assessment of accuracy on target – the hessian screens which were mounted on the foreshore faring rather ill from the onslaught.

Our CENTO nuclear role involved last-minute loading and target study. We had targets in the southern USSR, which were regarded as 'one-way tickets'. We flew constituted crews with the standard Combat and Combat Star classifications.

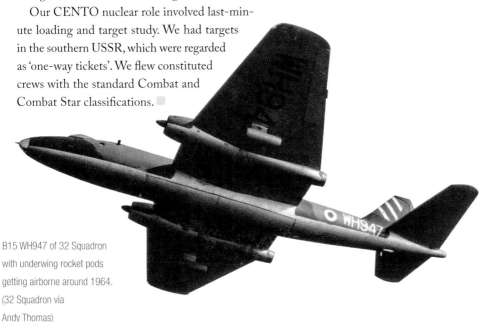

B15 WH947 of 32 Squadron with underwing rocket pods getting airborne around 1964. (32 Squadron via Andy Thomas)

In early February 1963, BRIAN 'BOZ' ROBINSON, his wife Ann and their babe in arms caught a Britannia transport of RAF Transport Command at RAF Lyneham for their move to the island of Cyprus.

73 Squadron was required to fulfil part of its worldwide troubleshooting role by taking part in an exercise in Kenya and I was able to persuade the boss, Colin Foale, the father of Britain's first astronaut, that he might find an experienced ground-attack pilot of value to him since the task for the Canberras would be to provide air support to the land force. I was by then a graduate of the Day Fighter Combat School and a pilot attack instructor so there was some merit in my case. However, I had only been on the squadron for a few weeks and was not qualified in all the roles that those Canberra B15s could perform, so my claim needed some hard-talking to get me involved, and I had to agree to escort the ground crew on the trip out. Arriving in Kenya after a memorable trip as officer i/c troops on one of Her Majesty's venerable Hastings transports, routing via El Adem and Khartoum where we refuelled, and over Lake Rudolf where we put up thousands of flamingo, I found myself attached to 70 Brigade, King's African Rifles, whose brigadier was Fitzalan-Howard, later Duke of Norfolk. My job was to be his brigade air support officer. That meant advising him on when and where to make use of the air assets available to him, namely my new colleagues on 73 Squadron with their capability to deliver 74 two-inch rockets in a shallow dive, or to drop six 1,000-lb bombs from level flight.

The crew of a B15 or a B16 at that time constituted a single pilot supported by a navigator sitting in the left-side ejection seat behind the pilot, and a navigator/observer in the right-hand bang seat. The latter's job was to move about from his bang seat either down the nose in a prone position to carry out level bombing runs, or to sit alongside the pilot in what was known as the rumble seat to effect a better lookout to the starboard side when combat became imminent. Travelling on the rumble seat was no great hardship; many a staff officer has been grateful for that mode of transport in

Microcell two-inch rocket pod as carried by the 39 B15s and 19 B16s. Each pod carried 37 rockets.

an emergency, and many an erk has been equally content to travel thus to reach a sick relative. We often took compassionate cases back to England at short notice, combining that errand of mercy with a training syllabus sortie that would have had to be flown sooner or later in any case. The Canberra when not carrying bombs could be used as a convenient transporter: fitted with two large panniers in the bomb bay, the aircraft could be used to move fruit, vegetables, milk and a variety of other goods around the Middle East during everyday navigation exercises. Wine and ham from Malta were popular in Cyprus, oranges and lemons from Cyprus went down well in the Gulf and in Aden, as did fresh milk. The Canberra was always a popular arrival. On the return trip from Embakasi in Kenya we had ample space for our bags full of the attractive wooden carvings from East Africa.

My two navigators were first tourists, meaning that they had just come straight from training. At Bassingbourn they had chosen me as their pilot because I had some 2,000 hours experience already, but despite their loyalty and their enthusiasm I knew that it would be a good idea to keep an eye on them for a while until they had got some time under their belts. As a professional pilot-navigator and instructor myself, it was relatively easy to keep a mental check on their navigation which I pretended to do using the tiny map to be found in a tin of Benson & Hedges cigarettes, but in those early days of our operations together I twice had to resort to drastic action to save the day, in the first case to save us all by not flying into the mountains of Crete as directed by the senior nav.

On another occasion, not long after the first, we were returning once again from a trip to El Adem at night. The time came in my calculations for us to be hearing a signal from the Akrotiri NDB to show that we were nearing home. Mike said he could hear nothing and on we flew to the north-east. Time passed and I became very uneasy – Mike could still hear nothing from the NDB, then suddenly he let out a cry of delight – he had the Akrotiri NDB at extreme range ahead. That seemed quite wrong to me so I began an orbit of the current position and got my own radio working to talk to Akrotiri myself although that was not standard practice on training missions. Akrotiri gave me a steer of 210° at great range so we were well over central Turkey and heading for Soviet airspace when I began the orbit, probably just in the nick of time or we would soon have been outside radio range from base. It transpired that the Russians had on several occasions duped aircraft with a false signal duplicating the Akrotiri beacon but positioned near Mount Ararat, and we had nearly fallen for it. It certainly taught me that freshly-trained navs had some problems with time and distance calculations and could easily jump to conclusions without sufficient double-checking.

Although my standing in the eyes of my own crew was on the up and up, I was certainly not making too good an impression elsewhere among the dyed-in-the-wool bomber pilots who at that time composed the majority of the Strike Wing. They were not keen to have their ideas about bombing tactics questioned by a young upstart from Fighter Command, sent to get them to point their little pink bodies toward the ground. No Sir! 'Let me carry on in level flight at 7,000 ft' was the prevailing attitude among the bomber boys, or in other words 'let me die from a surface-to-air missile long before reaching the target'. 73 Squadron had been active in the Middle East over many years, previously as a Vampire, then a Venom squadron, after considerable success in North Africa during WW2. However, when re-equipment with Canberras took place in the

B15 WH955 of 32 Squadron over the Himalayas. (Boz Robinson)

early 1960s, the squadron's operating area became much larger. In fact stores were held at Akrotiri to permit detachment to any trouble spot anywhere in the world at short notice. On one occasion we readied ourselves to whiz off to Belize but the orders were rescinded at the last moment just as we were about to fly to Gibraltar.

The Akrotiri Strike Wing was declared to CENTO which co-ordinated the forces of the Baghdad Pact nations, hence our deployment to Pakistan in May '63. But the only roles in which all those Canberras were able to operate were in level bombing and in low-altitude bombing system (LABS) designed for the release of a nuclear weapon. This despite the fact that the aircraft was able to carry two pods of two-inch rockets which could be released at very low altitude, or in a dive. Equally, the bombs in the bomb bay could be released in a dive but that method of delivery was neither recommended nor practised. Indeed, the aircraft carried no effective sighting device to enable shallow dive-bombing.

Our role in Pakistan was simply to provide high-level targets for the PAF to intercept which we did. The authorised routes took us way to the north of the country where we had magnificent views of the Kyber Pass and Himalayan mountains. The PAF requested that we remain below 40,000 ft but when the Canberra has used up half its fuel it can be cruise-climbed much higher. As a fighter pilot I thought it would be a good idea to even the score a little and despite the briefing, climbed with my No. 2 Dave Willis toward 48,000 ft. My navigators were working hard, one keeping us on track, the other helping me with lookout to spot the incoming fighters. Suddenly I saw two F-104s way below the left wing and thus without any hope of carrying out an intercept on us. In those days there was no air-to-air missile threat from those F-104s so their only chance of a kill would have been with guns. I decided to play a game with them and hard turned into the F-104s. Too late I remembered that the 100 series Avons fitted to the Canberra didn't like that sort of treatment. There were two loud pops and then silence. I had flamed out both engines and would now have to descend to below 20,000 ft to relight them. That did not worry me at all. Relighting is a very reliable procedure and rarely fails. Nor was I particularly concerned that we were far from any suitable diversion into which to glide the aircraft in case of inability to relight. In fact despite the alarm of my two navigators, I assured them that all would be well and please not to panic. Of course the event did mean that we would be an easy kill for the F-104s but happily they had exhausted their fuel and gone home. Therefore, I calmly told my No. 2 on the radio what had happened and asked him to be patient while I descended and relit. However, he had already noticed our sudden loss of height and being the well-trained Cranwellian that he was, had taken matters into his own hands by transmitting a Mayday call on the wing discreet frequency. Quite what he thought a Mayday call would do to help was beyond me, but it did at least create panic in the mind of our gallant wing commander who just happened to be ahead of us and listening out. Suddenly my earphones were filled with his questions – 'had I done this – had I done that?' All that he mentioned had already been completed and the last thing I wanted at that moment was to shorten the life of my battery by having to conduct a conversation with him so I told my No. 2 that I was turning off the radio to conserve battery power and therefore would be making no further calls until the engines were relit. That put the wing commander into a state of apoplexy. Having glided down to 19,000 ft we relit both engines and carried on with our task, climbing back to height and returning to Mauripur without further ado.

Needless to say, the wing commander was waiting for me on the tarmac, his anger little assuaged. I had to endure a very severe bollocking and a threat of dire punishment when we got back to base. Furthermore I was forbidden from any further flights during the exercise. During the course of yet another one-sided discussion with Wg Cdr Walker back at base I was tasked with preparing and delivering a lecture to the whole wing on the subject of the Avon engine's propensity to surge and flame-out if mishandled at high altitude. This I achieved with some help from the Rolls-Royce rep in

Boz Robinson at height. (Boz Robinson)

Cyprus, though I doubt that I gave a very convincing performance. Lecturing on technical matters has never been one of my strong points. Not that it mattered much because news of our escapade in northern Pakistan, coupled with the loss of a 6 Squadron B16 and its crew of three caught in a cumulonimbus in the vicinity of Khartoum, was evidence enough to convince my colleagues that the 100 series Avon required careful handling above 40,000 ft.

By this time, our presence as weapons instructors at Akrotiri was beginning to be taken more seriously and now began a positive attempt to make better use of the Canberra as a ground-attack vehicle. Even as early as 1963 our supposed targets in time of tension were the Syrian air force airfields and to destroy their aircraft before they could get airborne meant a surprise low-level attack using rocket projectiles. These were tactics that the predominantly 'bomber' guys at Akrotiri had never trained for and so now we had to bring everyone into the picture so they could operate at very low levels with confidence. Under the guidance of a very positive and gung-ho squadron commander of 32 Squadron, Mike Knight, Manx Kelly, Curly Hirst and I began the task of carrying out rocket delivery trials and later converting the wing pilots to low-level rocket delivery. This was a method of attacking parked aircraft by surprise and approaching at a speed of 300 kts or about 350 mph, and a height above ground of only 35 ft using the normally reliable radar altimeter. That is really fast and low and quite exciting! My first student was Mike Knight himself and we began the trials by running in toward the target at Larnaca range (now Larnaca airport) at a height of 60 feet above the ground. Moving lower to 35 ft came later when people felt happy at 60 ft. After a demonstration sortie, he flew the aircraft while I 'screened' him by sitting alongside on the Rumbold seat. Height was checked using the radar altimeter and when the pippa in the centre of the gunsight ran on to the target at a range of 1,000 yards in absolutely level flight and the firing button was pressed by the pilot, the rockets devastated the target and a 4g escape manoeuvre ensured that the aircraft flew well clear of any ricocheting rockets or debris. Well, that was the theory.

In practice this method generally worked well and very few ricochets were collected; the problem came with what we called 'twirlers', namely rockets that instead of following a direct path to the target, malfunctioned in some way and took a zigzag path into the ground much closer than 1,000 yards. They sometimes threw up debris or ricocheted directly into the path of the aircraft and called for exciting evasion techniques. It came about that the 4g escape manoeuvre sometimes became a 6g manoeuvre, and the usual transgressors in that respect were the instructors, especially me. I had for so long been accustomed to the Hunter and a 6g pull-out during ground attacks that it was not second nature to pull only 4g especially when I could see debris hurtling toward me. I cannot remember exactly how many times I overstressed an aircraft but it was a cause for concern to the boss, and of course to me as well because my reputation was at stake. Eventually I was cured before any aircraft suffered permanent damage as a result of my excessive use of force. The process of getting all the wing pilots except Wg Cdr Walker qualified at low-level RP delivery went on for almost a year until international tensions made our lives much more exciting with a move to the Far East that justified all our efforts.

At base in Cyprus, our flying pattern was to start with a met briefing at 0700 in the air-conditioned operations block then to disperse to the outlying squadron buildings scattered about the eastern end of the airfield. After passing 249's place you could turn right for 32 Squadron or left for 73 Squadron. Beyond lay 13 Squadron with their PR9s. The other famous ex-fighter squadron, 6 Squadron was the odd man out by being situated at the western end of the field, over a mile away from us and quite close to the transport aircraft dispersals and the helicopter zone. The temperature in the ops block was kept at 70°F. Early in the morning it seemed quite pleasant and much like ambient temperature but by lunchtime going in there felt like entering a fridge because the outside would be up to 90 plus (around 30°C). Our Canberra B15s and B16s did not have the opening canopy that the PR9, the B8 and the RNZAF B12s had, so our ground crew would station an air conditioner just outside the side door and put a type of large umbrella over the top of the cockpit some time before the crew arrived to conduct their pre-flight checks. However, although this procedure gave one a reasonably comfortable start to a trip, once the door had to be closed to start the engines, the cool air supply was cut off and the umbrella removed. Then the temperature inside the cabin became very hot very quickly and the crew began to sweat freely. We had a simple rule that if it became impossible to get into the air within seven minutes of shutting the door then the pilot could abort the sortie.

CHAPTER 15
AKROTIRI STRIKE WING

BARRY DOVE joined the RAF in 1961 and trained as a navigator. He flew Canberras in Cyprus, before converting to Buccaneers and then Tornados.

Although 13 Squadron had been the first Canberra unit to be based on Cyprus, my personal experience is of the period 1963-66 when, on my first tour, I was a navigator on 249 (Gold Coast) Squadron.

During 1957, 32, 73, 6 and 249 Squadrons had traded in their Venoms for Canberras. Unlike previous re-equipment exercises, when the pilots and ground crew had simply converted to a new type, this time the process involved complete replacement of all aircrews and many of the ground crew as well. Each squadron had an establishment of eight aircraft and ten crews. The technical personnel had a variable amount of experience: on 249 Squadron, for example, one-third were from the original unit; one-third came from other Canberra units on Cyprus, with the rest being posted-in direct from the UK. Of the total, only half were specifically Canberra-trained.

Life was fairly rugged in those early days as Akrotiri still lacked permanent buildings and most personnel were accommodated under canvas. 249 Squadron was particularly unlucky and had been given a piece of rocky ground on which to erect its tents, borrowing a pneumatic drill from the Royal Engineers to help in the task. It was not until 1959-60 that permanent air traffic control and air operations facilities for the multi-squadron Flying Wing were ready for occupation, permitting the tents, caravans and huts to be abandoned. For the newly-arrived squadrons there was a considerable gap to bridge between low-level ground attack and medium- and high-level bombing and they trained hard to achieve the necessary combat-ready status. There were frequent practice bombing sorties and navexes over Libya, deployments to RAF stations in the Persian Gulf and to air bases in Turkey and Iran, along with detachments to the staging posts at Habbaniya and Basra in Iraq.

One of 249 Squadron's first tasks was to send a Canberra to Nairobi to collect the squadron's silver and other property. Staging via El Adem and Khartoum, the aircraft returned with the hoard four days later, having been liberally decorated with mini-elephants – the squadron badge is a running elephant – courtesy of the ground staff at Eastleigh. In the last weeks of 1959, 6 and 249 Squadrons were re-equipped with ex-Bomber Command Canberra B6s; the other two squadrons retaining their Mk 2s for the time being. Training continued, the Canberras carrying out frequent bombexes in which they attacked Cyprus from all altitudes to provide interception practice for the visiting Hunter, Javelin and, later, Lightning squadrons from the UK. During long-range navigation training the emphasis was on locating pinpoint targets from medium and low level.

In 1956, when plans were being laid to develop Akrotiri as a forward base for V bomber detachments and a permanent home for Canberras, they included provision for nuclear weapons storage. As in the Far East, British planners saw nuclear weapons as the most cost-effective way of contributing to allied defence of the region. However, it was thought that the weapons would be used only in a global war between the Soviet Union and the Western allies. By 1960, facilities were available for 16 Red Beards to be brought to Akrotiri in a crisis and stored temporarily. On 28 November 1961, a permanent facility, the supplementary storage area (SSA) at nearby Cape Gata, became available to hold 32 Red Beards. These 15-kt weapons weighed 1,950 lbs apiece and each Canberra could carry one in the bomb bay. Two RAF Regiment squadrons defended the Cape Gata installation as part of their protection of the base. Although Akrotiri and Cape Gata were technically on British soil, this did not eliminate political sensitivities as the Cypriot government under Archbishop Makarios was neither especially pro-British nor a member of CENTO. A British Air Ministry official wrote in 1960, 'all possible measures should be taken in Cyprus to conceal the arrival and storage of nuclear bombs .... whether they be inert, drill or the real McCoy'. A few years later a plan of Akrotiri was published in a local newspaper; luckily the SSA was identified as 'Soldiers and Sailors Accommodation'.

The arrival of Canberra B15s and 16s in 1961 gave the Akrotiri squadrons a nuclear role, which was implicit in their collective title of the Akrotiri Strike Wing. The B15s were allocated to 32 and 73 Squadrons whilst 6 and 249 Squadrons received the B16s.

B16 on the 249 Squadron dispersal looking towards the runway at Akrotiri. (Barry Dove)

Both versions were modified B6 airframes strengthened for low-level operations in general but particularly for the nuclear delivery manoeuvre associated with LABS. Both aircraft had a crew of three: a pilot, a navigator/plotter and a navigator/observer. The nav/plotter sat behind the pilot in the 'Black Hole of Calcutta' with a Blue Silk Doppler, a ground position indicator (GPI Mk 4A), Rebecca/Eureka range and bearing equipment, a Marconi radio compass, an STR18 HF radio and an orange putter tail warning radar for company. The navigator/observer's role, lying prone in the nose of the aircraft, was map-reading at low level and operating the bombsight for medium-level bombing. The Mk 15 could carry its crew of three plus one, as it had three ejection seats and an occasional fold-down Rumbold seat alongside the pilot.

The Mk 16 had ejection seats only for the pilot and the nav/plotter, the nav/observer having to make do with the fold-down seat. With no ejection seat the observer relied on a flying suit, which had an integral parachute harness, and a chest parachute that clipped onto two hooks. His escape from the aircraft was via the entrance door which could be opened from the inside by turning a handle at least three-and-a-half turns clockwise. The third ejection seat had been removed from the Mk 16 to make way for the Blue Shadow sideways-looking radar. This new device was not popular with the navigators for several reasons. First, the navigation table had to be folded up to check that the system was working. This obscured the Blue Silk display and, inevitably, the Doppler would choose that moment to unlock, and thus drive the GPI read-out off the edge of the chart. Secondly, the radar output was burnt onto specially impregnated paper that had a nasty habit of producing clouds of smoke when it went wrong. Finally, it only looked to starboard, to a range of about 60 miles – consequently, to be of any use, the aircraft had to fly anti-clockwise around the Mediterranean, which meant that we became very familiar with the outline of the southern coast of Crete.

The re-equipment of all four squadrons with B15s and 16s was completed in early 1963 and marked the start of the period during which the Cyprus Wing possessed its greatest potential. The Canberra had a credible low-level strike (i.e. nuclear) capability, with the LABS-delivered Red Beard, and a wide range of attack (i.e. conventional) options, employing medium-level 1,000-lb bombing, shallow dive-bombing and low-level rocketing; in addition 249 Squadron had a target-marking role using 4½-inch parachute flares and target indicators. Allied to routine weapons training were regular squadron detachments and solo training exercises (known as lone rangers) to all points of the compass: west to Malta and Gibraltar, and occasionally the UK; north and east to Turkey, Iran (Tehran), Pakistan, Bahrain (Muharraq), the UAE (Sharjah), Oman (Masirah) and Aden; south and west to El Adem and Idris in Libya or on to Khartoum and Nairobi via the bottom left-hand corner of Egypt, known as 'Nasser's Corner'.

This is when I actually appeared on the scene, in August 1963, but that had not been the original plan for my future. Although originally earmarked for the single-navigator Canberra B(I)8 in Germany, my course on 231 OCU at Bassingbourn was reshuffled to meet the need for a three-man crew for Cyprus. I drew what I thought was the short straw and was posted to 249 Squadron as a navigator/observer. The nuclear weapons course at the Bomber Command Bombing School (BCBS) at Wittering followed the OCU and, as the observer, I had to learn how to carry out the last-minute loading of the Red Beard. This involved a large flask that contained the central core of the weapon, discreetly referred to as 'the physics package'. The whole thing was not dissimilar to the shape of the Jules Rimet World Cup trophy, i.e. a ball on the end of a pole with a flat bit at the bottom. To get this core from the flask into the weapon, a handle was attached to the base plate; the device was then lifted with great care out of the flask and offered up to the weapon. It was then locked into place and the handle removed. A tricky operation at the best of times but with the well-used equipment at BCBS the odd dummy physics package did occasionally end up on the hangar floor. The procedure was affectionately known as 'playing gynaecologist to an elephant'. Armed with this invaluable knowledge, I arrived at Nicosia in a British Eagle Britannia early one hot summer morning and thence by RAF 39-seater Bedford coach to Akrotiri ready to enjoy this seemingly idyllic location. However, the peace did not last long and hostilities between Greek and Turkish Cypriots erupted in late December 1963. The aftermath meant that there was a dusk-to-dawn curfew for most of the following year. For us, that was an inconvenience, rather than a real problem. We could, for instance, still travel to the north of the island and enjoy the delights of Kyrenia by day. Despite the continuing UN presence, the curfew had been lifted by 1965 and most of the previous freedoms had been restored. Generally speaking the situation remained that way for the rest of the Canberra era.

Back to 1963 and, with the B15/16 re-equipment complete, the wing settled into a training and exercise routine that was broadly similar on all four squadrons. The station worked six days a week, mornings only, from 0700 to 1300 hours. We flew Monday to Friday, with Saturday mornings devoted to target study, last-minute loading practice and lectures on the weapon in preparation for the annual visit by the Weapons Standardisation Team. Crews had targets in the so-called 'soft underbelly' of the Soviet Union but, unlike the Canberras stationed in Germany, there was no QRA. My crew had a target near Tashkent, in Uzbekistan, which would have involved a hi-lo sortie of about 1,500 miles; the planned recovery base was Peshawar, about 600 miles away in Pakistan's North-West Frontier Province. Night flying took place on a fairly regular basis and the crews' working day was adjusted accordingly. Most of the local area flying used the weapons ranges at Episkopi Bay and Larnaca. LABS by day, medium-level bombing and shallow dive-bombing (SDB) by both day and night took place at Episkopi using 25-lb practice bombs. LABS involved pre-computing the release param-eters before take-off, these being set by the navigator on the release computer at the rear of the aircraft. Approaching the target at 250 feet, at a pre-determined point the pilot began a 3g pull-up until the bomb was released automatically to be thrown

Barry Dove during the Lepus flare trial at RAF El Adem in 1965. (Barry Dove)

forward by about two miles. To gain maximum possible separation from the weapon before it detonated, the aircraft continued its looping manoeuvre before rolling off the top to recover to low level heading away from the target. Should the automatics fail, the technique was to proceed to the actual target before starting the manoeuvre, releasing the weapon about 120° into the loop in the so-called 'over the shoulder' mode before escaping. Medium-level bombing differed little from the techniques used during WW2; although the bombsight had improved, the same 1,000-lb bombs were in the inventory. Shallow dive-bombing started from a circuit height of 5,000 ft before diving towards the target at 30°. The navigator/plotter called out the heights in the dive down to the release point when the aircraft was recovered for another pass – quite exciting at night. Low-level rocketing was practised on the Larnaca range and was also an exciting event. From a circuit height of 1,000 ft the aircraft made a descending turn to 100 ft or less and accelerated to 350 kts for the run in. The fixed aiming point was lined up to track over the ground up to the target and when they coincided the firing button was pressed. Only single rockets were fired on the range but the operational load was two pods with frangible noses, one on each wing weapons station, each carrying 37 two-inch rockets. Firing a full salvo of 74 rockets in this attack profile produced an elliptical pattern of about 1,000 ft by 40 ft and was ideal for attacking lines of unprotected aircraft or vehicles. Following firing the aircraft turned away sharply to avoid ricochet damage as the rockets impacted.

Bombing practice with thousand pounders was carried out on El Adem range in the Libyan desert. This could be a single aircraft operating from El Adem or a bomber stream from Akrotiri led by 249 Squadron crews dropping 4½-inch parachute flares at medium level followed by coloured target indicators in true Pathfinder tradition. Weapons training locally was complemented by regular detachments to El Adem, Idris (for Tarhuna range) and Sharjah (Exercise Potage), using Rashid down the coast south of Dubai. There was involvement with CENTO nations, Iran and Pakistan, through Exercises Shahbaz and Shahin, and detachments to Tehran and Karachi (Mauripur) provided target practice for the local air defenders. Combined exercises were held to test the squadrons' efficiency in the nuclear and conventional roles. An example of this was Exercise Totem, a global alert exercise held in February 1965. Elements of the

Akrotiri Wing were required to assume the nuclear role for the first 48 hours of the exercise, with aircrew being brought to various states of readiness until phase one was completed. During phase two the aircraft were dispersed. My own logbook shows that on 25 February I flew to Masirah with OC 249 Squadron, John Sutton; we returned to Akrotiri, via Tehran, on the 27th. The lone ranger programme provided invaluable experience and taught the crews a great deal about operating alone away from home in some fairly remote parts of the world. Well before satellites and mobile phones allowed communication from almost anywhere, crews simply submitted their flight plans and set off to make use of the many RAF stations and international airports east of Suez.

Where possible we took full advantage of what the location had to offer. For example, Malta had smoked hams, Aden duty-free electrical goods and cameras, Masirah crayfish tails and swordfish steaks, and Nairobi carved wooden animals. Things did not always go according to plan however, and 6 Squadron lost an aircraft and crew returning from Nairobi. The aircraft suffered a major structural failure and crashed when it flew through an embedded cumulonimbus cloud while descending into Khartoum. Lone rangers to Nairobi were sensibly suspended for a while, the only downside being that it was my crew's turn next, so I never did sample the delights of that part of the world. As will have become clear by now, life for the Cyprus Canberra community was never dull, such was the scope of our normal activities and the variety of additional tasks, large and small, that regularly came our way. One of the biggest was in 1964-65 when the Cyprus squadrons replaced the Canberra B(I)8s from Germany that had been rotating through Kuantan for two months at a time as part of the UK's response to the Indonesian Confrontation. Operating from a tented camp on the east coast of Malaya was an entirely new experience for everyone. Apart from the Kuwait crisis of 1961, the Malaysian

The other chaps in Barry Dove's crew: pilot Flt Lt 'Mac' MacGregor and nav Sgt Dave Smith. (Barry Dove)

experience was the closest the Cyprus Canberra Wing ever came to going to war. Aircraft were loaded with 1,000-lb bombs, crews were briefed, issued with pistols and Maria Theresa dollars and put on standby – but they were never used. There were several other significant occurrences on the wing during the mid to late 1960s.

249 Squadron carried out trials with the new Lepus flare at El Adem in September 1964 and it eventually replaced the 4½-inch flare in 1967. Ground environmental and flying trials with the new nuclear weapon, the WE177, took place in 1964-65 when weapons were loaded and the aircraft taxied around the airfield to monitor temperature and vibration. Instrumented rounds, minus the 'physics package', were flown on a series of sorties nicknamed 'confectionary'. At much the same time, the French AS30 radio-guided air-to-ground missile was added to the B15's weapons inventory. The first squadron firing took place on 20 October 1965 when Brian Cable of 32 Squadron guided a missile to the target at El Adem range. Other innovations included 'pop-up' bombing and trials with the SFOM gun sight and, finally, the dogma of centralised servicing for the wing was introduced at the end of 1966 – but it did not last long. In mid-1968 the runway at Akrotiri was closed for repair and the central servicing force was split into four with each squadron being allocated its own personnel. Morale and serviceability soared and very few sorties were lost over the next four months or so, even though the squadrons spent much time away from Cyprus at a variety of places including Malta, Sharjah and Nicosia. These were Indian summer times for Akrotiri's Canberras but the end was in sight. It had been the intention to re-equip two of the squadrons with the TSR2 but that project was cancelled in 1965 and the US F-111 was ordered instead. That order was also cancelled and eventually Akrotiri's Strike Wing received two squadrons of Vulcans from the UK. The beginning of the end for the Canberra came on 10 January 1969 when a disbandment fly-past was held. Shortly afterwards 6 Squadron left to be re-established at Coningsby with Phantoms. 32 Squadron was next to go, disbanding on 3 February, followed by 249 Squadron on the 24th and 73 Squadron on 3 March.

CHAPTER 16
RAF GERMANY
GOES NUCLEAR

On 1 January 1958, 88 Squadron's Wildenrath-based Canberra B(I)8s and their two-man crews were formally committed to the nuclear strike role. In C-in-C 2TAF's words, 'their role is that of night interdictor, but they are also capable of high and "pylon" (low-level) bombing...Much of 88 Squadron's practice work is now carried out over Denmark. High-level attacks are made to test the air defences, followed by low-level ones on airfields to practise the LABS technique. 88 and the other Canberra B(I)8s occupy an important place in 2TAF and the morale of their crews is high. They have absolute trust in their aircraft and are confident of their ability to reach a target anywhere, however small it may be and however limited the visibility. In fact, 88 Squadron has claimed successful low-level practice attacks with only 450-yard visibility.

The B(I)8 conventional weapons load. (Tom Eeles)

DICK KIDNEY joined 88 Squadron as a first tour B(I)8 pilot with Martin Watts as his nav in July 1959.

Our primary role then was night ground attack (NGA). We operated as pairs using slow flares. The first B(I)8 would drop its flares while the other attacked the illuminated target, whereupon we would swap positions. The forward-firing 20-mm Hispano guns were awesome – the 525 rounds of ammunition weighed a ton before the gun pod went on. We also did day ground attack. We were to aim for the wooded areas of East Germany, looking for Scud missiles rising to the vertical so we could hammer them with cannon fire.

In August 1960, just over a year after Martin and I arrived at Wildenrath, the boss – Wg Cdr F. C. 'Sid' Dunmore – got permission to move us smoothly into QRA. We had one B(I)8 armed at all times with barbed wire around the blast wall in the south-east corner of Wildenrath. The QRA crew lived in the hangar together with the US alert duty officer (ADO). It was an 80-100 yard sprint to the aircraft so three service bicycles, each painted red, were positioned in the hangar, one for the pilot, one for the nav and one for the Yank. The other three strike squadrons followed suit in very quick succession. ▨

Canberra upgrading, combined with cutbacks generated by Duncan Sandys' 1957 Defence White Paper, resulted in the following Canberra B(I)6 and B(I)8 squadron number plates in RAF Germany:

3 Squadron	RAF Geilenkirchen	B(I)8	January 1961-January 1968
3 Squadron	RAF Laarbruch	B(I)8	January 1968-January 1972
14 Squadron	RAF Wildenrath	B(I)8	December 1962-June 1970
16 Squadron	RAF Laarbruch	B(I)8	March 1958-June 1972
59 Squadron	RAF Geilenkirchen	B(I)8	November 1957-January 1961 (Renumbered 3 Squadron)
88 Squadron	RAF Wildenrath	B(I)8	January 1956-December 1962 (Renumbered 14 Squadron)
213 Squadron	RAF Brüggen	B(I)6	August 1957-December 1969

A single Canberra from each squadron was on QRA initially. Ray Leach was a first tour nav on 16 Squadron and he was on QRA at the height of the Cuban crisis in 1962 when the QRA commitment was doubled up and stayed that way, with a requirement to be airborne within 15 minutes of an alert. With the assumption of the nuclear role, 88 Squadron should have relinquished its previously assigned roles of army cooperation and close air support but life was never that simple.

In **DICK KIDNEY'S** words:

We kept our ground-attack skills for deployments. For instance, in June 1961 I was woken at 0500 as Iraq was threatening Kuwait. We loaded up with 1,000-lb bombs and guns and set off for Akrotiri – the first half dozen or so aircraft to arrive in Cyprus had a quick rest and then flew in a straight line to Sharjah with no flight plan, no nav lights and no radio transmissions. The targets we were given included Iraqi radar sites and the MoD building in Baghdad. I was expected to strafe the fourth and fifth floors with cannon – I was told to avoid the lower floors which accommodated western female typists. People had great faith in our pinpoint capability. Most of our subsequent flying over Germany was without the gun pod fitted. It was a bit of a fag to install and remove the gun pack but we kept current over the Nordhorn range and the Stroehen range west of Brunswick.

After National Service as a fighter controller, **PHIL WILKINSON** graduated from Oxford and rejoined the RAF in 1961. He arrived on 14 Squadron at Wildenrath with his nav, Paddy O'Shea, in November 1963, by which time the nuclear strike role was well established.

Back in February 1957, Germany strike Canberras were being fed into the modification programme to install the Honeywell systems that were the core of the LABS attack system. Political and technical complications surrounded the progress to full operational status, not least the arrangements that had to be made for physical storage areas for the US weapon, and for separate accommodation for its technical support team, and for the security force that guarded it. But by September 1959, all four squadrons were each maintaining a single aircraft on QRA (increasing to two in 1962), with a requirement to be airborne within 15 minutes of the alert. The two crews were accompanied in the wired-off compound by a USAF alert duty officer (usually a lieutenant) who provided half of the two-man concept that governed all access to and handling of the weapon. The USAF air policemen similarly provided half of the security cordon, sharing the task with RAF police, both armed.

The concept of operations was straightforward: the QRA aircraft and equipment inside 14 Squadron's hangar at Wildenrath in 1965, showing the training ballistic 1,650-lb 'shape' store on a trolley in front of the middle aircraft, would provide

Phil Wilkinson (left) and his nav Paddy O'Shea at El Adem, Libya on 28 February 1966. (Phil Wilkinson)

immediate response to SACEUR's call for strikes, and would be able to do that either individually or as the vanguard of a fully generated force that had benefited from a period of alert state development allowing time for the weapon loading and crew preparation to make the whole squadron available for selective release against targets on SACEUR's strike programme. Given the Canberra's low-level radius of action – with 24,000 lbs of fuel, the B(I)8 could cover 600 nm out and back in a straight line at 420 kts (365 till the wing-tip tanks were jettisoned, or at least that is what the Pilot's Notes said) to dry tanks – the targets were almost all confined to tactical airfields in one or other of the Warsaw Pact satellite countries. The primary QRA target was the one exhaustively studied by crews in regular sessions in the Operations Wing vault – the day before a QRA duty started was a mandatory study day; other sessions were programmed in with all the other routine training requirements. The visit of the weapons standardisation team from the Armament Support Unit at Wittering was a regular challenge to the memory glands. And of course Taceval, and all the lower level alert and readiness tests, kept the edge permanently sharpened. With half the squadron assigned to each of the two QRA targets, it was never less than once a fortnight that a crew had a 24-hour shift in the compound. The weekend duty, covering 48 hours, came up six or seven times a year. The junior combat-ready crews could, of course, expect to have the several days of the Christmas break for their personal enjoyment.

That was the ground-based theory. What of the flying training for the role? In three years on 14 Squadron I fell just nine short of 1,000 hours. The role of the squadron was totally focused on low-level operation. Hence the vast majority of sorties were two-hour excursions around a relatively-unrestricted German airspace, including first-run attacks at the main ranges and academic practice-bomb sessions, almost invariably at Nordhorn. The other continental ranges were used – in Belgium, the Netherlands, and (occasionally) France – and regular runs were made to all the UK targets, but it will be the features and time checks along the LABS run to Nordhorn target that are probably still etched on the memories of anyone who served on one of the Germany squadrons of the period.

The attack was a trifle mechanical, and involved pre-computing release parameters prior to take-off, which were set by the navigator on the release computer at the rear of the aircraft before clambering aboard. In-flight adjustments were possible but only by over-riding the cues that the pilot followed to initiate the pull-up. For both the standard forward toss and the reversionary 'over-the-shoulder' attacks, the approach speed was calculated (from met data) to give an equivalent air speed of 434 kts; the pull-up was triggered by pickling the bomb release button at the final IP and waiting until the computer-driven timer ran down and gave the cue. On a manual ILS-type instrument the driver then gathered the horizontal needle back up to the centre and maintained the vertical needle vertical (hence the Hornchurch/Biggin Hill aptitude tests) which meant a modest application of +3.4g. Bomb release was also signalled to the driver and the mildly aerobatic escape recovery from 4,000+ ft back to the 250 ft approach height was carried out ready for another run in the academic pattern.

Proficiency in this manoeuvre was of fundamental importance, both for consistent weapon accuracy and for survival. Hence the regular detachments to better weather areas with range facilities on the doorstep, for intensive work-up of new crews and consolidation for the more experienced. Thus, in my second month in the squadron, three crews and two aircraft left the murk of north Germany in December and worked for a five-day period at RAF Idris, 20 miles south of Tripoli, and with Tarhuna range just minutes off the end of the runway. Flying started at 0600 or asap after sunrise and was as intensive as the ramp heat and the cockpit air conditioning would allow the ground and aircrew to achieve.

A typical day's flying was, therefore, a four-bomb detail, with the first being a first run attack (FRA), returning to Idris after perhaps only 25 minutes for an engines-running re-arm with four more 25-lb practice bombs on the wing pylons ready for the same again. That would be repeated twice more before lunchtime. Each crew would thus drop 24 bombs a day; 70+ per crew per detachment. The third crew split; one man to the range as the range safety officer, the other to manage the ground activities at Idris and keep the orange juice cool for the quick turn-rounds. Range work was usually built in to the exercise sorties flown within the overall pattern of NATO training: major ATAF-wide air defence events such as Blue Moon or Cold Fire; smaller-scale Canberra B(I)8 in the conventional role fit; air defence exercises such as Brown Falcon over Denmark; Highwood and the smaller-scale Priory versus the UK Air Defence Region; Round Robin, later Ample Gain, to check cross-servicing facilities at other NATO bases; even Datex – for the benefit of the French; and, with due political correctness, Cloggy Emotion to exercise the Dutch forward air controllers. These, and many others, remained fixed points in authorisation sheets and logbooks.

The versatility of the Canberra meant inevitably that it would be asked to do more than hold alert for nuclear response and the associated training. Thus the regular reversion to conventional fit – with the four × 20-mm gun pack fitted in the bomb bay and all conventional weapon options available from wing pylons and the remaining forward sector of the bomb bay. Operational actuality was regularly the cause: 59 Squadron went to British Honduras (Belize) in 1958 to discourage Guatemalan advances; 213 and 88 deployed to the Gulf in mid-1961 for an early version of the Kuwait crisis; in 1963 all RAF Germany Canberra squadrons were rotating through Kuantan in Malaya to reinforce the UK response to the Indonesian Confrontation. To remain at least semi-prepared for these short-notice excursions, all Canberra squadrons had at least one three-week detachment to (usually) Cyprus, in the conventional fit – Exercise Citrus Grove. Dive-bombing was against the raft targets in Episkopi Bay; strafe was at Larnaca, against targets on the salt marsh that now supports the international airport. The highly agreeable solution to the need for readiness for these exotic deployments

B(I)8 XM278 of 14 Squadron flown by Phil Wilkinson on 10 June 1966 over Germany as photographed by Dickie Lees from a PR7 of 17 Squadron. (Phil Wilkinson)

was simply to practise exotic deployments: this was Exercise Lone Ranger. There was hardly a day on any of the squadrons when there was not a singleton aircraft and crew somewhere down the Southern or Extended Southern Ranger route; via Cyprus, the Gulf (Sharjah, Bahrain, Masirah, or even Djibouti), through Aden and on to Nairobi and (then) Salisbury. Return routes often staged via Tehran and then had extended low-level sectors across Iran before climbing out to overfly Turkey back into Cyprus. Sometimes, too, the last homeward stage would take in some Libyan desert low-level flying, using El Adem as a refuel/re-arming point, prior to some range runs or an attempt to find the wreck of the 'Lady Be Good' B-24 before climbing out on fuel minima.

In mid-1966 there had been a change of strike profile: the Mk 7 LABS weapon delivery being replaced by laydown with a US Mk 43 2,100-lb weapon. Work-up had gone well and the CEP for strike had been radically improved from LABS scores of around 200 yards to laydown scores of 60 to 80 feet. The US Mk 43 2,100-lb weapon could be dropped from a high-speed laydown attack by parachute retardation. After a short pause from QRA while ground procedures and practice weapon loading had been exercised, the squadron resumed QRA with the new weapon on 4 November. Just to prove the point, HQ RAF Germany and the station commander called us out for three alert and generation exercises in the next ten days. This was very percipient since the NATO Taceval team arrived on 14 November – the squadron received an across-the-board rating of '1' – the first for a strike unit in RAFG.

I don't think we were ever told what the time delay was to be before detonation – which strikes me today as a little worrying. We began to get quite clever with the SFOM sight fitted in the bomb-aimer's position (and even more so with the essential Chinagraph marks placed on the widescreen).

The navigation fit consisted of a first generation Doppler known as Blue Silk, which was the precursor of Green Satin. It was then decided to add the Decca Mk 8, and RAY LEACH flew on the trials.

We added an extra navigator and flew hi-lo-hi to and from Germany to attack Henstridge airfield in Somerset. One nav map-read down the nose, while the other plotted on the desk. The trial proved the Decca to be ideal for flying a trawler but it was fitted anyway. I spent most of my time navigating the B(I)8 by map-reading down the nose. I flew Laarbruch – Bahrain – Sharjah – Aden – and back via El Adem and Malta using dead reckoning, a pair of binoculars and a set of topos (1:50,000 topographical charts). On interdiction sorties, the nav turned the pilot towards the target and left him to fire the gun. ▮

ED ELTON joined the RAF as a pilot in 1966 and his first tour was on the B(I)8 with 16 Squadron:

We were based at RAF Laarbruch and our major role was nuclear strike. As such we held QRA 24/7 365 days a year with four aircraft, two from 16 Squadron and two from 3 Squadron. We were regularly locked in the QRA pen for 24 hours, most usually after a full day of work, whiling away the time with *Playboy*, bridge, eating, moaning and sleeping and occasionally doing some target study.

Our weapon was actually an American weapon, and therefore 'owned' by an American special weapons officer, most of whom saw the specific trade as a way of avoiding service in Vietnam. Whenever access to the nuclear-loaded aircraft was required, which was parked in a hangarette within what was called a 'no-lone' zone, literally marked around the aircraft with a painted line, the aircraft captain, the American custodian and the American guard all had to enter the zone together, alongside whoever might need access to the aircraft.

From time to time we would participate in a 'scrambled' exercise to check our procedures. When the hooter blew there was a mad rush to exit the domestic site, we gathered the minimum three and together with the ground crew stepped across the line, to prepare for release. Meanwhile the navigators had to open the safe and withdraw their target bags and follow on as fast as they could. Once strapped in we had to have release from both the UK and American authorities, UK for the aircraft and American for the weapon. To maintain the two-man concept the pilot had certain actions and the navigator others. I should say engines were never started and it was the job of the American guards to shoot one if you tried. Once this was done the ops centre would stand you down, presumably report the response time up the chain and we could return to boredom. Civilisation could sleep easy.

On one occasion (and it wasn't me), the hooter blew and the usual mad rush ensued. Three aircraft checked in but with the fourth – no navigator! Great consternation but eventually the exercise scramble was declared over (post-mortem to follow) and we returned to our accommodation to find No. 4 navigator flat on his back totally unconscious but still clutching his target bag. He had been last in the queue and as he rushed to leave the building had received the heavy swinging doors full in the face! I cannot remember what happened subsequently. Nuclear strike is a deadly serious matter but I think it had to be regarded as a one-off. ▮

16 Squadron in May 1972. The boss was Ken Appelboom. (Steve Fisher)

PHIL WILKINSON again:

In June 1967 the AFCENT Tactical Weapons Meet saw the squadron just beaten by a Canadian F-104 team; the USAFE F-4Es were a long way behind. A 14 Squadron crew won the night strike competition by a wide margin. Given that the navigation equipment fit still consisted of just a steam-driven Doppler (Blue Silk) and the Decca Mk 8 (conceived as a navigation system for shipping, and quite good at that sort of speed!), the abilities of the navigator fraternity were remarkable. Their working environment – in the B(I)8 – was testing to say the least: 90 per cent of the time stretched out in the nose map-reading, contorting back at regular intervals to update the navigation equipment from the most recent visual fix. There was no ejection seat for him, just the normal entry/exit hatch and a chest parachute. My own partner was 6'1" tall and as solid as you could wish (very Irish, too). The aviation medicine people were concerned! But – especially if you were very small – escape was possible. On 11 June 1968 Flt Lt Stu Stringer decided to leave after his driver had had an airborne coming-together with another of the squadron's aircraft. The driver ejected successfully at just 200 ft, no doubt still astonished at seeing Stu roll up and dive for the ground some 800 ft earlier.

In an emergency the navigator had to jettison the door and roll out of the doomed Canberra. When a Canberra went in at low level it usually claimed the lives of all on board. Out of 57 production B(I)8s, 51 were to be divided between three RAFG squadrons and of these, 12 were lost and 15 aircrew died. Even worse was the loss rate of the B(I)6s, which were flown only by 213 Squadron. Of the 19 taken in strength, eight were lost and as the B(I)6 carried a crew of three – all with ejection seats – 20 aircrew still died.

All good things have to come to an end. The first of 2 TAF's Canberra strike/interdictors to disband was 213 Squadron on 31 December 1969. For the 18 crews still keeping 14 Squadron at full strength until the last moment, 31 May 1970 saw 14 Squadron come off state as a Canberra strike squadron. 14 Squadron converted to the Phantom FGR2 but they could not maintain the Canberra pace. In January 1967, 475 hours were flown by 13 B(I)8 Canberras manned by 18 crews: in January 1972, there were 10 F-4s for the squadron's 15 crews but they only shared 175 hours.

3 Squadron converted to the Harrier GR1 at the end of 1971. Dick Kidney had been a flight commander on 31 Squadron when it folded and then he was sent to do the same job for nine months on 3 Squadron. In June 1972, 16 Squadron began converting to the Buccaneer S2. The retirement of 16 Squadron's B(I)8s marked the end of the 21-year strike career of the RAF's first jet bomber.

Steve Fisher and Mike Gee taking off on 14 September 1971 on a bombing competition sortie. The pylon, capable of carrying a 1,000-lb bomb, is clearly visible under the outer wing. Gerry Kingwell had written 'Watch the flak chaps' at bottom right. Gerry was killed in a flying club accident shortly afterwards. (Steve Fisher)

The Canberra B(I)8 made an impression to the very end, as STEVE FISHER of 16 Squadron recalls:

It was around the summer of 1971 when the buzz of a court martial being held at HQ RAFG caught the attention of the crew room at Laarbruch. Although some of the fine detail might be lost in the sands of time, the gist is as follows.

A gaggle of largely reluctant aircrew officers were undergoing ski training on the slopes of Bad Kohlgrub in Bavaria in preparation for the rigours of escape and evasion (and inevitable interrogation) training. On the day in question, a Canberra crew from one of our sister squadrons found fit to buzz a couple of their pals struggling with their first foray into Alpine skiing. The aircraft first appeared at the low end of the hill, and flew up the piste at impressively low level, culminating in a sporting wing-over at the crest. Unfortunately this feat of derring-do was not appreciated by a wing commander participant on the course, who felt obliged to report the incident to the flight safety cell at Rheindahlen.

At a critical point in what then became the subsequent court martial proceedings, the witness wing commander was asked the following question: 'In your opinion wing commander, was what you saw on the slopes that day dangerous?' 'Not really,' he replied, 'but then again I consider myself a highly competent skier.' I believe the Canberra crew walked!

CHAPTER 17
FEAF OFFENSIVE
SUPPORT WING

B2 WH853 'D-Dog' dropping a salvo of 1,000-lb bombs during anti-terrorist operations in Malaya.

JEFF JEFFORD joined the RAF in 1959 as a pilot but was soon remustered as a navigator. He flew on Canberras with 45 Squadron in Singapore before joining the Vulcan force.

Canberras were first deployed to the Far East in 1955 when they replaced the previous detachments of Lincolns as Bomber Command's contribution to the Malayan Emergency – Operation Firedog. First up were 101 Squadron followed in turn by 617, 12, 9 and 101 again until September 1956 when the Suez affair disrupted this arrangement. The answer was to provide the Far East Air Force (FEAF) with some Canberras of its own and in late 1957 45 Squadron, then based at Butterworth, began to dispose of its Venoms while a new eight-aircraft Canberra air echelon was being assembled at Coningsby. The squadron began to deploy to Singapore-Tengah in December and the first strike by in-house FEAF Canberras, Operation Ginger, was flown on 18 March 1958 when four aircraft each dropped six 500 pounders. Compared to the squadron's earlier aeroplanes, its Canberras could lift a lot more bombs, carry them a lot further, fly a lot higher and go a lot faster. In September 1958, for instance, they dropped 60 1,000 pounders in the course of ten sorties. It is a measure of the considerable increase

B6 WH968 of 12 Squadron dropping bombs during the Malayan Emergency. (Peter Green Collection)

in offensive capability conferred by the Canberra that for the squadron to have delivered 60,000 lbs of bombs with its Hornets would have required 60 sorties, or 30 by Venoms.

So progress – of a kind – because a Canberra crew in 1958 was no better able to see terrorists in the jungle than a Beaufighter pilot of 1948. Apart from visual aiming, which was very rarely employed, as jungle targets were hardly discernible, the squadron used three basic methods of bombing, all of which were already well-established in-theatre. The first was the flare datum technique. In short, this involved overflying, at about 12,000 feet and precisely on track for the nominated target co-ordinates, an army patrol, who indicated their presence by a flare or smoke, and simply doing a timed run to release. The system was inherently inaccurate and was of real use only against area targets, the bombers flying on slightly diverging tracks to scatter the bombs within a one-kilometre square. A more accurate method of assisted bombing employed a target director post (TDP). A TDP was a gun-laying radar (specifically an AA radar No. 3, Mk 7) adapted from its original role to work in the reverse sense – instead of aiming at the aeroplane it was used to guide it. Knowing both its own position and that of the target, and using its best guess at the wind, the TDP was able to project a narrow beam of energy in the direction of the target, but aimed off to allow for crosstrail.

The aircraft flew over the TDP, already heading in the right direction, and then proceeded outbound, kept on track by the director on the ground until told to release the bombs. It was much like a visual bomb-run except that the bomb aimer wasn't in

CHAPTER 18
CONFRONTATION

In JEFF JEFFORD's words:

The first ripples to disturb this period of relative calm had been made when the plan for the establishment of the sovereign state of Malaysia had come to fruition in September of 1963. Always opposed to, what he chose to represent as, an 'imperial plot', President Sukarno of Indonesia began to promote what came to be known as 'Confrontation', a state of armed political and economic hostility, sometimes including direct military action, but stopping short of outright war. Bands of guerrillas began to make incursions across the border from Indonesian Kalimantan and the frequency of these steadily increased. By this time, the New Zealanders had handed back their RAF B2s and gone home to take delivery of their own B(I)12s which were to be based at Ohakea, although the squadron was still committed to return to Singapore as and when circumstances dictated. By 1964 circumstances did so dictate and 14 Squadron RNZAF flew up to Singapore in April. Their presence at Tengah provided an opportunity to compare tactical notes informally and these discussions provide an interesting commentary on the state of low-level bombing in the mid-1960s. The New Zealanders were practising straight-in attacks at 250 ft. When it was pointed out that their bombs would almost certainly skip and go off underneath them, they countered that this would not be the case if the bombs were retarded. This was true but, although retarded tail units were just beginning to become available, there were none in the Far East. Unperturbed, the Kiwis wanted to be ready for when they did arrive and anyway, they said it was 'more fun that way'.

The Australians, up at Butterworth, favoured a low-level approach and a pop-up to 2,000 feet. This would certainly reduce the incidence of bombs skipping but, using 1,000 pounders, there was a significant risk of self-damage and at this relatively low altitude the aircraft would be very vulnerable to the target's defences, including small-arms fire. As 2(B) Squadron had only eight aeroplanes, it was questionable whether any such risks were acceptable. For its part, 45 Squadron was advocating a pop-up to 3,500 or even 7,000 ft which would guarantee that the bombs would stay put where they hit, eliminate any risk of self-damage and avoid the threat from all but AAA, with which the Indonesians were not well provided (and in the mid-1960s they lacked any form of surface-to-air missile). On the other hand, bombing accuracy obviously degrades with height and there was a significant chance that the aeroplane would climb into cloud. I should stress that none of the squadrons were practising one tactic to the total exclusion of all others; nevertheless they all tended to have different starting points in crew room discussions. As the controlling formation, one might have expected HQ 224 Group to have laid down the law, but the wide range of prevalent opinion was symptomatic of the fact that wholesale low-level tactics had been introduced only recently. In 1964, in the absence of appropriate weapons, there were a number of alternative solutions to the problem of low-level bombing, but there was no right answer.

In the summer of 1964 the Offensive Support Wing finally perfected joint strike. Using four Canberras and two four-ships of Hunters, various combinations were tried, but a typical strike would involve the Canberras saturating the area with a barrage of 296 two-inch rockets followed by the two sections of Hunters with their heavier 60-lb rockets. As the last of these cleared the area the Canberras ran back in to drop 24,000 lbs of bombs and the Hunters then returned to rake the target with cannon fire. It was tried out on Exercise Raven in July, using the inland range at Asahan, the usual venue for live FAC training, and if nothing else it certainly raised a lot of dust. Although the opposition had some Tu-16 Badgers and late-model MiGs, the most likely threat to Tengah was a strike by MiG-17s and WW2-vintage B-26s and P-51s. All of these were potent enough as ground-attack aircraft and a low-level approach from Indonesian airspace, which was only fifteen miles south of Tengah, would have provided minimal warning. As a counter to this, a survival scramble procedure was introduced, and when the tension began to ramp up in December 1963 it was exercised for the first time, which – since it involved a variety of reinforcement aircraft, including a number of Victors, in addition to the four-squadron home team of Javelins, Hunters and Canberras – was quite 'exciting'.

There was considerable concern over the vulnerability of our aeroplanes, which were routinely parked in neat rows, more often than not supplemented by a long line of naval aircraft whenever a carrier air group was ashore, topped off by several Victors. In an effort to reduce the risk of losing all of one type to a single strafing run, we tried mixing them up so that a dispersal might contain two or three Hunters, a couple of Canberras, a Victor, a Javelin and the odd Britannia or Hastings that was passing through. It proved to be quite impractical, as the increased demand for MT simply could not be sustained. If a fitter needed to collect a grommet or a widget, his squadron's stores was no longer just across the pan. It was now likely to be a couple of miles away on the far side of the busiest runway in the RAF, which could be crossed only during rare intervals in the intensive flying programme. The alternative meant going off camp through one gate and in through another, which involved laborious security checks, and then retracing one's steps. Minor engineering snags could take hours to clear.

Aerial sharp end during Confrontation – 45 Squadron B15 leading a 64 Squadron Javelin FAW9 and a Hunter FGA9 of 20 Squadron.

There were even cases of aeroplanes being 'lost' because they had been parked on a different dispersal from the one from which they had taken off. After a few days of this chaos the aircraft all returned to their own pans but, where space permitted, they were no longer parked in neat rows but staggered, with aircraft sometimes being pushed right back onto the grass.

By mid-1964 Tengah had been provided with an active defence system with an outer ring of radar-laid army-operated AA and an RAF Regiment Bofors squadron within the airfield perimeter. In addition, a few 20-mm Oerlikons had been sited at random locations for use by anyone in the mood to engage the enemy. The overall plan for the air defence of Singapore was conducted under the nickname 'Franciscan' and from time to time the alert state called for dawn and dusk patrols to the south of the island. Usually conducted by Javelins and/or Hunters, on occasion 45 Squadron was co-opted into the system and rocket-armed Canberra 'fighters' flew a number of these sorties during 1964. Another element of the Franciscan plan called for the Strike Force to be dispersed and, following seaborne and parachute landings on the Malayan peninsula by Indonesian commandos in August and September, 45 Squadron moved up-country to Kuantan where it lived under canvas, while maintaining a dawn-to-dusk stand-by for about a month with armed aircraft.

Canberra bomber reinforcement of FEAF during Confrontation was as follows:

Who?	When?	Where?
73 Squadron	September-November 1964	Tengah
3/14 Squadron	October-November 1964	Kuantan
32 Squadron	November 1964-February 1965	Tengah

Who?	When?	Where?
16 Squadron	February-June 1965	Kuantan
249 Squadron	June-August 1965	Kuantan
6 Squadron	August-September 1965	Kuantan
73 Squadron	September-November 1965	Kuantan
32 Squadron	Nov-Dec 65	Kuantan

At much the same time FEAF was reinforced by 73 Squadron from Akrotiri and a month later an eight-aircraft detachment of B(I)8s flew in from Germany to relieve 45 Squadron up at Kuantan. The B(I)8s were withdrawn after a few weeks, leaving just one additional squadron in-theatre but that level of reinforcement was sustained for the next fifteen months.

A word about what FEAF's bombers were going to do. As I have indicated, the B15 was nuclear-capable and 45 Squadron crews maintained currency with LABS but, as a very junior flying officer, no one ever saw fit to tell me why. We surely weren't going to 'nuke' Djakarta, so I imagine that there must have been some sort of plan for 'doing it' to China. I have a vague recollection that there may have been some highly classified stuff relating to China held in the ops block vault – but I was never given access to any of that. What we did have squirreled away in the vault was a selection of mission folders, which we drew up ourselves, for various conventional targets in Indonesia. My personal war plan involved an attack, so far as I was aware, by just one Canberra on Djakarta airport after which we were to recover to Labuan where we were to re-arm, refuel and do it again on the way home after lunch, this time to something at Pontianak in Kalimantan. When radars were installed at Kuching and Labuan in 1964 my crew was sent across to Borneo for a week to do the calibration sorties. Our aeroplane had a bomb beam, triple carriers and empty, but operational, rocket pods and we were at the disposal of Comairbor for offensive tasking as required. We were far more interested in bombing or shooting someone than droning about for the benefit of the radar guys so, as soon as we landed at Kuching, we asked where the bomb dump was – there wasn't one. We asked about rockets, but there were none of those either. We insisted that they must be there somewhere, because it was 'in the plan'. We eventually had to accept that the only reload capability at Kuching amounted to a few Firestreak missiles and some Aden gun packs, and we found the same situation at Labuan. When we got back to Tengah we reported this to Ian Pedder, who looked a trifle concerned and told us to keep it under our hats. So we did.

At the end of 1964, the Indonesians infiltrated some more troops into the south-western tip of Malaya – on Kukup Island. Operation Birdsong was mounted to dislodge them. This involved simulated strikes by Hunters and Canberras on 23 and 24 December, followed by a four-ship Hunter attack using live ordnance on the 24th and, on Boxing Day, a rocket attack by one of 45 Squadron's Canberras controlled by an FAC in a helicopter, which finally did the trick. This was the last live offensive sortie to be flown by an RAF Canberra.

From January 1965 onwards the squadron had one or two aeroplanes more or less permanently deployed to Labuan and/or Kuching for much of the next eighteen months, indeed from April to June the whole squadron was at Labuan while Tengah's runway was being patched up. While in Borneo the Canberras flew numerous border patrols, exercised with FACs and dropped some 1,000 pounders on a new weapons range that had been hastily laid out and licensed at Balambangan – so OC Offensive Support Wing had evidently managed to paper over the bomb-availability crack by then. By this time, President Sukarno was becoming increasingly isolated in diplomatic circles and Indonesia had become increasingly preoccupied with internal affairs. Confrontation had been Sukarno's baby and as his personal influence began to wane, the steam began to go out of his campaign and it was finally brought to a close by a treaty signed in Bangkok on 11 August 1966.

This was the beginning of the end for the Canberra in FEAF. The New Zealanders flew back to Ohakea in November 1966 and in the following April the Australians redeployed from Butterworth to Phan Rang to participate in the fighting in Vietnam; by the time that they were withdrawn in 1971 they had racked up some 12,000 sorties. But 45 Squadron still had one more shot in its locker – the AS30. The AS30 had been in prospect since the end of 1964 but it took a long time to materialise. As always, FEAF had to wait until the Cypriots had had a go and the first AS30-capable aeroplane didn't reach Tengah until June 1966. Thereafter four Exercise Hotshots were mounted, two from Labuan and two from

45 Squadron's 50th birthday formation at Tengah in 1966 including a T4.

AS30 missile being loaded onto a 45 Squadron B15 at Labuan.

Woomera, during which no fewer than 128 missiles were fired – which seems to have been a remarkably generous allocation of what must have been fairly expensive toys.

Before 45 Squadron began to run down, it mounted a series of five FAC training detachments to Kai Tak, whence it had also flown three slightly unusual tasks in 1965, '66 and '67 under Operations Monomania and Tennon. These involved air sampling sorties, following Chinese nuclear tests, sometimes employing B6s that had been provided for that purpose. The squadron had had a good run, but it managed to write off nine Canberras in 14 years, which was probably about par for the course in those days.

BOZ ROBINSON, detached from Akrotiri with 73 Squadron, recalls:

Off the coast of Malaya at Kuantan from a height of 5,000 ft one could look down and see the ghostly shapes of the *Prince of Wales* and *Repulse* lying about 5 nm offshore. Our targets were Indonesian airfields where their aircraft were dispersed. My target was Djakarta airport which had both civil and military aircraft, and we did not wish to inflict damage on the civil guys. After much deliberation we agreed that I would lead six aircraft at very low level – 50 ft or lower – and I and my wingman would spread 148 two-inch rocket projectiles against the lined-up MiGs and Tupolevs. Thereafter, while the other four aircraft did the same but from different angles, we (the first pair) would pull up to 6,000 ft in a continuous climbing turn and roll in for a 30° dive attack against the same aircraft or others that became visible in the manoeuvre, diving back down to 50 ft to make our getaway. The other two pairs would do the same so that we would have delivered 444 two-inch rockets and 36 1,000-lb bombs to make President Sukarno's eyes water. The nearest we on 73 Squadron got was to be brought to two minutes readiness which lasted for about six hours. That certainly concentrated the mind!

ANTHONY WRIGHT was a V Force nav radar at the time:

After a tour on Valiants I found myself on Vulcans at RAF Cottesmore. In November 1965, now fully prepared, we flew out to join the other half of a detachment of a squadron already based at Tengah as part of the RAF's contribution to defending Malaysia in the conflict formally known as the Indonesian Confrontation.

During that period Tengah accommodated a large number of different types of aircraft but Vulcan bomber crews had more in common with the RAF and RNZAF crews of the Canberras. At Tengah we were accommodated in the officer's mess. Not, I may add, in the 'new' accommodation, with air-conditioned sealed rooms, tailor-made specifically for the V Force and people like us on detachment. Those single rooms had been purloined by the non-detachment bachelor officers serving on the station, some of whom were the Canberra crews. We had to double up in the old original rooms that had open slatted doors and were clearly designed to allow the mosquitoes to feast on us.

Flying a Vulcan at low level in the Far East was something to be remembered. The heat in the cabin was stifling and sweat used to pour off us all. On the ground at Tengah cold air was pumped into the cockpit through a long flexible pipe. We envied the Canberra crews who also had portable, removable shades placed over the large glass canopy of their cockpits when they were parked (see photo page 121). Although tailor-made for the Canberra, and not designed for a Vulcan, they would have afforded extra protection from the sun for our pilots and rear crew compartment.

As part of our requirement to drop conventional bombs both Vulcan and Canberra crews used two air weapons ranges (AWR) in west Malaysia to drop 1,000-lb bombs at namely: Song Song, a sea range up the west coast off Kedah, near the Thai border, and China Rock situated off the south-eastern tip of the Malay Peninsula in the South China Sea. We dropped all our bombs from high level in the Far East unlike the Canberra crews who dropped bombs and fired rockets at various heights. I heard later that 14 months earlier a RNZAF Canberra of 14 Squadron from Tengah, also on detachment for Confrontation, crashed into the sea during a simulated low-level rocket attack at the China Rock bombing range. The aircraft, one of a six-ship formation, completed its low-level rocket run and was pulling away in a banked turn when a wing tip hit the water. Both crew members were killed.

After our detachment ended we'd only been back in the UK for a month when news reached us of another Canberra aircraft accident that had occurred on 6 April. It involved a Canberra B15 of 45 Squadron that rolled and then dived into the ground after loss of control. This was while carrying out a fly-past over a jungle camp in west Malaysia for other members of the squadron who were on an expedition. All three crew were killed. This latter accident was a bit of a blow to my nav plotter and I as we had got to know all three of that particular crew over our four-month detachment.

When the V Force came off QRA in 1969, I applied for the staff navigation course but to my surprise, and to the envy of my colleagues, I was posted to RAF Tengah on a ground tour as station intelligence officer. The month that I arrived, a 45 Squadron Canberra had an accident on landing. Not long after that, in May, an 81 Squadron Canberra had a starboard engine flame-out and the pilot had to abandon the take-off. Apparently the engine then relit, whereupon the aircraft left the runway and continued across the grass. I understood that it eventually came to rest in a monsoon drain with a collapsed undercarriage.

Whilst I never wanted to go onto Canberras and, as a navigator radar, went directly into the V Force, a number of navigator plotters did start off on Canberras. My other crew navigator was one such example. Therefore, it should have come as no surprise to a number of the Far East Canberra navigators when they found themselves posted to the V Force. To swap life in the Far East RAF for the RAF in Lincolnshire was also a shock. Speaking to one 45 Squadron navigator he was nearly in tears when he heard of his posting.

CHAPTER 19
FEAF PR

GORDON GILBERT was CO of 81 Squadron from 1963-1966.

The first Canberra, T4 WH641, arrived on 81 Squadron in January 1960 followed in February by PR7 WH777 and in August by WH780. The Pembrokes (which had been used for low-level work since 1956) and the last two Meteor 10s departed in July 1961. 81 Squadron achieved its full complement of six PR7s in 1962.

Initially the squadron was engaged in the Thai Survey. The whole country had been surveyed by PR Valiants based at Butterworth but 81 had been employed to fill in gaps ranging from the Burmese border in the west to the Laotian border in the north and the Cambodian border in the east. It was a popular commitment; one aircraft deployed from Tengah twice a week with the crew staying overnight in Bangkok. On conclusion of the survey the Royal Thai survey department of the army invited all 81 Squadron aircrew and a selection of the ground crew to a party in Bangkok.

The survey of North Borneo, Sarawak and Brunei continued to figure with increasing importance during 1962 and 1963. To the south, Indonesia was apparently eyeing the territories of British Borneo and it was essential to complete the survey before trouble broke out in that area. There were frequent deployments to RAF Labuan although the Borneo weather hampered progress.

When the Brunei insurrection broke out in December 1962, 81 Squadron was tasked to reconnoitre the area of fighting and to watch the frontier with Indonesia. This led to the British Borneo survey being given the highest priority and from May until September 1963, the whole effort of 81 Squadron was directed to this end, working at times seven days a week. By the time worsening weather made further effort wasteful about 80 per cent of the area had been covered.

81 had been engaged in the Malay and Borneo Surveys since the late 1940s but the weather in high humidity tropical rainforest areas had always been a limiting factor. The maximum cloud cover acceptable for mapping was ⅛th and it was often difficult to find an area which was clearer than that. The most likely window of opportunity occurred early in the morning when overnight mist started to clear and before the sun's heat had begun to trigger the development of convection cloud and thunderstorms. The aim, therefore, was to reach the designated target area at first photo light to seek

out clear patches. If there were none the crew could either loiter in the vicinity to wait for a clearance or, if that did not look promising, divert to an alternative target area.

Before and during Confrontation, Borneo Survey sorties were mounted on a daily basis from Tengah generally requiring pre-dawn take-offs to arrive overhead by first photo light. If the weather proved unfavourable but there was the possibility of a clearance later in the day, crews would land either at Labuan or at Kuching to refuel and to make a second attempt in the afternoon before returning to Tengah where the films would be processed immediately and evaluated by a JARIC (Far East) detachment permanently located near the squadron HQ. Results which met the required criteria were passed to 84 Survey Squadron Royal Engineers based in Singapore which produced the maps needed to support operations.

Tactical reconnaissance of the border areas in Borneo where our ground forces were engaging the enemy followed the same pattern. The aim was to get the photography back to Tengah as soon as possible for processing and onward transmission to the front line. With the onset of Confrontation, Borneo Survey provided a convenient cover for carrying out photo reconnaissance across the border. Dense rainforest did not lend itself readily to oblique photography and it was occasionally necessary to overfly suspected insurgent sites and lines of communication.

For both survey and intelligence tasks, the PR7 was equipped with one F49 survey camera, for mapping, and a fan of six 36-inch F52 cameras. Photographic runs were flown at 30,000 ft to yield a precise scale called for by the map makers and, equally specifically, a scale of 1:10,000 from the vertical F52 cameras for analysis by photographic interpreters.

Less conveniently however, 30,000 feet was an altitude at and above which the aircraft could be expected to produce condensation trails. For survey work this was not a problem but it could prove embarrassing on clandestine tasks. Checks for trailing could be made by periscope from the navigator's station but not at the critical stage when he would be prone in the nose of the aircraft to ensure that it was on track over the target. On one deep penetration sortie, trailing was assumed to have prompted a ground station to ask for the aircraft's call sign while it was overflying an active airfield. It was a slightly disconcerting moment for the navigator, Pete Desmond, who had vacated his ejector seat to go forward as we approached the target.

Whitehall kept a very tight grip on clandestine activity and incursions over the border had to be cleared at Cabinet level. To maintain a tight grasp on security, Headquarters Far East Air Force tasked the squadron direct via dedicated secure link, by-passing the normal chain of command. Long-range overflights, mainly to cover airfields which posed a potential threat, were particularly sensitive. However, crews on Tengah's Offensive Support Wing probably drew their own conclusions when recent photography appeared among their targeting material. Most of these sorties were uneventful but on one occasion the crew concerned suspected that there had been too much cloud cover over the target and promptly carried out a procedure turn to make a second attempt on the way home. When the film was processed both runs proved successful. The first one revealed no activity on the airfield but the second pass detected two MiGs taxiing in, leading to the uncomfortable conclusion that they must have been airborne nearby when the first run had been made a few minutes earlier.

On 12 September 1964 a very welcome reinforcement by two PR7s and crews from 58 Squadron led by their flight commander Tony Vasey arrived from Wyton. This was the first of a succession of detachments provided on rotation from the UK and Malta for the duration of Confrontation. At one stage we were reinforced by two PR9s. Unfortunately, because HQ FEAF was adamant that clandestine sorties could only be flown by resident crews, we were unable to use them to our best advantage. They provided invaluable support for our other tasks but, despite their superior performance and being designed to operate at much higher altitudes, they were not best suited for our Borneo Survey mode of operation which favoured an aircraft which could loiter for some time at around 30,000 ft waiting for a break in cloud cover.

Meanwhile, 81's crews were also planning for immediate low-level post-strike reconnaissance of targets which had been designated for attack by Tengah's Offensive Support Wing in the event of an escalation of hostilities.

81 continued to meet ongoing tasks throughout Confrontation including outstanding elements of the Malay Survey, remnants of the old Firedog campaign, and periodic photographic detachments to Addu Atoll and Hong Kong. Other commitments included the SEATO exercise Air Boon Choo in Thailand, a 'Joss Stick' exchange visit with a USAF squadron based in the Philippines and deployments to Darwin for air defence exercises Hot Squirrel and High Rigel.

Looking back, it was a very interesting and enjoyable tour for all of us. For me it also prompted a strong sense of déjà vu. Ten years earlier during the Malayan Emergency, I had been on the Far East Flying Boat Wing alongside 81 Squadron and JARIC (FE) at Seletar. It may seem bizarre, but the Sunderlands were actively involved in

Alan Harrison and Mike Bell being presented to Prince Bernard of the Netherlands after Royal Flush XII, 1967. Mike was the shortest person on 31 Squadron and Alan was the tallest. (Alan Harrison)

ground-attack operations against the communist terrorists and relied heavily on 81's photography to identify target areas. We also used to crawl along the Hong Kong border occasionally with a 46-inch F52 camera mounted in the beam gun position to peer into China and adjacent islands. ◼

ALAN HARRISON was an 81 Squadron navigator.

I joined the RAF in 1962 with the aim of becoming a pilot. I was posted to Acklington, in Northumberland, to start pilot training but I was 'chopped' for taking unnecessary risks. At the beginning of 1964 I found myself at Hullavington to start navigator training – of the 14 students on my course, 12 were chopped pilots. Next stop was Stradishall for advanced training and on graduation to Bassingbourn to become a recce navigator on Canberra PR7s. Both Acklington and Stradishall became prisons shortly after I left. In 1965, it was unusual to be posted to recce on your first tour. My first squadron was 31 at Laarbruch in Germany. At 23, I was about 12 years below the average.

I flew with Mike Bell on 31 and we ended up as the most successful RAF team in Royal Flush XII, 1967, which was the premier NATO flying competition. The squadron was first and Mike and I came an individual second.

At the end of my tour I was posted to 98 Squadron, RAF Watton, to hold for 18 months until the recce Phantom arrived. 98 was a flight checking unit and one day whilst we were away (having landed for lunch) a message came in that we were to return to Watton and I was to report to the boss immediately on landing. With some trepidation, wondering whether this was a 'Hats On' or 'Hats Off' interview I went to see the boss. Relief! A navigator had failed the recce course at Bassingbourn and they wanted a volunteer to replace him and go to Singapore. Hence, towards the end of 1968 I joined 81 Squadron.

81 was unusual in that it had a squadron leader boss, Chick Henderson – most other squadrons had wing commander bosses. Approaching our withdrawal from Singapore it was policy to post only bachelors, if possible, to the Far East. This did lead to some riotous parties. However, I did find time to pass my promotion exams and was gazetted as a flight lieutenant.

I was crewed with a first tour pilot, Godfrey Hugh Cornish-Underwood, 'Noddy' to his friends. He was a great pilot but could be a disaster on the ground. After four months the boss called me in and said that he was splitting us up as I was a bad influence on him. Two months later he realised that I had actually been a restraining influence on Noddy.

After the tense regime of 2ATAF in Germany with constant alerts, it was a very pleasant change to be on 81 with the mix of high- and low-level flying and many detachments. During my 14 months on the squadron I went to Gan, in the Maldives, Malaya, Borneo, Hong Kong, New Zealand, Australia, the Cocos Keeling Islands, Bali and Jakarta in

Indonesia. There were some differences flying in FEAF, especially with the weather. We had to have coolers in the cockpit before and during start-up. Once the coolers were removed and the door shut we had 20 minutes to get airborne or abort the sortie due to the heat. Once off the ground we immediately climbed to 20,000 ft to cool down. We also had to contend with the thunderstorms. On one occasion during climb out from Butterworth we were told to hold at 20,000 ft as an Australian Mirage was recovering after being hit by lightning. The climb and descent gauge was off the clock with the up and down drafts whist the hail stones hitting the aircraft were so loud that we could not hear one another over the intercom. Once back at Tengah we saw that the paint had been stripped from all the leading edges and most of the top surfaces.

One of my first sorties was to Labuan in Brunei. Before being allowed to navigate on my own, I had to be shown the border so that I would not infringe Indonesian airspace – this was shortly after Confrontation. With an experienced crew in the back doing the navigation, I was lying in the nose enjoying my first sight of Borneo. I then saw an airfield coming up with the odd MiG on it. We had strayed 20 miles over the border. So much for showing me where I was not to go!

We eventually finished the survey and the Malay mapping office produced the first two ¼ million scale maps which they proudly came to show us. Unfortunately, as the nav leader pointed out, they did not abut one another and in the gap between them was Mount Kinabalu, the highest mountain in South East Asia!

81 Squadron PR7 on final approach to Kai Tak airport, Hong Kong. (Alan Harrison)

We then started the survey of southern Borneo, known as Kalimantan to the Indonesians. At this time, 1969, all the maps had on them was the coast line. Therefore, we would pick a spot on the coast, fly inland for 200 miles with the F49 survey camera clicking away in the rear camera bay, execute a 180° turn and fly back to the coast with the satisfaction that we had taken the first survey photographs of this part of the world. This was carried out at 20,000 ft.

Somewhat higher, with a minimum height of 50,000 ft, was the job in Hong Kong. This was flown with an F52 oblique with a 48-inch lens, in the front camera bay, which could record objects out to 60 miles. We were given a track to fly over the ground and points to switch the camera on and off. On landing, the film was whisked away and, although we had taken the film, we were not allowed to see the results. Hong Kong was another place where you had to be shown the border before you could fly. This was at 500 ft in an army helicopter. What relevance this had to the heights we were flying I have yet to discover.

These were the days when one could 'borrow' an aircraft for the weekend. The most popular destinations were Gan for snorkelling and Penang. For Penang, we would leave the aircraft at Butterworth, the Australian base, and take the ferry across to Penang Island. The only place to stay was The Runnymede, the army guest house which had nearly 30 schoolteachers in residence and no bachelors on the island. Life could be tough at times.

Australia was a frequent place to visit to take part in exercises and carry out surveys. On one visit we had the opportunity to visit New Zealand. We nursed a fuel leak all the way across the Tasman Sea to RNZAF Ohakea where it took five days to repair.

One of the problems in Singapore were the snakes. One night, a Lightning of 74 Squadron was taxiing in when the pilot saw a snake on the taxiway. He stopped and called the tower who dispatched Crash 1. Nothing was seen so he continued to the dispersal and shut down. As the ground crew were affixing the tow bar they saw a snake wrapped around the nose oleo. The local snake man was summoned and, with the help of a CO_2 fire extinguisher, removed the snake which was deposited in the station zoo behind 81 Squadron. It was a half grown Reticulated Python. At half size it was still 15 ft long and weighed 190 lbs. Three days later it escaped and we all walked around the squadron very carefully for some days.

Another trip was to bring back an aircraft that had been repaired at Darwin in the Northern Territories. At the base of the pilot's control column is an explosive charge called the 'snatch unit'. Its purpose is to snap the control column forward should the pilot eject – otherwise he is likely to lose his lower legs. Dick Shuster was descending into Darwin when the snatch unit fired. The aircraft had just had a major service in Hong Kong and a piece of swarf is likely to have been the cause. The upshot was that Dick still had aileron control but no elevator. The runway at Darwin looks like a couple of waves with a 50ft rise and fall. Just using the trim button, Dick made a successful landing. Three or four weeks later Dick had a bad landing at Tengah and swerved off the runway which resulted in a Cat 4. A few weeks after this Dick was summoned to the station commander where, in the same interview, he was 'bollocked' for the semi-crash at Tengah and awarded an AFC for Darwin!

One further trip saw us going from Perth in Western Australia to the Cocos Keeling Islands in the South Indian Ocean. This is a flight of about 1,700 nm with our diversion being Singapore, 1,000 nm, or Butterworth – another 300 nm. To make this we had to use the cruise-climb technique where you use a constant throttle setting and as the fuel burns off and the aircraft get lighter, so it rises and you use less fuel. We arrived over the islands at 48,000 ft to find good weather.

It was not all medium- and high-level flying. Some days we were tasked with patrolling the Malacca Straits looking for smugglers or tankers discharging their tanks illegally. On one such sortie we saw a submarine on the surface. Time to have fun with the navy and some extremely low passes were made – 20 ft max. It was on the third pass that I realised that the sub was not flying a white ensign. A more sedate pass followed and we then realised that the Soviet navy flag was white with a red hammer and sickle. It was a Soviet Foxtrot Class sub!

And then came the day, 16 January 1970, when the squadron was disbanded. The ceremony was timed to end at sunset and the fly-past to coincide so that we flew out of the setting sun and into the night. As you would expect of 81, the formation was immaculate as was the timing.

However, the story did not finish here as we had to fly the aircraft back to the UK. We were scheduled to fly in pairs, which was just as well. Communications over the Indian Ocean with ground stations was by HF radio. By the time we had rounded the top of Sumatra we had lost the receive function and the other aircraft had only transmit. Therefore, they passed the message to us on UHF and I made the reply. In this way we made our way to RAF Gan. The next day we were to continue to RAF Muharraq in Bahrain. Climbing through 10,000 ft there was a sudden judder and one engine started to wind down. The Canberra PR7 fuel system fed to the number nine tank in the belly, which acted as a collector and from there to the engines. It soon became apparent that the fuel was not flowing from number nine and by switching our tanks the engines would keep going. We returned to Gan for repairs.

Luckily, the one fuel pump we had in our spares pack was for the belly tank. Unluckily, the ground crew forgot to empty the tank before removal and were hit by 4,000 lbs of fuel and they in turn hit the trestle with the new pump on it. Disaster! But our luck changed as they found just one Canberra fuel pump in the stores and it was for a belly tank. So, it was off to Bahrain. As usual things started to break and we encountered a jet stream on our nose as we got to the Gulf. After five-and-a-half hours we landed with only our UHF radio working between the two aircraft. Spares had to be flown out from the UK. Bahrain was not the most salubrious place in those days, especially in the winter. Three days later we took off for Cyprus. Just the place to have a breakage, but everything on both aircraft was perfect. Next, and final, stop was St Athan where the aircraft were to be stored and nobody cared what state they were in. So, it was off on leave and then to RAF Coningsby to learn the Recce Phantom. A powerful beast, but not a patch on the Queen of the Skies. ▨

Farewell formation on 16 January 1970 to mark the disbandment of 81 Squadron. Alan Harrison was the navigator in WH797 (No 2 on the left of the photo) with Mike Phillips as pilot. (Alan Harrison)

CHAPTER 20
FROM LAARBRUCH
TO KUANTAN

TOM EELES attended the RAF College at Cranwell followed by advanced flying training on the Gnat at Valley. After the Canberra OCU he joined 16 Squadron at Laarbruch in September 1964.

My first task was to become qualified to go into QRA. This involved many hours of low flying in Germany and the UK, practising navigation and IP-to-target runs as a two-man crew. There was also the requirement to have delivered a certain number of practice bombs in both methods of LABS deliveries on weapons ranges. Peacetime rules for practice LABS bombing were very restrictive; we were not allowed to enter any significant cloud during the LABS manoeuvre and we were not allowed to do LABS bombing at night. This in my view had a significant effect on our operational capability and I am sure the other side was well aware of these limitations placed upon us. With the weather generally being poor in the winter in Germany we spent a lot of time doing LABS bombing on the ranges in Libya, where the weather was much better, but not representative of our likely area of operations in war. It took me three months to work up to an operational status allowing me to go on QRA.

We were required to study our war targets extensively, each crew having a primary and secondary target. Target folders with full mission details were kept in secure hardened accommodation and targets were generally large features such as airfields, air defence command and control facilities and military installations; they were located in East Germany, Poland and the Baltic area. We were not expected to return from these war missions

Tom Eeles with his 16 Squadron B(I)8.
(Tom Eeles)

When we were young. (Tom Eeles)

and the navigation information in the folders ceased at the target. Another nuclear mission considered to be quite likely was known as 'Selective Release'. This envisaged launching a nuclear strike into the land battle if Soviet forces had broken through; the procedures for this were regularly practised during tactical evaluation exercises. In that era there was no concept of flexible response within NATO; if the Soviets crossed the Inner German Border we would have gone into nuclear warfare straight away. It was interesting that we were never briefed on what to do if attacked by an enemy fighter; the Canberra could have a rearward-looking radar in the tail but none of our aircraft had it fitted. We carried no form of chaff and the SAM threat was considered to be minimal at the heights we were expecting to fly. AAA would have been a major threat. At least our squadron commander, who had flown Hunters, gave us some unofficial tips on what to do if bounced by a fighter. We also were not given any form of eye protection against nuclear flash, nor did we have any form of NBC equipment or personal sidearms.

So how effective were we? The fact that the RAF fielded eight nuclear-armed aircraft on QRA all the time was a fair deterrent against adventurism by the Warsaw Pact. (Other NATO nations also contributed to this posture.) Had a shooting war started some of us would have got through by day given the likely fog of war, but many would have fallen to AAA. Fighters and SAM might have got one or two but not many. By night or in poor weather our chances of success were very much reduced. None of us would have got back but there would not have been much to get back to. Another question, never answered, was whether the 'dual key' release arrangements would ever have worked, given the need for both US and UK governments to agree, in what would have been a time of great confusion and tension.

Our conventional capability, only ever used for purely the UK national tasks, was not very impressive. Although the B(I)8 was capable of carrying three 1,000-lb bombs in the forward half of the bomb bay, they could only be delivered in straight and level flight, using a bombsight in the visual nose position. No such bombsight was fitted; the only delivery mode was a shallow-dive attack and bombs in the bomb bay would not fall clear of the aircraft in a shallow dive. Thus we were limited to the two 1,000-lb bombs carried on the wing pylons, which could be dropped from a shallow-dive attack. The forward part of the bomb bay was only used for the 16 flares employed to illuminate targets at night, dropped from a straight and level over-flight of the target. True, we had 2,000 rounds of WW2 vintage 20-mm ammunition, but doing night air-to-ground gunnery or dive-bombing under our ineffective flares, most of which dated from the 1940s, was hairy to say the least. A very simple 'ring and bead' display gunsight was provided for weapon aiming.

In early 1965 the squadron was actually stood down from its QRA commitment and deployed nine aircraft in the conventional role to reinforce the RAF in Singapore during the Indonesian Confrontation. Being the most junior member of the squadron I thought it highly unlikely that I would be able to take part in this detachment into

what might turn out to be a war zone, but I pleaded with the squadron commander to let me go and to my astonishment he allowed me to join the detachment.

I travelled out to Malaya courtesy of RAF Transport Command in a Britannia, stopping en route at Malta, Cyprus and Bahrain, where I was bumped off the aircraft in favour of a more senior officer, not difficult in my case. Thus there was no likelihood of suffering from jet lag. I finally got on a Comet, which delivered me via Gan to Changi, where I was met by some of the squadron members and taken downtown to Bugis Street, quite an introduction to the fleshpots of Singapore.

Next day, it was off to the squadron's base, the airfield at Kuantan, some 150 miles north-east of Singapore close to the east

TOP: Kuantan airfield. (Tom Eeles)

BELOW: Officer's mess tent with grumpy flight commander. (Tom Eeles)

coast. The airfield had one runway 6,000 ft long, a short taxiway allowing access from the dispersals to the northern threshold and no permanent accommodation. There was no formal air traffic control and the nearest diversion airfields were in Singapore, 150 miles away. Flying operations were very much VFR, and night flying was particularly challenging. There was a primitive electric lighting system marking the runway edges, hardly visible from the air. Gooseneck flares were used to supplement this, but there were only enough to mark one side of the runway so one had to remember which side was marked. There were some very tall trees in the jungle not far from either end of the runway so an engine failure after take-off was not a pleasant prospect. Communication with the outside world was by two phone lines routed to the nearby town of Kuantan's telephone exchange. We lived in two man tents, had a large marquee for an officer's mess, the gents was a bucket surrounded by a canvas awning and the ablution facilities were somewhat primitive when compared to what we had left behind at Laarbruch. There were many slit trenches, surrounded by sandbags, which filled up with rainwater every afternoon after the inevitable downpour, making quite reasonable baths. They presented a significant hazard to the unwary officer wandering back to his tent in the pitch-black tropical night after consuming a few cans of Tiger in the mess tent.

Night work consisted of flare-illuminated dive-bombing and air-to-ground firing on China Rock range. The first time this was attempted there was no range safety officer at China Rock because the range party had been withdrawn at night, the area being considered at high risk from Indonesian infiltrators. Clear range procedure was the order of the day, the crew being required to ensure they delivered their flares and bombs into the correct range area. Sadly, with the rudimentary navigation aids in the B(I)8, the gallant crew was not really sure where their flares had gone so were unable to identify the target. Next morning all hell broke loose when the 16 parachutes were found in the trees on the mainland some way from the range; initial reaction was they had been part of a supply drop from Indonesia to infiltrators in the jungle. Some explaining had to be done down at HQ FEAF.

Off-duty activities consisted of visits to the local town of Kuantan, which had not changed much since the great days of the British Empire, swimming from the local beaches and occasional trips to Singapore for the weekend. On base we played volley ball, watched films in the make-shift open air cinema, drank Tiger in the mess tent and sometimes went exploring in the jungle which came right up to the airfield boundary. We were re-supplied by air from Singapore on a regular basis, the Bristol Freighters of the RNZAF being regular visitors. Because of the unique up-country nature of Kuantan airfield numerous visitors from HQ FEAF would appear; on one occasion we made the day for the visiting command fire officer by setting fire to the cookhouse facility. On only one occasion was the squadron called upon to conduct live offensive support operations. A task came in to provide three aircraft loaded with full gun packs of HE ammunition, to strafe an area of jungle in Johore Bahru where

TOP: The pilot. (Tom Eeles)

BELOW: The navigator. (Tom Eeles)

it was believed there were Indonesian infiltrators. A Pioneer aircraft from Tengah provided forward air control. Naturally the squadron commander and the next two most senior pilots flew this mission, leaving us junior members of the squadron frustrated on the ground. It was the first time 16 Squadron had been in action since 1945.

Eventually it was time to go home to Germany, as we were to be replaced by a Canberra squadron from Cyprus. To commemorate this detachment so far away from the squadron's normal home base we commissioned some Selangor pewter beer mugs, each marked individually. Mine is inscribed 'JP' – for junior pilot, and is still much used today. By this time the state of the navigation aids in the aircraft was not good, as there were few spares in the Far East for the Doppler navigation system, which was different to the one used in locally-based Canberras. The other aid we had was Decca and there were no Decca chains outside Europe apart from one in the Persian Gulf. Our route home involved some long ocean crossings without diversions so represented quite a challenge for the navigators. It was Kuantan – Butterworth – Gan – Bahrain – Akrotiri – Malta – Laarbruch, with night stops at each location so again no chance of suffering jet lag. The ground crew followed us each day in a Britannia. I flew as No. 2 to the squadron commander. On the Gan to Bahrain leg he announced that we were diverting to Masirah. I asked my navigator, a much older and wiser man than I, why we were doing this. 'I suspect the boss needs a new pair of desert boots,' he replied, 'Masirah has the best selection in the Middle East.' After a couple of low passes to clear the goats and camels off the runway we landed at this remote RAF outpost and bought our desert boots. After lunch in the officer's mess, where we were shown the door to the BBC TV room, which opened out onto the desert, we continued on over the forbidding territory of the Sultanate of Oman to Bahrain. The final leg from Malta to Laarbruch was flown as a diamond nine formation, the first time I had been in such a large formation in such a large aircraft, a memorable if somewhat alarming way to cross France at high level.

Looking back, the time spent at Kuantan was really an unforgettable experience for a very inexperienced first tour pilot. Flying in Germany and QRA seemed very mundane after the exciting times at Kuantan and it was not long before I volunteered for loan service with the Fleet Air Arm.

CHAPTER 21
AUSSIE CANBERRAS

The Royal Australian Air Force (RAAF) acquired 48 Canberras, with the first Aussie-built version getting airborne on 29 May 1953. These Canberras was based on the B2 but with increased internal fuel capacity in a redesigned wing leading edge, a revised radio fit and a reduction in crew from three to pilot and navigator/bomb aimer. Australian-built aircraft were designated the Canberra Mk 20. 2 Squadron was the first to receive the Canberra Mk 20 followed by 6 Squadron in 1955 and 1 Squadron in 1958. The 48th Canberra Mk 20 was delivered in September 1958. Five aircraft were converted to dual control Mk 21 trainers.

JOHN BUSHELL attended the navigator course at East Sale in Victoria and on graduation, he was posted to 82 Wing at RAAF Amberley to convert to the Canberra Mk 20.

Despite not getting my first preference for Neptunes, I was extremely happy to be posted to do the Canberra conversion. This promised to be interesting flying, and I had enjoyed a couple of Vampire trips – my first experience of jet aircraft. I was teamed up for the conversion with Wg Cdr Rolf Aronsen, an experienced pilot who had seen service in WW2 flying Sunderlands and, more recently, Lincolns. Rolf was later the CO of 2 Squadron when it deployed from Butterworth, Malaysia to Phan Rang, Republic of South Vietnam. The instructor on our first flight was Flt Lt John Downing.

Pilot and navigator flew together on every sortie in the conversion course. For the first half dozen trips the nav had little to do apart from reading the checklist, calling speeds on take-off and around the circuit and keeping an eye on whether we were in the assigned airspace. These were all about the instructor pilot going through flying procedures and techniques. Demonstrating some of the more interesting habits of the Canberra like: pulling an engine soon after take-off and practising flying on one engine, stalling, feeling the effects of compression at Mach 0.82 and general handling. First 'solo' was when the crew under training went for the first time without an instructor in the right seat of the Mk 21.

The Canberra Mk 21 had dual controls and several other differences from the Mk 20 bomber. Neither of the pilots had ejection seats, but the navigator did. The same antique Martin-Baker Mk 1 that was fitted front and rear in the Mk 20. The instructor's seat could slide to a position beside the navigator's seat, or to the front where the

An ex-59 Squadron aircraft flying with 2 Squadron RAAF.

controls were located beside the pilot's seat. It could be locked in either position for flight, or even moved back and forth if required. The Mk 21 had no Doppler, whereas the Mk 20 had Green Satin to drive the GPI Mk IV. No bombing was possible from the Mk 21 because it was not fitted with the 12/24 Way bomb selection panel, and there was no bomb sight in the nose.

After the pilot was more or less trained to fly the aircraft, the crew took off for their first flight in the Mk 20. This was Conversion 8, and was a one-and-a-half hour in the local area around Amberley. The first navigation exercise on the course was the 20th flight. By then the pilot had an instrument rating and we had about 30 hours flying around the Amberley area and across to Brisbane to practise ILS approaches. At that time the RAAF used ground-controlled approach as the primary landing approach system, but the Canberra was equipped with ILS, so we used civilian airfield facilities to practise that system.

The phase of the course after the pilots had an instrument rating was a reasonably concentrated sequence of navigation exercises, each flight about three hours. Initially they were high-level sorties just getting used to the amount of ground covered. Remember I had trained at about 150 kts at 10,000 ft, so around 400 kts at 30,000-40,000 ft was an impressive advance. In the Dakota we had kept meticulous logs of height, speed and heading changes. The Canberra crews used an abbreviated log written on the plotting chart. The vital information was noted in a small box that we drew on the chart to record fix positions, altitude, ETA and fuel. This was kept only while at altitude – when we descended to low level the nav would map-read from a topographical map in much the same way as a pilot would navigate in a single-seat aircraft.

The Mk 20 Canberra was fitted with Green Satin Doppler which fed ground speed and drift to a GPI Mk IV, which also received heading from the G4B compass. This was the primary dead reckoning system, and visual map-reading, ADF bearings and distance-measuring equipment ranges were used to correct the GPI errors. There was also an air position indicator, but that was pretty much useless because of the errors induced by the effects of compressibility. There was a periscopic sextant, but we could not use it because rotation was limited by the Green Satin and GPI IV being mounted beside the navigator. At that stage the Canberra was not fitted with TACAN – that was retrofitted for Vietnam.

On the fourth navigation exercise we flew over the Evans Head bombing range and took a photo of the target. This was to be sure that we had identified the right place to aim our bombs. Following that we did a two-and-a-half-hour trip from Amberley to Evans Head and return after dropping six 25-lb practice bombs (one at a time). They were the first bombs I dropped – 9 June 1965. I honestly do not remember the results, but they all fell within the danger area. As I recall those bombs were dropped from 1,000 ft, but just flying level rather than pulling up from low level, levelling at 1,000 ft using the bomb doors to help stop at the right level and acquiring the target while attempting to get the aircraft stable on height and speed. It was much easier to drop from level flight at 1,000 ft.

That night after dropping our first bombs we went night flying for one-and-a-half hours around the circuit, then the next day we flew two sorties again. The first was low flying with an instructor pilot, then the second was down to the range to drop eight 25 pounders. Over the following days we had a range sortie each day to drop eight practice bombs – 25 pounders. Then on 24 June we flew our first navex that went via the range and we dropped two practice bombs off the navex. This was becoming more like the flying I would do for the next few years – a navigation exercise that went past the bombing range and required bombs to be dropped as part of the flight – not the whole object of the flight.

The next milestone was a maritime exercise and on that flight we dropped one 500-lb bomb on Evans Head. My first HE bomb dropped on 29 June. For obvious reasons we did not drop HE on the same target we used day-in, day-out for practice bombs. Practice bombs were dropped on the north range where the range safety officer had his primary working area of quadrant huts and radio equipment. For the southern range he had less accurate sighting equipment, but when a 500 pounder goes off you can see pretty much where it hit. The main thing is to get all the switches right in any case.

In this period we began flying high-low-high profile navigation exercises. The idea was to climb to a high level from base then cruise for long range, but before entering the enemy's radar network descend to low level for approach to the target. After dropping the bombs escape at low level until clear of the radar, then climb to high level for a long-range cruise back to base. This was the operational tactic that the Canberras were intended to fly in the mid-1960s. Cruise at high level would be Mach 0.74, or what might be needed to achieve time on target (TOT). At low level the planned speed was 300 kts, leaving a possibility for an increase to make up time if late for TOT. Low level was authorised as 500 ft above ground level (AGL) to the initial point, then 150 ft AGL from IP to target. However, the aircraft had no means of measuring height above terrain, so in general we flew much closer to the ground.

At the time Darwin was envisaged as the most likely operational base, so later in the conversion course we flew to the northern base. On the deployment we did a cruise climb, and even though we went overhead Townsville to make the route a little longer, we arrived at Darwin with lots of fuel remaining. One unusual exercise I recall was dropping six 500-lb bombs from 17,000 ft. We rarely dropped from medium level, and rarely carried so many HE bombs, so it was not your normal trip. I recall one of my mates made an incorrect selection which meant the bombs he dropped should not have been armed. They all went off, which might not enhance one's faith in the safety system, but at least the range party did not have to go looking for them.

15 July 1965 saw the end of 19 Canberra Conversion course, and I was posted to 1 Squadron. During the course I had flown 90 hours and 50 minutes day and 12 hours and 10 minutes night on conversion training. I also had three hours and 30 minutes 'other' flying which was a couple of trips to Canberra for the weekend. Rolf had left his family in Canberra so was keen to get home for the odd weekend.

Flying in 1 Squadron was similar to a continuation of the conversion course, except that some variety of missions began to be mixed in. The odd air test, which could be a comprehensive test after a major servicing, or just a short sortie to check some rectification. Occasionally an air defence exercise was flown, which was really for the benefit of the ground control intercept controllers and the fighter force. We flew at high level so that they could see us and did not evade. Our primary operational training was the high-low-high profile flight to achieve long range, but avoid detection by radar.

Most months I was flying 30 to 40 hours and while I was with 1 Squadron from 16 July 1965 to 8 April 1967, I flew 661 hours and 30 minutes day and 43 hours 35 minutes night.

LANCE HALVORSON was a Canberra Mk 20 navigator on 2 Squadron from November 1964 to November 1967.

2 Squadron deployed from Butterworth, Malaysia to Phan Rang air base, 35 km south of Cam Ranh Bay, a large USAF base in the far east of South Vietnam, on 19 April 1967. 2 Squadron 'Magpies' were part of the 35th Tactical Fighter Wing and were tasked by HQ 7th Air Force in Saigon, for eight sorties per day, seven days a week, in all areas of South Vietnam from 23 April 1967 until they returned to Australia in 1971.

The Canberra filled a gap in the USAF inventory as it was the only tactical aircraft in South Vietnam which bombed, visually, from straight and level flight, albeit at 350 kts. Often, the Canberra could fly below the cloud while the dive-attack aircraft could not see the ground to acquire the target because of the low cloud base.

For the first few months, the squadron carried out night combat Skyspot missions where aircraft were guided on the bombing run by ground-based precision radar. The first low-level day missions started in September 1967, with FACs marking the targets with smoke. Most sorties were in support of the Australian Task Force in the IV Corps area. Flying at about 3,000 ft AGL to avoid ground fire, the crews achieved accuracies of about 45 metres. On a number of occasions, aircraft released their bombs from as low as 800 ft, followed by a rapid pull-up to a height outside the fragmentation envelope. However, a number of aircraft were damaged by bomb fragments (shrapnel) and some navigators suffered minor injuries as a result.

HQ Seventh Air Force was impressed with the bombing accuracies of the Canberras when operating with FACs in close support of ground troops and by November 1967, we were being tasked with four-day low-level sorties. However, greater accuracy was necessary to achieve the required damage levels on the targets being attacked. Bombing accuracies were improved to 20 metres CEP.

Flying about five per cent of the wing's sorties, 2 Squadron was credited with 16 per cent of the bomb damage assessment. Initially, bombs released were ex-WW2 war stocks. Typical aircraft loads varied from 10 x 500-lb bombs to six x 1,000-lb bombs. All the war stocks were exhausted in 15 months and 2 Squadron changed over to the USAF M117 bombs; four in the bomb bay and two on the wing tips. More reliable fuses in these bombs resulted in few of the problems experienced with the earlier British-designed bombs.

2 Squadron's aircraft serviceability was high. Eight aircraft were kept on-line and maintenance personnel worked two x 12-hour shifts to meet the daily tasking rate of eight sorties. The squadron achieved a 97 per cent serviceability rate. ▪

North Vietnamese troops unleashed a heavy mortar, artillery and rocket attack on the marine base at Khe Sanh on 21 January 1968, before the Tet offensive. Khe Sanh was an important strategic post and its capture would give the North Vietnamese an almost unobstructed invasion route in the northernmost provinces, from where they could outflank American positions south of the DMZ.

Operation Niagara deployed the Australians to bomb around the besieged Americans at Khe Sanh. One pilot even recorded an 'accidental' 260-km incursion into North Vietnam. Fg Off McGregor recalled the start of another mission in 1 Corps right on the DMZ. On rendezvous with a madly weaving FAC he was given the following ground fire report. 'Heavy small-arms and LMG fire to 1,000 ft, HMG and Quad 20-mm cannon fire to 2,500 ft, AAA and possible SAM activity at higher altitude.' In this busy scene, Fg Off

McGregor and Fg Off Jim Aiken were bombing from only 800 ft; the crew achieved excellent results but they received bomb shrapnel in the tailplane of their Canberra.

2 Squadron Canberras were involved in day and night operations, usually in pairs, and carried out visual bombing (daylight) and Skyspot missions in support of the siege. The most dangerous missions to the Khe Sanh area were flown at night when aircraft were often held in racetrack holding patterns at 20-25,000 ft with numerous (up to 30 or 40) USAF, USN and US Marine Corps aircraft.

Recalling one mission, **PLT OFF J. KENNEDY** and **FLT LT N. DUUS** commented:

> On reaching the target area, a bunker system in V Corps, the crew found the cloud base was down to 1,000 ft. We were forbidden to bomb below 1,000 ft but 2 Squadron had a reputation for not bringing any bombs home. (Canberras could land with a full load of bombs. The Americans would not do this.) As a result we decided to bomb from 800 ft. We dropped the bomb and through the Perspex window I watched it fall. I saw it explode, then almost immediately the window disintegrated. We thought we'd been hit by ground fire. By now we were quite angry with the VC and advised the FAC that we wanted to drop the rest of the bombs on the target. This was done and we headed for home.

Fg Off Michael Herbert (left), and his navigator, Flt Lt Ron Aitken (right) with a M117 US general purpose bomb, attached to the right wing hard point of Canberra bomber A84-241, flying as 'Magpie 21'. The bomb inscription commemorates the 60,000th bomb dropped by 2 Squadron RAAF in Vietnam. Michael Herbert and navigator Robert Carver were lost on operations on 3 November 1970. (Australian War Memorial)

On the way back I inspected the damage in the bomb site area. I had not been wearing flying gloves and received small cuts on my hands. I then glanced up and around for the first time and saw a large piece of shrapnel (from our own bomb) which had penetrated through the nose cone and was now protruding through the upper skin of the aircraft. After landing at Phang Rang the realisation that I had almost been killed hit home hard. The moral of the story is if one is going to drop bombs, one must reach safety height. ▓

On 3 November 1970, the first Canberra was lost during a Skyspot mission in the Danang area. The aircraft was not found until February 2009 and the cause of its loss has not been determined. Another aircraft was lost in March 1971 in the Khe Sanh area. The crew, Wg Cdr John Downing (who taught John Bushell in 1964) and Flt Lt Al Pinches, ejected. Following their rescue the next day by a 'dustoff' UH-1H rescue chopper, they confirmed that they had been hit by a SA-2 missile which blew the right wing off.

The last RAAF Canberra mission in Vietnam was on 31 May 1971 and it was tasked in support of the US 101st Airborne Division in the A Shau Valley, an area visited by 2 Squadron many times over the previous two years. 2 Squadron released a total of 76,389 bombs during its time in Vietnam.

CHAPTER 22
USAF B-57s

The Canberra was sold to the USAF before it entered RAF service, making it the first British military aircraft to be built in the US since the DH4 in 1917. Throughout its life in the USAF, the Canberra was known as the B-57. A total of 403 B-57s were produced by the Martin Company in six different versions with the first B-57A making its maiden flight on 20 July 1953.

The Canberra/B-57 was unforgiving if its engines weren't handled properly and a perennial 'gotcha' was practice asymmetric flying.

On 1 June 1955 JOHN HARRIS piloted one of five B-57s from Warner-Robbins AFB, GA to Laon, France.

We made a first stop at Dover AFB, Delaware to refuel and to pick up sea-survival and other gear for our adventure across the cold North Atlantic. Dick McCullough was another of the pilots and he had some difficulty with his airplane on the way to Dover. When the maintenance was finished, he flew a test hop to make sure it was OK for the trip. 'Rock' Miserocchi volunteered to go along for the experience, since we were all inexperienced in the airplane. On his landing attempt, a need for a go-around became apparent late in the approach. Dick tried to hurry the power application and got the throttles too far ahead of the engine acceleration. One engine accelerated faster than the other and caused the airplane to start a rapid roll to the left. Dick retarded the throttles, but the damage had been done. He was able to level the wings, but heading about 30 degrees away from the runway heading.

The airplane hit hard, causing the nose gear to separate from the aircraft. The bottom of the nose was crushed in enough to drive the pilot seat up and forward – the top of the seat penetrated the canopy. The pilot's head was driven up and forward. Originally, the magnetic compass was firmly attached (probably could have lifted the nose by it) to the canopy bow above and forward of the pilot's head. Dick's head hit the compass, smashing a hole in his helmet and rendering him unconscious for a short while. The canopy opening mechanism was also wrecked. The airplane continued to roll for about 2,000 ft across 'the boonies' toward the gun club and skeet range. The pilot was blissfully unaware, but Rock was pretty frantic. It finally stopped a short distance from the club building, where a sergeant was dashing from one window to another to see if the possibility of collision looked any better or worse. Rock couldn't get his pilot to respond.

He couldn't see it, but Dick was clawing for the throttle to shut it down, but couldn't find it. They had moved aft relatively, and Dick was still about half out of it. He probably also tried the canopy open switch, because the fire crew were able to open it by putting an axe in the crack under the canopy and prying. Meantime, Rock was trying desperately to open the canopy. He pulled the emergency T-handle and the shell blew up in the cockpit. Didn't cause any more damage, but added to Rock's considerable fright, when the smoke and smell of the explosive became so apparent. He located the crash axe and proceeded to try to chop his way out. The curve of the axe pretty well fit the curve of the canopy and Rock only managed to peck a small hole in the tough plastic material. The airplane sat there for a while with both engines at idle, treating everyone present with the beautiful sound of a B-57, just waiting. The fire crew, after trying everything decided to get physical. A big guy swung his axe at the seam below the canopy where it closes. It worked. He prized the canopy up and things went well after that.

Dick got a couple stitches, and found another way to France. If his career suffered any, it wasn't apparent. After his France tour, he wound up in the long-wing B-57s. A lot of us learned the hard way about asymmetrical thrust in the B-57.

At the other extreme, Operation Heart Throb was a high-altitude B-57 reconnaissance programme to photograph 'non-friendly areas of the Asian mainland' in 1955. Four RB-57A-1s were deployed to Yokota AB, Japan in September 1955 as part of the 6021st

RB-57 with camera fits. (US Archive)

Reconnaissance Squadron. Heart Throb RB-57s differed from the production aircraft in several ways. The missions were to be single-pilot reconnaissance so the navigator's seat was removed. Most of the modifications served to lighten the aircraft and make it suitable for very high-altitude performance. All navigation equipment and armour was removed. The rotating bomb door and associated hydraulics and racks were removed and the bomb bay skinned over. An optical viewfinder was installed and pilot 'intervalometer' controls for the cameras, and for setting shutter speeds and time between picture exposures, thus producing the necessary picture overlap for the photo interpreters. Navigation was to be aided by the viewfinder which looked through the nose, making positioning the aircraft on course and over targets easier. Because of the altitude the RB-57s were to operate at, a pressure suit ventilator system was installed. The recce suite installed within a pressurized camera compartment was one T-11 vertical mapping camera, and two K-38, 36-inch focal length oblique cameras with 10-15 per cent overlap.

B-57B instructor pilot CAPTAIN JOE GUTHRIE was one of four pilots assigned to Heart Throb in Japan. None of them had any reconnaissance background so for two months they learned how to take pictures. Come mid-November they were ready to go. In Joe Guthrie's words:

It was to be a complete radio silence mission. If radio silence was broken within the first 30 minutes the back-up aircraft would be launched. The mission profile was briefed to fly north from Chitose and along the eastern side of the island of Sakhalin far enough seaward and at an altitude of 100 ft to avoid radar detection. This profile was to continue to a point abreast the northern portion of the island where the tip tanks would be jettisoned and a climb initiated to the maximum obtainable altitude. Somewhere in the climb a 180° turn would be started in order to arrive over the northern tip of the island headed south at an altitude of about 55,000 ft. At this point a reconnaissance run would be flown down the entire length of the island with specific pinpoint targets and lines. The flight would then continue on to Hokkaido, break radio silence, and land at Chitose. The aircraft would be refuelled and the film left in place for an immediate return to Yokota. There, the film would be downloaded for processing and photo interpretation.

The day of the mission arrived and the weather was excellent. We gathered early for the briefing. We had a controlled take-off time, so it was imperative that I get dressed and get strapped in the aircraft in time to get airborne right on time. I went to the aircraft and completed the walk around inspection, then back inside to get suited up. This was quite a task. I put on a pressure suit, an air vent suit, a padded suit, a water survival suit and a Mae West. Looking like the Pillsbury Dough Boy and moving with the dexterity of a robot made me wonder if I could still fly the aircraft. As a result of worrying about the controlled take-off time, I got dressed too early. It did not take long for me to get way too hot, so I went outside into the frigid Hokkaido weather to cool off. Finally, it was time to get aboard the aircraft. With all the equipment I was wearing it took a personnel equipment technician to stuff me into the pilot's seat. Then he spent some time getting my parachute buckled and everything hooked up before checking everything out thoroughly. At this point, for the first time in my life I really wished I were someplace else. The feeling did not last long…as soon as I got the engines started I was raring to go.

We had a man in the control tower and as soon as he saw I was ready to taxi he told the tower operator to issue taxi instructions. Two minutes before take-off time, I was cleared on the runway and cleared for take-off.

Exactly on time, I rolled down the runway, lifted off and took up my first heading. I passed over the northern part of Hokkaido and was soon over the ocean east of Sakhalin flying 100 ft above the water. However, it was not long before I ran into low clouds and I was completely IFR. I was flying about 350 kts indicated and this made for a sporty ride over the ocean. I decided I had better get a little altitude before I ended up in the drink, so I climbed to 200 ft and held that altitude the rest of the way north. I could not see anything. I went completely on dead reckoning. At the appropriate time on the flight card I punched off the tips, and initiated the climb. During the time I was in the clouds I was worried that the mission would be a washout because of the weather. But I was quickly on top of the clouds and as I gained altitude I could see that Sakhalin was completely clear the entire length of the island. I continued my climb a little north of the island and turned back south at a little over 55,000 ft. I had checked the cameras out previously so I was ready to start taking pictures. Everything looked just the way it had during mission preparation and I was going great until I saw that I was too far east to photograph an airfield. Not knowing any better, I made a 360° turn and picked it up. As a result I got every target assigned – but not without consequences later.

There were many airports and as best as I could see plenty of MiGs on them. Also there was no doubt that they knew I was there. We had a warning device that told us when we were being tracked by radar. We could discriminate between airborne and ground radars by the tone of the oral warning – a high-piercing tone meant airborne radar. I looked around a lot and changed headings when I could, but I never saw anything. When I changed headings I would lose the airborne tone, but then it would come back. There wasn't much I could do but head south. In frustration, I turned the warning device off and kept heading south.

It was good to see the island of Hokkaido slip under the nose and I broke radio silence and called Chitose for landing instructions. I made an uneventful landing and logged four hours and 40 minutes. After a quick turn around and a change into a normal flight suit we returned to Yokota, landing just before dark.

After Heart Throb ended in Japan, two USAF pilots went to Okinawa to train four Tai-wanese pilots in high-altitude recce. They had with them two RB-57As. From Okinawa they moved to Taipei and Taoyuan air base. On the third mission over Red China, one of the aircraft was shot down over the Shantung Peninsula and the project was abandoned.

Ten years later and there were 96 B-57s assigned to bombing South East Asia during the Vietnam War. One of these was flown by **CHARLES 'CHUCK' RAMSEY**:

My memories (or what's left of them) are that sometime in late February 1965, the VC blew up something, so we were going to retaliate. In early March the air force came up with a strike on a supply depot in the southern part of North Vietnam. The B-57s were included in this strike. At that time, the 57s were operating out of Bien Hoa. There were two squadrons (8th and 13th) stationed at Clark AFB. Both squadrons were rotating crews on an individual basis, so we had a mixture of both squadrons at Bien Hoa. As far as I can remember this was the first time the B-57s had been in an operation like this. There were to be four or five different types of aircraft taking part in the mission.

As the luck of the draw would happen, I was at Bien Hoa when this took place. This means I was fortunate to be a part of this historic event. Yeah, right!

The briefing was pretty straightforward and we headed for the aircraft. The aircraft were full of fuel; bombs loaded and gun cans were full. What more could you have asked for? Steel plating around the cockpit comes to mind. We were putting 12, 16, or 20 aircraft on the mission – I don't remember the exact number. (It's that memory thing.) Needless to say the 'pucker factor' was pretty high. We were to be the last of the aircraft to hit the target. What we weren't told was that the higher ups had calcu-lated that the big, slow, B-57s would experience a 50 per cent loss. Had this titbit of information been passed down, the pucker factor would have been off the scale.

USAF B-57s on the
45 Squadron pan at
Tengah. (Alec Audley)

Take-off, climb and cruise were normal. Except the take-off roll was a little long (an understatement). North of Danang, we started our descent down to the tree tops. Just north of the DMZ, we switched over to the strike frequency. Much to our consternation, rescue operations were already in full swing and we hadn't even gotten to the target. Remember that pucker factor, it really shot up at that moment. Now we were at the point of getting all the switches in the right positions for the bomb drop. Rotate the selector switch to 'bombs internal'– fly formation; arm the bombs – fly formation; bomb bay switches on – fly formation; get gun sight set – fly formation; rotate bomb door – fly formation; and watch out for the trees. OK – the last bit is an exaggeration – but we were *low*.

Planned attack was to use what I call the 'Thunderbird Reversal'. Pop up from the deck, do sort of a wing-over, establish the dive-bomb angle, drop the bombs and get 'the hell out of Dodge'. This manoeuvre makes it a little more difficult for the gunners on the ground to track you. Altitude, airspeed and heading are all being changed at the same time. Being No. 4, there wasn't anything on the ground to aim at because of all the smoke, so I just aimed for the middle of the smoke. There was some AAA because I'm sure I felt the tail of the aircraft lift up a couple of times as I was coming over the top. After bomb release, it was full throttle and head for the deck and close the bomb door.

Levelling off I picked up No.3 and fell in behind, about one to two miles back. After a couple of miles, I realised that I was not gaining on anybody and that was because they also had their throttles bent around the wide-open position. Down the road, lead backed off a little on the power, we joined up and started the climb out.

Now, in the pilot's handbook (Dash One), there is a little obscure note that says, 'If the beak of the aileron comes in contact with the wing, a vibration will occur throughout the aircraft' (or something to that effect). About the only way this can happen, is to come off the hot jungle floor and make a rapid climb to altitude, which results in the metal of the aircraft contracting at different rates. Going through about 35,000 ft, guess what, the airplane starts vibrating. Since we had encountered some triple A, I just knew I had taken some hits. The other members of the flight checked me out and said everything looked good. Since the engines were running good and the aircraft was controllable, I stayed with formation. That way if anything bad had happened, they could at least mark the spot. Passing through 40,000 ft the vibrations eased off and shortly after level off it went away.

Fortunately, the remainder of the flight was uneventful with recovery at Bien Hoa. No aircraft had been lost and only a couple of aircraft had damage. Earlier I had mentioned that the higher ups had calculated that we would lose a bunch of airplanes. Since we had not, each aircrew had to write a narrative of what we had done, to avoid being shot down. So ended the first strike, if you don't include a trip to the bar.

CHAPTER 23
LIFE IN THE OLD DOG

ANDREW BROOKES recalls:

Back in the 1970s a Phantom cost about £3,000 per hour to fly, whereas a Canberra came in at something like £400. Since we had hangars full of redundant Canberras squirreled away at places like Wroughton, it made sense to use them to enable a newly-trained pilot to acquire a little more situational awareness or confidence before moving on to front-line fast jets. It was not uncommon to have as many as a dozen Canberras on the flight line in those days. If the one you had been allocated was disinclined to start, you took the next one instead. Unimaginable on a Typhoon squadron today? Virtually every young navigator I flew with went on to Buccaneers or Phantoms.

What were these second-line outfits, and what did they do? There was 7 Squadron at St Mawgan which had TT18s, with a big Rushton winch under each wing from which they could tow either a target 'dart' or a sleeve which other folk would then shoot at – often the Royal Navy, which is probably why 7 Squadron was where it was. Then there were 85 and 100 Squadrons at West Raynham, which were also in the target facilities game. Alongside the OCU at Cottesmore there were 98 Squadron, which spent its time calibrating navigation aids, and 360 Squadron whose aim in life was to spoil the day for all sorts of people, but mainly those trying to operate air defence radars on the ground and/or on HM ships. In the mid-1970s 360 Squadron moved to Wyton where it joined 51 Squadron, another part-Canberra operator, although one that was engaged in more mysterious SIGINT activities and which was not inclined to seek publicity.

Apart from being a useful way to provide newly-trained aviators with some additional flying hours, the Canberra was also one way for experienced guys who had been on ground tours to get back up to speed, and that was where I came in. I spent my first tour as a co-pilot on strategic reconnaissance Victor Mk 2s at Wyton. When it was my turn for a captaincy, there were no vacancies, so I was put out to grass on a ground tour. By the time that had expired, I was somewhat behind the drag curve in terms of flying hours. So I finished up on 85 Squadron at West Raynham which had B2s, T4s and T19s – T11s with the original AI 17 replaced by a lump of concrete (we called it the Blue Circle radar). The T19 had no drop tanks, which limited its range a bit. We couldn't make Malta in one go, so we used to night stop at Istres, jug up on cheap vino at the Routier Café and carry on to Luqa the next day. Someone had to do it!

Typically, 85 Squadron Canberras would work in pairs, exercising with one of 8 Squadron's Shackletons or the radar station at Neatishead, where fighter controllers were trained. One Canberra would act as the target while the other one was vectored in to an interception by the third party. Once it had all ended in the inevitable stern chase, you broke off, switched roles and did it again until the fuel began to run low – about an hour and a half as a rule. Given the Shackleton connection, for a few years we were given a Lo-Pro war role whereby a Canberra would be sent to visually identify Soviet ships picked up by the maritime patrol fraternity. I suppose that if we didn't come back, that would have told the powers to be that something was afoot.

Andrew Brookes with Canberra B2 WJ603.

Flying was quite fun actually because we were in 11 Group and that meant fighter-style rules, so formation flying was standard procedure. If you were briefed as a pair, you took off together, if it was a threesome, same thing, and when you came home, it would be a fly-past in formation or a run-in and break – all of which was great fun and a good way to do business. There was always somebody who wanted someone to play the bad guy, and that was our trade – we were the professional bad guys. Apart from these routine training events, there were more formal fixtures, two or three JMCs (joint maritime courses) every year, for instance, and the occasional major air defence exercise. For exercises we might deploy to somewhere in Denmark for a couple of weeks – under canvas sometimes. And from there we would fly back to the UK to 'attack' it at low level to provide the air defenders with something to do. They would have all these unidentified radar responses popping up on their screens, because we didn't file flight plans, and if 360 Squadron was playing, as they usually did, that made it all the more difficult because our blips were hidden in a lot of 'noise'.

Another occasional activity involved escorting Hunters to and from Gibraltar. This was still General Franco's era and relations with Spain were a bit tense, so we used to maintain a couple of Hunters at North Front and, because fighter pilots have a limited range (intellectually) we used to look after navigation and radio traffic for them between Gib and Brawdy – down on Friday, back on Monday.

Towards the end of 1975 there was one of those periodic culls to trim off a bit more fat in the name of 'cost effectiveness'. This time the MoD had 85 Squadron in its sights and we got our marching orders. Fondly imagining that Defence Minister Roy Mason might be persuaded to change his mind, we wrote asking him to reconsider – we even sent him a squadron tie, with our famous hexagon motif – as if that would have made any difference. It didn't, of course, and shortly before Christmas we lost our identity.

I was part of the rump of 85 Squadron that was absorbed into 100 Squadron, which almost immediately relocated to Marham. That meant that we had been transferred from 11 Group to 1 Group – and what a culture shock that was. 1 Group rules were really – what? – ponderous – that's the word. In December we could fly in formation; in January we couldn't. Life just wasn't such fun anymore. The clamp on formation flying is just an example, but it is a good one, because formation flying is good for you – it focuses the mind, sharpens your judgement, hones your skills and generally makes you a better pilot and that, to a significant extent, is what these second-line Canberra outfits were really about.

98 Squadron had been disbanded at much the same time so we inherited some of their E15s along with the calibration task – and what a bore that was. On the other hand the E15 had a lot more poke than the rest of the fleet, which were all B2 derivatives, and it was much more fun to fly. I loved it. It could go a long way – no problem getting to Malta, and we used to do low levels over Sicily.

I eventually left in May 1977 to become a Vulcan captain. I mention this because the Canberra could be more difficult to fly than the Vulcan. I took the place of another captain who wanted a change and had moved over to Canberras. He was back within six months after being chopped because he couldn't handle the asymmetry.

What of 360 Squadron? It is best to let AEO RICHARD 'DICK' TURPIN tell the story:

The Canberra had first become associated with the EW community as early as 1953 when Watton's 192 Squadron had been provided with a couple of B2s. Interestingly, these aeroplanes, which were intended for electronic intelligence (ELINT) duties, were the first Canberras to be fitted with a Green Satin Doppler radar. They were succeeded by quite extensively modified B6s from 1954 onwards, these aircraft operating around the Baltic and elsewhere monitoring and recording electronic emissions. It was possible to make duplicate tapes from which aircrew could be taught to recognise the audio signatures of specific equipment and thus to evaluate the level of threat they represented.

Meanwhile, Canberras began to be issued to other units within 90 Group. Most of these were concerned with the calibration of early warning, GCI and missile fire control radars, IFF and so on but in the early 1960s 97 Squadron acquired a limited jamming capability which permitted it to offer a degree of practical EW training. Having established the Canberra's pedigree in the signals world, from 1964 24 surplus Canberra B2s

360 Squadron T17s (with knobbly EW noses) and officers. 360 was a joint RAF/RN squadron and the CO at this time was Cdr G. Oxley RN. (360 Squadron Association)

began to be fed through Samlesbury where they were turned into T Mk 17s. The conversion involved the installation of a range of equipment in the bomb bay and the provision of sundry aerials, resulting in the distinctive bulbous and 'warty' nose that was so characteristic of the breed. Twelve of these aircraft were assigned to 360 Squadron (the rest were to go to 361 Squadron in the Far East but that plan didn't survive long) to provide a realistic ECM training capability for both the RAF and the RN. The squadron moved to Cottesmore in 1969 and in 1975 to Wyton where it remained for the next 20 years.

The T17 had a comms noise jammer, covering the VHF/UHF bands, and two E/F-Band (or, alternatively, one D-Band and one E/F-Band) jammers, and an I-Band jammer; the latter could transmit from either front or rear aerials but not both. There was also an I-Band CW Pulse Doppler repeater jammer. It could sometimes be difficult to be certain that the jammers were tuned to the appropriate frequencies because the operator was obliged to work with an APR-9 of some considerable vintage, this having a 'window' covering only 20 MHz.

The squadron flew a variety of sortie profiles according to a weekly programme which was prepared by the Electronic Warfare Training Cell (EWTC), a part of Wyton's Ops Wing and where I first became personally involved in this business in 1980-82. The squadron's principal bread and butter missions ranged from so-called 'coffee deltas', which exercised the radars of the UK's air defence ground environment, 'profits', against either singletons or pairs of fighters, and flag officer sea training's (FOST) weekly 'war' off the south coast. Larger-scale exercises often entailed multi-aircraft detachments to Scotland for joint maritime courses (JMC), or to a variety of airfields in Germany, Belgium, Holland, Italy, Norway, Portugal and France to participate in NATO or bi-national events. Another range of major tasks involved Mediterranean Fleet exercises flown from Gibraltar and naval exercises sponsored by NATO.

Over the years I am sure that 360 Squadron accomplished a great deal in providing RN and RAF personnel with an insight into the problems that ECM could cause them in their operational roles, whether on land, at sea or in the air. By the mid-1980s, however, in order to reflect changes in the Warsaw Pact's electronic ORBAT, it was becoming increasingly necessary to update the Canberra's EW fit and there was a corresponding need to modernise the original navigational aids. In 1985, therefore, WD955 was flown back to Samlesbury to act as a trial aircraft for a new electronics suite. This time we could afford to update only half-a-dozen aeroplanes to the new T Mk 17A standard but, with their much enhanced capability, they served the squadron well for the rest of its life. The T17A had a wide-band spectrum analyser, its 20 GHz window permitting the operators to cope with the frequency agile radars which used to be able to 'hop' outside the mere 20 MHz covered by the old APR-9s. The new active equipment included a 1-Kw communications jammer, a 3-Kw frequency-controlled I-Band jammer (which actually went just into J-Band) and an enhanced noise/repeater jammer. The installation involved the replacement of all of the original wave guides and the provision of new aerials. The new E/F-antenna in the nose, for instance, produced a more sharply focussed 17.5° beam giving a much higher effective radiated power (ERP) while a new omni-directional D-Band aerial beneath the aircraft gave a respectable 15 db gain.

Despite its limitations, the T17's kit permitted us to play some relatively sophisticated tricks. I recall, for instance, visiting UK radar sites to show the operators that, even with their ECCM features operating, they could be deceived into believing that they were not actually being jammed. It was, perhaps, a pity that 360 Squadron never had a formal war role. I am sure that it could have made a useful contribution to an offensive and, had it been seen in that light, the funding of updates might have been easier. Had the chips really gone down I suppose that they might well have been pressed into service, even if only as command and control relay aircraft, and the squadron certainly became involved in some urgent trials work in connection with attempting to counter the Exocet threat during Operation Corporate. As it was, the squadron did not long survive the end of the Cold War and it was disbanded in 1994. Like so many other military functions, the EW training role has now been put out to civilian contract.

LESLIE STEPHENS recalls the view from higher up:

Here I was, at 40,000 ft in a Canberra T Mk 17 and pretending to be a helicopter. My throat microphone was the only genuine article about me. I found a frequency that the US aircraft carrier was using – pure luck, as we didn't carry the opposition's frequencies – and started to talk to the carrier. I pretended to be a helicopter en route to the carrier with some senior officers from 'our' group of RN ships. The man to whom I was speaking bought it and, contrary to normal procedure, cleared me to approach and land on board. Well, that was too good to pass up – I then stretched probability still further and 'saw' a periscope; where there's one of those, there's a submarine, see. Ooh, I was so excited, so only just in possession of myself and fighting to get the words out. He continued to believe my impromptu performance and, in a voice dripping with exaggerated calmness, told me to break off my approach and go back to my parent ship. In the meantime, he (and his aircraft carrier, with their escort ships) broke away from the course he was steering in order to launch and land his jets – and went away from 'my' submarine at top speed. His aircraft all had to land at a not-so-nearby Norwegian air force airfield.

At the subsequent exercise 'wash-up', our (360 Squadron) representative offered to 'shed a little light upon this incident', finishing with a reminder to take back to the US nuclear-powered aircraft carrier, the USS *Nimitz*. The reminder was, 'Never believe all that you may hear – especially when you haven't authenticated incoming communications – from a Canberra T Mk 17!'

RON SAUNDERS was a nav instructor on 231 OCU at Bassingbourn in 1958.

I flew with QFI Flt Lt Ron Crawford taking a Canberra B2 to Sola airfield, Stavanger, to perform a display for the RNoAF Day. Our display routine ended with a fast, low-level run along the runway, pulling-up into a loop with a roll off the top into a downwind position for landing. Approaching the inverted position the undercarriage was selected so that it appeared while still in an unconventional attitude; alas on this occasion three greens failed to show.

Unstrapping from my ejector seat, I moved forward alongside the pilot to attempt to pump the undercarriage down manually, doing so without much confidence. On my previous tour, on 44 (Rhodesia) Squadron at RAF Honington, I had experienced two wheels-up landings following hydraulic failures; however, this time the system worked and we landed uneventfully. We soon learnt that the Norwegian commentator had made something of a verbal drama out of the incident and we were minor celebrities when later we attended the hangar dance.

Nineteen years later, I returned to Canberras to command 360 RN/RAF Squadron, equipped with the T17 (Warthog) variant. Our major area of operation was the North Sea, probing the UK air defences. One night we received a weather diversion to Sola and after landing and putting the aircraft 'to bed', which routinely comprised putting the chocks, engine blanks and covers in place, we lumbered off to the mess in our immersion suits. During the night the storm hit Sola with such force that it rocked our aircraft back onto its tail, damaging the tail cone. Once again the RNoAF workshop saved the situation and repaired the damage. Back at Wyton it was forcefully pointed out to me that the rear hatch of the aircraft contained a device known as a 'pogo stick' which, if fitted to a plate to the rear of the fuselage, prevented such accidents. Picketing an aircraft in inclement weather had never been mentioned at the OCU or anywhere else, and even after examining the profile of the pogo stick I was not fully convinced: the image of a sausage on a cocktail stick always came to mind.

I can only conclude that the trolls of Norse mythology did not enjoy Canberras of any type muscling-in on their territory.

But right to very end, the Canberra could not be trifled with. When I worked in the RAF Inspectorate of Flight Safety, we calculated that more Canberras were lost from practice asymmetric flying than from actual engine failures themselves. The last of these took place in March 1991 when the station commander of RAF Wyton asked to perform a simulated engine failure after take-off (SEFATO) in a T4 for his currency training. Start-up and take-off were normal until just abeam the ATC tower, where the undercarriage had just retracted when the station commander called for a SEFATO on the starboard engine. The T4 was seen to roll slightly left and then right but then hold a slight right bank at about 200 ft AGL. The T4 then began to roll and turn to the right at an alarming rate before descending. It then struck a road sweeper that was parked between two buildings before hitting a small garage and bursting into flames. None of the three aircrew on board survived.

CHAPTER 24
INDO-PAKISTAN CANBERRAS

The Indian air force (IAF) was the third largest Canberra operator after the UK and USA. The IAF initially ordered 80 Canberras (65 B(I)58s, eight PR57s and seven T4s) to replace its B-24 Liberators. The T4s were standard trainers while the others were based on the B(I)8 and the PR7 respectively, though modified to Indian specifications. Final deliveries of the 80 Canberras were made in the autumn of 1959 and a further six were ordered in 1961. India placed an order for three more Canberras is 1962 – a T4 and two PR57s. During 1970 India bought eight B(I)12s and two T13 ex-Kiwi Canberras.

On 1 September 1957, 5 Squadron (the Tuskers) became the first IAF squadron to re-equip with the B(I)58 bomber-interdictor version of the Canberra. Other IAF units to convert to the Canberra were 16 Squadron (the Black Cobras) at Gorakhpur, and 35 Squadron at Puna. 106 Squadron (equipped with the PR Mk57) and the Jet Bomber Conversion Unit were at Agra.

AMRIK SINGH AHLUWALIA was a DC-3 navigator who was sent to Bassingbourn in August 1957 to convert to the Canberra. On his return he was posted to 5 Squadron.

The main initial role of the Canberra for which she was built was high-altitude bombing and that was what the RAF taught us during the conversion – straight and level bombing from different heights. That role had to drastically change because of the threat from surface-to-air missiles (SAMs) and by the time the Indian air force acquired the Canberra, this threat was real and always looming large.

Along with some other crews I was now engaged in developing operating procedures for using the Canberra in different roles which involved penetrating enemy airspace without being detected by radar or ground observers by day and by night. My squadron had 16 aircraft divided into two flights – A Flight with eight bomber aircraft and B Flight with eight interdictor aircraft. All crews had to fly both roles but they had to become experts in one role and proficient in the other. However, over time the bomber role was slowly overshadowed by the requirements of interdiction. In the hills of Rajasthan, and in the foothills of the Himalayas in the Shimla-Deharadun area we flew the same schedule of day flying at 1,000 ft AGL in the valleys far below the high peaks, and as we gained experience we stepped down to 700 ft, then 500 ft and eventually to 200 ft before similar low-flying training in the hills at night. ▪

While the standard IAF Canberra bomber squadron had 16 Canberra bombers and two trainers, 106 Squadron had between five and seven PR aircraft and no trainers. Of the original PR Canberras provided for the IAF, a PR57 was shot down by a Pakistani AF F-86F Sabre on 10 April 1959 at 47,500 feet over Rawat, near Rawalpindi. Both Canberra crew members – Sqn Ldr J. C. Sen Gupta (pilot) and Flt Lt S. N. Rampal (navigator) – ejected and were repatriated the next day. The Canberra was reportedly on a weather mission when it became lost, drifted off course, and strayed over the border.

IAF Canberras first went into offensive action in 1961 during the 'liberation' of Goa. 16 and 35 Squadrons were launched against Dabolim airport on 18 December with 12 Canberras dropping 1,000-lb bombs. It was a pretty one-sided affair but good bombing practice in staying clear of terminals and civilian facilities. At the other extreme, IAF Canberras were moved north during the 1962 confrontation with China. No combat missions resulted but 22 PR Canberra missions were flown over disputed areas of Aksai Chin and the Eastern sector to monitor encroachments.

When the former Belgian Congo started to come apart in 1961, the UN sought international intervention and India responded by sending six 5 Squadron Canberras, 12 aircrew and 90 support personnel from Agra to Ndjili airport, Leopoldville. This 6,000-km detachment staged through Jamnagar and Nairobi. The Canberra was selected in preference to other aircraft because of its relatively long range and endurance, having a navigator and airborne navigation aids, all deemed essential because of the frequent tropical storms and lack of ground-based navigation aids. The 5 Squadron detachment represented the only long-range attack capability available to the UN for its military mission in the Congo.

Among the first missions, on 5 December 1961, was a long-range counter-air operation at 1,300 km range, to attack the main Katangan rebel air base at Kolwezi, which the Katangans had thought too far from UN airfields to be attacked. Canberras destroyed a number of aircraft of the Force Aérienne Katangaise (FAK) on the ground, among which were Fouga Magisters that had been flown by European mercenary pilots to harass UN ground forces. The Canberras also destroyed a number of FAK transport aircraft and during a second strike on Kolwezi, they destroyed fuel storage tanks. These Canberra attacks were carried out in the face of hostile fire, and OC 5 Squadron's navigator, Flt Lt M. M. Takle, was wounded. Destruction of most of the Katangan aircraft, hitherto regarded as safely out of range, caused many mercenary aircrew to abandon their contracts and decamp to Angola.

In exchange for permission to allow U-2 flights to operate out of their air space over the USSR, the US supplied the Pakistan air force (PAF) with 25 Martin B-57s (including two trainers) to equip 7 Squadron (Bandits) and 8 Squadron (Haiders) of the 31st Bomber Wing on 11 May 1960. Subsequently, the PAF also received two modified Martin RB-57F high-altitude reconnaissance aircraft. The PAF became the first to form a regular formation aerobatics team of four B-57s.

Pakistan air force B-57. (PAF)

Both India and Pakistan used Canberras to attack each other's airfields and installations with iron bombs during the short wars of September 1965 and December 1971. During the former IAF Canberras attacked the PAF base at Peshawar. This base was closer to the Afghan border than the Indian so that PAF was using it to disperse its B-57 strategic assets. Led by Senior Flt Cdr J. C. Boss Verma, and bombing on TI flares just like the RAF at Suez, 5 Squadron damaged Peshawar runway and threatened the entire PAF B-57 force. Due to poor visibility, a road outside the base was bombed instead of the runway where PAF B-57 bombers were parked. Again, just like Suez.

The Tuskers flew around 300 sorties during the 1965 war for the loss of one Canberra, while returning from a raid on Sargodha, to a Sidewinder attack by a PAF F-104, on the penultimate day of the war. One of the IAF's worst combat loss incidents occurred on 1 September 1965, when four IAF Canberras were destroyed on the ground at Kalaikunda by PAF fighters operating out of East Pakistan.

An unknown PAF B-57 pilot was nicknamed 'Eight-Pass Charlie' by IAF pilots stationed at Adampur air base during the 1965 war. The nickname was derived from the number of passes the B-57 would make in each raid. Tactically it made sense for a B-57 to deposit its load of eight 500-lb bombs at one go before the defences could react. But 'Eight-Pass Charlie' would make eight different runs and drop just one bomb on each selected target by moonlight.

IAF fighter pilot **PADDY EARLE** paid tribute to the unknown Pakistani pilot:

> I had the utmost respect for the Pakistani Canberra bloke who loved to ruin the equanimity of our dreary lives. Eight-Pass Charlie was an ace, but he had this nasty habit of turning up about 30 minutes after moonrise, just as we were downing our first drink! Seriously, he was a cool dude and a professional of the highest order. To disguise the direction of his run, he used to cut throttles before entering a dive and by the time the ack-ack opened up he was beneath the umbrella of fire. After dropping his load he'd apply full throttle and climb out above the umbrella.

By the time of the 1971 Indo-Pakistan conflict, the Canberra/B-57s which undertook night attacks against airfields and strategic targets were becoming increasingly vulnerable against aircraft such as the Mirage and so losses were greater than in 1965. The highlight of the 1971 war from India's point of view was the bombing of the Karachi oil refinery which resulted, according to a recce pilot, in 'the biggest blaze ever seen over South Asia'. That said, the IAF lost a Canberra over Karachi.

Several PAF Canberra pilots and navigators who had moved across to Pakistan International Airlines re-joined their squadron when war became imminent. On 6 December, Sqn Ldr Khusro and his navigator Peter Christy failed to return after a bombing mission to Jamnagar. Sqn Ldr Ishfaq Hameed Qureshi, who was also recalled from PIA and his navigator Flt Lt Zulfiqar Ahmad failed to return from their second mission of the war on 5 December. Flt Lts Javed Iqbal and his navigator Ghulam Murtaza Malik flew two missions against heavily-defended Indian airfields until on 5 December, they failed to return from bombing Amritsar airfield.

In the mid-1960s the IAF took delivery of two ex-RAF PR7s, which were upgraded to become known as PR67s. 106 Squadron PR57/67s were involved in a number of strategic photo-reconnaissance missions, including refuting reports of Chinese troops and materiel moving into Pakistan along the Karakorum Highway. One sortie on 8 December 1971 to Longewala produced a notable photograph of crossed and inter-twined tracks of the Pakistani armour as they manoeuvred to avoid destruction by the Hunters of the Operational Training Unit. The squadron flew a number of missions over PAF airfields.

During the 1970s the dwindling PAF spares situation, exacerbated by a US arms embargo, led to 8 Squadron amalgamating with 7 Squadron. On 27 December 1983, a ceremony was held at Masroor air base, the erstwhile home of the B-57s, to mark their retirement from PAF service. Two B-57s in close line astern flew past to mark the end of an era.

Although the IAF's need for a Canberra replacement had been evident from before the 1971 conflict, delays in awarding a contract to meet the deep penetration strike aircraft resulted in 5 Squadron operating attack Canberras at Agra until 1981. A target-towing version was added to the IAF inventory

Indian air force Canberra crews.
(IAF library)

in 1975. 35 Squadron continued to use modified Canberra B(I)58s with MiG-21Ms in the electronic warfare role at Bareilly. The squadron phased out its Canberra B(I)58s in 2001.

Which left 106 Strategic Reconnaissance Squadron. In 1999, a PR57 on a low-level mission over Kargil was hit by a Stinger infrared missile. Although one engine was taken out, Wg Cdr Perumal and Flt Lt Jha landed the aircraft safely at a nearby air base. On 19 December 2005, the same aircraft suffered an engine failure forcing it to return to base, but it crashed 5 km short of the runway, killing both aircrew. After this, all remaining IAF Canberras were grounded and then finally retired on 11 May 2007. The fact that the PR Canberra had continued in IAF for so long was explained by a previous CO of 106 Squadron, Wg Cdr Jaggi Nath, when he said that, '106 Squadron (with the Canberra PR57/PR67) was not just an air force asset, it was a national asset'.

Journalist VIJAY MOHAN witnessed the passing of the Indian Canberra era:

On 7 March 2007 at Chandigarh, as the supreme commander of the armed forces, IAF personnel and selected guests on the airfield gazed skywards, the vulnerable Canberra made its last public appearance in the Indian skies.

With IAF standards and colours fluttering on the tarmac and an array of aircraft and missiles keeping a stoic vigil, the Canberra, flown by Wg Cdr S. K. Mathur, flying a figure of eight, signed off on a chequered career spanning 58 years.

Once the mainstay of the IAF's bomber fleet, only a handful of Canberras remain in service today (2007). At present, they are being flown by 106 Strategic PR Squadron at Bareilly. As the commentator put it during the Fleet Review: 'The unique features of the Canberra made the aircraft relevant even today in an otherwise modern air force'.

The IAF first expressed its interest in the Canberra during the visit of the then Defence Secretary, M. K. Vellodi, to the UK in June 1956. A few IAF pilots had already flown the Canberra by then. One of them was the Indian air attaché to the UK, Gp Capt H. Moolgavkar, who had flown the Canberra as early as 1954 as part of an evaluation team led by the then Air Cdre P.C. Lal, who was the air chief during the 1971 Indo-Pak war.

Two of the IAF's most highly decorated officers, Wg Cdr Jaggi Nath and Wg Cdr P. Gautam, both of whom have been awarded the Maha Vir Chakra twice in different wars, have been Canberra pilots. ▨

CHAPTER 25
'ARGY-BARGY'

Two FAA B62s in close formation. The photo was taken from a Lear Jet 35R during a visit
to the 2nd Air Brigade. (Juan Cicalesi)

Venezuela was the first South American customer for the Canberra. The initial Fuerza
Aerea Venezolana (FAV) order was placed in 1953 for six B2s with the first aircraft arriving
at Maracay on 1 April 1953. Civilian delivery crews were supplied by Silver City Airways
but some of the Canberras were delivered by aircrews from 12 Squadron at Binbrook. A
further eight B(I)8 Canberras were ordered in 1957 (with gun-packs) as well as two three-
seat T4 trainers. These Canberras equipped Esc 38 and Esc 39 of the Grupo de Bombardeo
13 at Barcelona and over the years the FAV accumulated no fewer than seven marks including
the PR3/PR83. In late 1990, the Grupo de Bombardeo 13 finally withdrew its remaining
seven B82s, one PR83, two T84s and one B(I)88. FAV crews liked the Canberra and it
served them well in its primary roles of low-level interdiction and close air support (CAS).

The Fuerza Aérea Argentina (FAA) placed a contract at the end of 1967 for ten ex-RAF B2 and two T4 aircraft to replace the Avro Lincoln in the bomber role. These were refurbished and modified at Samlesbury and delivered as B62s and T64s between November 1970 and September 1971. A second contract for a further two ex-RAF Canberras was embargoed by the 1982 Falklands conflict.

During the Falklands conflict eight FAA Canberras of Grupo de Bombardeo 2 (six B62s plus two T64s) were deployed to naval air station Almirante Zar at Trelew in Chubut province, over 1,000 km from the islands to avoid congestion on the closer southern airfields.

CAPTAIN JOSÉ AGUSTIN ORSI flew 50 missions as a Canberra pilot and around 40 as a bombing navigator.

> The Argentinian air force had, for many years, incorporated a modified engine-starting system for the Canberra due to the shortage of the starter cartridges. This modified system was designed by a Group 2 Technician of the II Air Brigade, based in the city of Paraná. The operation of this system was based on compressed air which, although not as instantaneous as the starter cartridge, gave a longer useful life to the starter turbine. Another benefit was that the air-start system didn't produce the high temperatures of the starter cartridge which meant that the starter turbines were less stressed which prolonged their useful working life. ▮

On the afternoon of 1 May, following the first Black Buck Vulcan raid on Port Stanley, the FAA mounted a concerted attack on the British naval task force. The FAA knew that their Canberras would be extremely vulnerable to RN Sea Harriers and their Sidewinder missiles so, in CAPTAIN ORSI'S words:

> Squadron commanders came up with an idea to confuse the British missile guidance systems to defend the B62s and surprise the nation who designed the Canberra. If the Harrier had chaff and flares, why not the Canberra? Because we had never intended to procure these defensive elements, we had to manufacture defensive aids and launchers. The head of intelligence provided the broadcast frequency of the Marconi 909 radar which controlled the Sea Dart and, after assessing the Sidewinder seeker head, we calculated the required chaff length and flares. The problem was how to make them.
>
> Having given a roll of paper, aluminium and scissors to children at the local secondary school, it became clear that a faster and more efficient method was needed to create the considerable volume of chaff that would be needed. Argentine talent then emerged. Each metallic chaff strip had the width of a noodle and in the II Brigade storeroom were large rolls of thick metallic paper sent by the British to line the jet tube and dissipate heat. The staff of the pasta factory, Vía Nápoli of the city of Paraná, were surprised one day when squadron personnel arrived with one of the rolls and

commandeered the pasta-cutting machine. Having proved this method, a noodle cutter was provided to brigade and work began to cut longitudinal strips on an industrial scale on large tables by female staff.

Meanwhile, Commodore Valenzuela worked on the design of the launchers and in the preparation of flares for the infrared-guided missiles. Canberra starter cartridges were placed in seven units on a horizontal drum that was located in the tail of the Canberra. Fabricaciones Militares developed a grain of powder which burned evenly at 500°C, a temperature slightly higher than that of the Canberra jet pipe efflux.

The cartridges contained a parachute flare, chaff strips and finally a plastic lid. An electric starter was connected to the initiator with cables that reached a cockpit panel which numbered one to seven launchers: each had an activation key and a red light indicating that it had been fired. Chaff or flare could not be selected together.

The technical head at Trelew was Major Fernando Rezoagli. A trials team moved to Trelew, tested the launcher and infrared flares and by 1 May, everything was installed. The pilot could trigger the system when he saw a missile being fired, either from the illumination on the ship's deck or if he saw, in the darkness of the night, a halo with black heading for the Canberra's centre. ▦

Some 40 FAA sorties were launched on the afternoon of 1 May. It was dusk as six Canberras of Grupo 2 approached in two flights of three at very low altitude from the north-west, on almost the direct line from Trelew. As the bombers were descending to low level they were observed on one of the ship's radars and Lt Cdr Mike Broadwater and Lt Al Curtiss of 801 Squadron were vectored out to intercept. Searching with radar at an altitude of 5,000 ft, the Sea Harriers made contact with first flight, call sign 'Route', and curved round to engage. The B62s did a brisk 180 while launching chaff.

Curtiss launched a Sidewinder at one Canberra about 50 ft above the waves. At the controls of the leading Canberra was Captain Alberto Baigorri. 'We were intercepted about 150 miles before reaching Puerto Argentino (the Argentinian name for Port Stanley),' he later recalled. 'No. 3 in my flight called that there was a missile heading my way.

FAA B62 which was shot down on 1 May 1982. B-110 started off life in 1954 as an RAF B2. (José Augustin Orsi)

I looked to my right and saw it hit the No. 2 aircraft, piloted by Lt Eduardo de Ibanez and with Lt Mario Gonzales as navigator. The bomber continued flying with an engine on fire then, as it started to go down, I saw de Ibanez and Gonzales eject before it hit the water.' From behind, Curtiss saw his Sidewinder explode close to the Canberra and pieces fall clear; but when the bomber continued on he launched a second missile, which was still in flight when the Canberra crashed into the sea. Broadwater loosed off both of his missiles at an evading Canberra but shortage of fuel forced the two Sea Harriers to return to *Invincible.* Baigorri returned to the scene of the crash but found no sign of his comrades.

After the abortive action on 1 May, Canberras of Grupo 2 were tasked with night operations which were little more than nuisance raids against the beachhead. Attacking from altitudes around 500 ft or way up at 40,000 ft, and in the absence of modern-targeting equipment, the FAA Canberra crews made what amounted to area bombing raids on San Carlos where military and civilian targets were few and far between. From the British point of view, the chances of a useful military result from such raids were extremely slender and in the event they achieved nothing.

From the Argentinian perspective, Canberras were chosen to perform missions that no other Argentine aircraft was able to carry out: night bombing. The flights began on 26 May and for five days, the troops landed at San Carlos were bombarded, night after night, by old aircraft that performed stoically. Every night, Puerto Argentino observers could see the mountains illuminated by explosions and so the almost besieged did not feel alone. At these times, the performance of the Canberra squadron was of great importance, not only for damaging the enemy but also to raise the morale of Argentine troops. 31 May would see the last mission in that area because the meteorological situation – almost always adverse – ensured that the releases did not have the desired accuracy, and the place was full of Argentine prisoners of war captured after the fall of Darwin.

The last FAA mission over Malvinas involved B62 Canberra bombers plus a couple of Mirage III interceptors for top cover on the night of 13 June. One Canberra was taken down at 39,000 ft by a long-range, high-altitude shot from HMS *Exeter's* Sea Dart. The pilot of the B62, Capt Roberto Pastrán, described the incident:

> After release of the bombs on Mount Kent from 40,000 feet, the missile struck our aircraft. We went into a spin and I kept calling the navigator, Capt Fernando Casado, to eject. I waited as long as I could, but after four turns I realized that for some reason he could not get out and I ejected at about 6,000 feet. Casado never did get out; I think the explosion of the missile might have caused his seat not to function.

Pastrán came down in the sea, released his parachute, and boarded his dinghy. Fortunately for him there was a northerly wind, and a few hours later he was blown ashore on the north coast of East Falkland. Argentine forces surrendered the next day.

The other Canberra pilot, **FIRST LT JORGE RIVOLIER**, recalled:

That last mission was tasked because our troops were fighting for Puerto Argentino. Shortly before ten in the evening, Baco 1 flown by Captains Pastrán and Casado together with Rivolier and Annino in Baco 2 took off from Rio Gallegos. Fifteen minutes later the Mirage IIIs, flown by Major Sanchez and Captain González, followed. The B62s carried the usual load of 500-kg bombs while the Mirages had air-to-air Matra R-550 Magic 2 missiles.

As planned, we passed the southern end of the Strait of San Carlos and over Bougainville Island before veering northward to reach the target, which was located about 7 km from Puerto Argentino. Up to now the British left us alone, maybe because they saw us as a diversionary manoeuvre. I was about 300 m behind the leader and I asked Malvinas radar for a fix – they confirmed for me the position which we had estimated by instruments.

It was about eleven o'clock and we were about five miles from the free-fall weapon-release point. I was the first to drop but when we exited back the way we came I saw five intense glares and explosions followed a few seconds by another series of glows. It was the other Canberra which had been hit. Until then everything had gone great *(bárbaro)*, the Mirage was taking care of us and suddenly when the English realised that we weren't there for fun, we had really dropped bombs so there began the drama of missiles. The Mirage section leader counted five missiles, but I personally only saw one.

I released the supplementary fuel tanks and saw a red light coming from the right, which undoubtedly was a missile. I told the navigator to take defensive measures and he did, but the missile did not reach us because it had exceeded its reach and run out of propellant.

After several changes of direction, radar Malvinas sings that there was a British CAP (combat air patrol) airborne, but it was about 80 miles away. Malvinas radar reported that something had happened to one of the Canberras. I answered that I was Baco 2 and he asks if I can make contact with Baco 1 on that radio frequency. I tried on our two designated frequencies but received no answer. They ordered me then return to base.

The Mirage pair landed back in Argentina at 2355 hours and Capt Rivolier's Canberra landed shortly afterwards on 14 June.

Group 2 carried out 35 missions during the Falklands conflict of which 25 were night-bombing missions. FAA Canberras delivered 45 tons of bombs in the process for the loss of two B62s and three aircrew members. Canberras were retired from 2 Group in April 2000 by which time the FAA was operating just two aircraft. In the words of one devoted fan, 'for the Argentinian air force and pilots who flew their beloved Canberras, they landed for a well-deserved rest after 30 years and a war'.

CHAPTER 26
CANBERRA TALES

CLIVE ELTON – 139 Squadron.

It was normal practice for squadron aircrew to be allocated an extra duty in addition to their normal flying. Such uninteresting roles as barrack block inventories were to be avoided but I was lucky to be given the highly responsible and demanding post of squadron entertainment officer. Needless to say a great deal is expected with the maximum enjoyment being provided at the minimum cost.

As no party is worthy of the name without a very plentiful supply of suitable alcoholic drinks it was our habit to combine a lone ranger which was a perfectly legitimate training flight with a visit to Gibraltar. At Saccone & Speed in Main Street it was possible to purchase considerable quantities of whisky and gin out of bond and have it delivered to the aircraft immediately prior to departure. The cost of a case of three bottles was less than a pound which even in those days was most certainly a bargain.

In April 1958, we, that is 139 (Jamaica) Squadron, took our turn in the rotation of so-called 'Sunspot Detachments'. These came round every six months and we were very fortunate to have a month or so in the Mediterranean each spring and autumn. On this occasion we were based at Luqa, Malta. The alternative would have been Idris later to be renamed Tripoli International. There we were able to practise our primary role as the Bomber Command marker squadron using targets at El Adem, Tarhuna and the tiny island of Filfla just off the south coast of Malta.

A squadron party was planned to take place prior to our return to our home base of Binbrook scheduled for 7 May. So it was that on Saturday 26 April two Canberras departed from Luqa for Gibraltar. What was neither expected nor forecast was that the Levant, a strong easterly wind, was blowing low cloud over Gib and landing there was out of the question. We were instructed to divert to Oran in Algeria. A second attempt also failed as the low cloud and visibility closed in again. A night stop in the transit mess at the French air base followed and in fact it was two days later before we were able to land at Gib.

We were adamant that the operation should be successful and decided to wait for a weather improvement at Gib. To make the most of our stay in Oran we urgently required some local currency and with this in mind we went to the home of the British consul having found that his office was closed for the weekend. We were informed that he could be found on a British cargo ship, the 10,000-ton *Hesperides* which it turned out was moored some distance from the quay in Oran harbour. We persuaded a friendly Arab boatman to row us out to the ship.

None of the crew seemed bothered as we boarded the ship but instead kindly directed us to the captain's cabin where we found not only the captain but the local agent of the shipping line accompanied by the British consul. Judging by the number of empty bottles to be seen, they had been there for some time and were most hospitable. Better still the consul kindly handed over a wad of notes which enabled us to have a most pleasant evening in town.

It was the Monday before we could finally land in Gibraltar. On top of everything else we had encountered a problem with the fuel which concerned us due to its relatively high freezing point. To be absolutely sure we flew at low level and on arrival immediately proceeded to Saccone & Speed to order the essential supplies.

Now it could be assumed that we would immediately set off for Luqa. However, we were having such fun that we took the clearly rather irresponsible decision to spend a night in the officer's mess at North Front on the grounds that all that French food at Oran had caused some members of the party to be suffering stomach disorders.

So it was three days after departing Luqa that two Canberras with six aircrew plus very important cargo finally landed back on Malta. Depriving the squadron of two aircraft had not gone down well with the powers that be so I suppose I got off lightly as the leader of the expedition in just having to write a full report.

Fortunately I was able to take part in a target marking exercise at El Adem that evening which was entirely successful. Equally important the squadron party was thoroughly enjoyed by all. Finally a happy ending was made even better by repayment of the loan from the consul in Oran never being demanded. ▥

STEVE FISHER – 16 Squadron.

It was in May 1972, and my navigator Mike and I had just been pronounced 'operational' as a Canberra B(I)8 crew on 16 Squadron. We were both aged just 22. We were summoned to the boss's office and informed that due to our diligence over the past six months we were being rewarded with a week-long 'ranger' flight to the Med. We would fly to Gibraltar for a three-night stay, then on to Luqa in Malta for a refuelling stop, and then on to Akrotiri, Cyprus for a further night stop. The return would be direct to Luqa, then back to Laarbruch. This was as good as it gets! The outbound sectors passed with little incident, other than losing our only reliable navigation aid, the radio compass, inbound to Akrotiri. Further investigation determined that this was a 'no-go' item to transit over the ocean. This had the pleasing prospect of an extended time in Cyprus, waiting for a spare part to make its way to us from RAFG.

But that evening we fell in with four Hunter pilots making their way back to the UK following disbandment of their squadron in the Far East. Over just a few beers that evening we hatched a plan to be escorted by the Hunters as far as Malta, after which we would have an acceptable (largely overland) transit back to base. A quick pass by station operations, and an HF patch to RAFG, and all was approved.

The following morning, our pre-order of demijohns of local Kokinelli wine secure in the luggage rack in the bomb bay, we launched ahead of the four-ship, with a pre-arranged rendezvous point about 100 nm short of Malta. After a brief conversation on a discreet air-to-air frequency, we set up for our approach into Luqa. The weather at Malta was poor, with a cloud-base of 5-600 feet in moderate rain. We would need to let down over the sea, well short of the airfield. With two Hunters on each wing I signalled a descent and then gave the visual signal for airbrakes. This was the point at which things started to go horribly wrong. The Canberra brakes deployed straight away, and we rapidly fell behind the formation I was supposed to be leading. I quickly stowed the airbrakes at just the point where the Hunters' brakes started 'biting', and as a result shot forward through the middle of the four. We then decided to continue the descent without the use of airbrakes.

We broke cloud at around 700 ft in driving rain, but on the extended centreline of the runway. Permission was granted by Luqa ATC to run in for a visual break and low-level left-hand circuit. Our plan, to take account of disparity of performance between the two aircraft types, was for me to call the break, at which point I would pull up slightly, and the Hunters would break below, after which I would join them downwind.

The cloud-base lowered a little on the run in, and the rain persisted. Nevertheless, halfway down the runway I called the break, and raised the nose. Not to miss the action I shot a glance to the left, and saw the spectacle of the four jets peeling off into the circuit. Suddenly it went quite dark as I re-entered the cloud, so speedily back on to instruments. Unfortunately the head snapping had now caused a severe bout of the 'leans', and I fought to keep the aircraft under control whilst trying to wrestle it onto a downwind heading and re-establishing visual conditions. During this tussle I sliced out from the clouds, only partially in control.

Fortune favours the stupid, and I caught glimpse of another aircraft ahead and in the gloom, and to him I riveted my eyes. We turned finals with a pounding heart, at which point Mike said: 'Remember we're well overweight for the bomb bay rack, and we don't want Kokinelli dripping all over the ramp!' So I decided to 'grease' it on to the runway. We touched down with just a squeak from the tyres, and a satisfied look on my face. I remember being surprised at the four braking parachutes that I could see ahead of me, and so applied my own brakes. Nothing! We were happily aquaplaning on what was now a flooded runway, and the Hunters were getting much larger by the second. A myriad of thoughts passed through my mind, none of them pleasant, and, none of them concerning nine times the square root of the tyre pressure aquaplaning formula! But suddenly we were decelerating, and at around 100 ft behind Hunter number four we were back in control. Parked on the ramp the Hunter boys legged it straight to the mess, and I can only cringe at what the content of their conversation was.

As we were getting out of the aircraft a lone officer came striding over to us, probably OC Ops or the station commander I thought. Luckily it was an ex-member of 16 Squadron. 'Very impressive', he said, and I wilted at his sarcasm. He then described the 'punchy' run in; the break; the Canberra disappearing, then joining the formation, perfectly spaced downwind etc. etc. What he didn't know! But I knew and Mike knew, and we both learned a lot about flying that day.

PHIL WILKINSON – 85 Squadron.

'You're on Fire!' Not what you want to hear as the nosewheel is raised and the short runway is looking shorter every second, and especially when it's a hot May day and the aircraft is full of fuel at max AUW for a B2, WJ567, C for Charlie, of 85 Squadron.

But is that what the ATC fellow had said? Surely not, I thought, as the main wheels left the ground and we approached safety speed. So: 'HEX 19, say again'. The reply was swift and clear – 'your port engine is on fire'. But inside there were no abnormalities on the gauges, and certainly no fire warning light. However I closed the port throttle and concentrated on handling the aircraft, still not quite at safety speed. There was now considerable airframe vibration. So I shut the engine down and headed for the coast, knowing that I would have to divert to Marham, with West Raynham's 6,000 ft runway not recommended for a heavyweight asymmetric landing.

Bob Tracy, highly-experienced Canberra operator with 100 Squadron, was airborne and joined up very quickly to give me an assessment of the presumed damage. He confirmed no sign of fire but said the port side fuselage and tailplane looked 'a bit scorched'. Then came a call from West Raynham tower to say that debris had been found on the runway and it might be undercarriage fragments, and I should have a full undercarriage function check before the final approach. By now I was at the coast, north of West Raynham, 12 miles or so from take-off, and just creeping up to 1,000 feet and a reasonable and manageable speed.

So equipped, and with Bob Tracy in close for a visual check of undercarriage up and down and no bits missing, the function check was done and all was OK. So, into the visual pattern for Marham, and a safe landing was made after just 30 minutes airborne. The damage to the engine cowling and the wing, when I got to look at it, was considerable.

The incident report was filled out and processed, and it was found that the force of the rupture of a flame can – for that was the cause of the problem – as well as opening up the top of the engine cowling, had blown away the fire detector wire so quickly that it had not had time to heat up and give a warning. So, a 'fail unsafe' system, which – it was recommended – should be put right. Good idea, for an airframe already over 20 years old. The write-ups by my squadron and station commanders led to the award of a Strike Command Flight Safety 'Good Show' certificate. Suitable for framing!

I'm bound to say that I was pleased it had happened to me – as a flight commander and squadron QFI, I had been through the emergency drills for engine failure and practised handling at critical speed and safety speed a good few times. With just short of 900 Canberra hours on the squadron, and almost 2,000 hours on type in all, I felt I could have handled the emergency better than most. And I was tourex in a couple of weeks, posted to a desk in MOD. This is why there's another aspect to the story.

The sortie was to be a routine target facility affair – providing a single low-level target for some 11 Squadron Lightnings to play with, out over the North Sea, cleared for evasive manoeuvres up to the maximum permitted for both target and fighters at low level. One of the squadron armourers, Cpl Les Landers, had always said he really didn't fancy flying, but he thought he ought to, at least once. He said, 'If you're leaving soon, I think I'd better make my trip with you, because you're not likely to have any upsets'. So he was briefed and strapped into the right hand of the two rear compartment ejection seats, with my navigator of the day, Fg Off Rick Suffolk, keeping a close eye on him. As the excitement began, and I was dealing with the problem, I managed a quick look over my shoulder and Les Landers' eyes were out on stalks over the face mask – seriously bulging. I felt instinctively – and I was having to consider the possibility, if we didn't get up to safety speed – that a call to eject might have been a touch too much for this reluctant flyer! So he was pretty pleased that I got him back on the ground, and I doubt he ever flew again.

28 May 1975 – for sure a day he'll remember. I do.

Mean machine – a B(I)8 with
offset canopy at Wildenrath in 1956.
(National Aerospace Library)

ED ELTON – 16 Squadron.

Sadly this tale is very much hearsay – I was not involved but found it entertaining. I'm sure it has improved with the telling!

Canberra B(I)8 on a dark winter night at 250 ft over a cold North Sea on its way to Wainfleet range. Suddenly the aircraft pitches up quite violently and the navigator who is unstrapped in the nose slides back towards the bulkhead.

'What's up?' he shouts.

'Flame out,' comes the strangled reply from the pilot.

'Well this thing will fly on one won't it,' says the nav.

'I'll let you know if I can get one going!' came the reply.

Story was it was severe icing and one assumes the pilot succeeded...

CHAPTER 27
THE ULTIMATE PR9

On 1 March 1954, a Canberra PR3 was flown to the US by a 58 Squadron crew. It was to be modified at Hanscom AFB near Boston to accept a 240-inch focal length framing camera that had been specially designed for long-range oblique photography (LOROP). Known colloquially as 'the bomb camera', it must have been designed specifically for the B-57/Canberra because it fitted neatly into the bomb bay using the existing lugs. After the PR3 returned to the UK, it was used by 58 Squadron to take pictures through a large optical window cut in the aircraft's port lower fuselage. While a second Canberra was alongside to warn of contrails, the modified PR3 flew at least nine LOROP missions in Central Europe and Eastern Mediterranean, returning with useful imagery of 'denied territory' taken from high inside friendly airspace.

PR9 in 'low conspicuity' hemp finish. The navigator entered through the open nose and he sat ahead of the pilot in the enclosed nose where two very small windows on either side at head level were jokingly described as 'day-night indicators'. The navigator controlled three of the four sensor systems, the exception being the F95 low-level cameras with 4- or 12-inch lenses and 70mm film, three of which looked left, right and ahead from their fixed positions in the nose. The pilot controlled these reminders that the PR9 could perform the 'tactical' as well as the 'strategic' reconnaissance role. But they were only used occasionally towards the end. (39 Squadron Association)

Which leads nicely to the Formula 1 version of the Canberra, the PR9. With powered flying controls, autopilot, bigger wing and much more powerful Avon 206 engines (11,250 lbs each), the PR9 was designed to operate at 60,000 ft plus. It had a redesigned nose similar to the B(I)8 but with an opening pilot's canopy which was a boon in hot climates. Access to the navigator's forward station was through a sideways-opening nose, and he had an ejection seat from the second production aircraft onwards. Production of 23 PR9s were subcontracted to Shorts at Belfast, of which 21 were delivered to the RAF. In 1959 a flight of Canberra PR9s was established on 58 Squadron at Wyton from where trained crews and aircraft moved out to 13 Squadron in Cyprus in 1961 and 39 Squadron in Malta in 1962. 58 Squadron disbanded in 1970.

VERNON HARDING had three squadron tours as navigator on the PR9.

In the early days, the PR9 was well able to sustain level flight at 60,000-plus-a-bit feet but later on, probably because of increases in its weight and dents and twists in the airframe, 58,000 ft became a more realistic figure. Flying at high levels meant that degradation of the image due to the effects of the atmosphere was greater. Therefore the PR9 was equipped with a much developed and improved suite of cameras. The F49 Mk4 survey camera was gyro-stabilised and mounted in a nitrogen-filled pod. It marked the first occasion on which a camera was pod-mounted on the PR9, a system which was to prove very successful with later sensor fits. For high-level reconnaissance, the PR9 had a number of F96 cameras mounted either in a fan of two or four, providing a wide-angle of cover or, in the oblique mode, set across the aircraft at angles of 15° or 18° below the horizontal. These F96 cameras were fitted with lenses of either 24- or 48-inch focal length and they had an image movement compensation system which improved resolution. For low-level operations, the PR9 had three of the same F95 cameras that were fitted to the PR7. It also had a night low-level camera.

13 Squadron flip-flopped between Cyprus and Malta as political imperatives changed. Despite spending much flying time over Italy and Greece, there was a constant demand for high-level national reconnaissance tasking from Near East out to the Far East. There was also a fair amount of tasking in North Africa and the occasional trip to Hong Kong. Make no mistake – the living was good!

39 Squadron was rather more static: it was based at Wyton from 1 October 1970 from where it was assigned to support NATO's Northern Flank in the low-level recce role. After a tour on the B(I)8, ED ELTON moved across to the PR9.

In my time on 39 Squadron our wartime operations would have been in support of AFNORTH and as such we had two major detachments a year to Norway. Our operating base was RNoAF base, Ørland which was located at the mouth of Trondheim fiord, quite a remote base though still south of the Arctic Circle. Our nearest diversion was at Trondheim itself at the inland end of the fiord. Our visits were very popular with the Norwegians as in an effort to maintain morale at this far flung outpost, our 'chalks' on the deployment Hercules included a considerable amount of alcohol and cigarettes – both to consume when away and to provide our 'bottle and 200' on return to the UK. UK Customs were happy, the booze was held in bond then exported, so no UK duty was payable. Fortunately, only one Noggie customs officer covered both airfields and travelled by boat between the two – a lengthy undertaking. If he was at Ørland a suitable codeword would be used by ATC and the Hercules would develop a fault that required diversion to Trondheim. Once the customs officer had departed for Trondheim by boat the 'fault' would miraculously rectify itself and the C130 would land at its intended destination. The speed with which the Hercules was offloaded and its cargo removed to a safe location had to be wondered at.

The squadron also mounted if I remember correctly about 24 individual detachments to Norway per year – so about two per crew. These lasted from Monday to Friday and involved operating from a number of AFNORTH airfields being tasked by AFNORTH and having our imagery exploited by Norwegian or Danish photographic interpreters. Again a useful trade developed. Demijohns of brandy in particular would be brought back from Cyprus – not the cheap stuff, the 10/- a bottle variety. We had a helpful customs man at Wyton who would place it in bond and release it to the individual crew as they set off to points north. Here it would be traded for what the Norwegians had – in particular fish. Not just run of the mill Pollack – I had a freezer full (I exaggerate) of smoked salmon. The exchange rate seemed to be one demijohn = one smoked salmon.

Winters could be harsh and the runway covered in snow. In the UK the 'snow plan' would have involved snowploughs, snowblowers, scrapers and tons of urea and usually rendered the runways unusable until the thaw, which then took longer due to the heaps of snow adjacent to the runway and the hard-packed ice ridges where the snow clearing vehicles had been. The Norwegians had a novel solution. A rig, the first part of which was effectively a flame thrower, drove slowly down the runway melting the snow. The second part of the rig (it may have been two vehicles – I can't remember) followed closely behind the first and scattered cinders on the now wet runway which then immediately turned back to ice. This was the surface we were expected to operate from and with a heavy Canberra with no reverse thrust, brake parachute or other aids to slowing down other than normal brakes you were very gentle with the aircraft on your first sortie off, what looked like, sheet ice. Surprisingly the friction was amazingly good.

The PR9, like the Hunter and Lightning, used Avpin for starting. Avpin or Isopropyl Nitrate to give it its proper name was nasty stuff. Extremely flammable, it burnt with no visible flame and could be self-igniting, if not explosive, if mixed with air. The PR9 had a tank on each engine which contained enough for several starts. Again I can't remember how many – so let's say four or five. This was fine when operating from base or locations with Avpin stores, but in the early days of operating in Norway and

Denmark there were no such, and operating 'down route' to the Far East could also provide difficulties. So we used to strap a five-litre can (sealed – we weren't stupid) into the pannier in the flare bay with lashing tape, and when the engine tanks were empty, top up from our onboard supply. I have seen many a Norwegian ground crew member tiptoe gently away with the remains of a not quite empty can – never found out what he did with it.

All was well until one Taceval when the team engineer discovered what we had been doing and promptly went very, very white. The outcome was a whole series of secure Avpin stores being built at all of our deployment bases in Scandinavia which had to be replenished about every six months – the best-before life of Avpin. This was accomplished by a special dedicated Hercules sortie carrying minimum crew as Avpin was designated dangerous air cargo (DC). ▪

13 Squadron joined 39 Squadron at Wyton in October 1978, by which time 13 Squadron was operating a mixed fleet of PR7s and PR9s. This arrangement allowed some PR9s to be put into storage to preserve their fatigue life and by the time 13 Squadron disbanded in January 1982, it was operating PR7s only. 39 Squadron was now the only unit flying the PR9 and when it too disbanded on 1 June 1982, five of their aircraft were used to reform 1 Photographic Reconnaissance Unit (PRU).

Between 1978-1980, 12 of the surviving 16 PR9 aircraft were given a better Doppler along with Decca TANS to improve track keeping. An updated radar warning system was simultaneously mounted on the tail. Much later, a very accurate embedded GPS/INS was added. This was essential if the new EO sensor, with its very long focal length, was to be accurately pointed at its pre-planned targets. In RAF service, this EO sensor was known as the rapid deployment electro-optical system (RADEOS). Manufactured by Goodrich in the US, this was also carried by USAF U-2s. For the Canberra, a new gimbal and crate assembly was built so that the sensor could be carried in the PR9's former photo-flare bay. (This bay once housed either the IRLS or System III, a 36-inch focal length camera with seven 'stop-and-shoot' positions that was also derived from the U-2. By Gulf War 2, both these sensors had been retired.) The 'fantastic' EOS in the flare bay weighed 1,500 lbs and measured 8 ft by 3 ft. EO imagery was datalinked to a ground station and was inter-operable with US systems. When the PR9 flew beyond the ground station's line of sight (as over Afghanistan), the imagery was recorded onboard for later relay, or replay on the ground.

The EO sensor brought the Canberra into the modern world of 'real-time' reconnaissance, and it cut through haze to produce very high-quality daytime imagery at very long stand-off range. But its field of view was very narrow, which made the fourth item in the PR9's sensor suite so useful. The KA-93 panoramic camera, made by Recon/Optical, provided wide-angle coverage from the horizon to the vertical on both sides of the flight path using a 24-inch focal length lens. It occupied the Canberra's forward camera bay, beneath which were small sliding doors that opened in flight so that the camera's scanning element (a rotating prism) could be lowered into position. A huge amount of territory could be captured on the KA-93's five-inch roll film, at high resolution, with stereo overlap. The overall PR9 system was both successful and popular, and in its final years many UK and US commanders would put 'Preferred Sensor Canberra PR9' on their recce request forms.

SIMON BALDWIN was a navigator who served as station commander at Wyton from 1985-87.

The PR9 was such a generational jump that it shouldn't have been called a Canberra. It had much better performance and kit compared with what had gone before. Varied tasks were flown by PR9 crews at high altitude, and low level, and provided good training for whatever tasks they might have to fly in war. In addition to the cameras, the ex-Phantom infra-red line scan (IRLS) was fitted in the former F49 camera pod and could be used at low level, though crews frequently flew along the East German border at high altitude. The PR9 was the only aircraft I have flown that was built around the navigator, with everything (apart from the IFF selector) in the right places. I was air attaché in Washington during Gulf War I and the PR9s brought great imagery back which was shown to General Colin Powell. 'Why can't we do this?' was his response. 'Why do I have to get this from the RAF?'

I PRU later moved to Marham and low-level flying virtually ceased to extend PR9 fatigue life. The weakest point was the pressure bulkhead at the back of the cockpit and as one of the PRU's PR9s reached the end of its fatigue life, it was replaced by another taken out of storage. The unit was renamed 39 (1PRU) Squadron on 1 July 1992. While extensive surveys were flown over Zimbabwe and Kenya, national tasking steadily increased and operations were flown over the Former Republic of Yugoslavia on behalf of the UN and NATO. Operations were also mounted over Afghanistan, Bosnia, Iraq and Somalia. Once the Lightning retired, the PR9 still climbed faster than anything else in the RAF until the Typhoon arrived.

39 (1PRU) Squadron deployed six times to Kenya and Zimbabwe between 1996 and 2001 for photo-mapping, though the Zeiss camera was used over Afghanistan, Iraq and Somalia for military purposes. The navigator had a 'recce sight' – a periscope with fore-and-aft steering – which presented the ground beneath to him through a nosecone in the middle of the front panel. Correcting for velocity and height, he called out small course corrections to the pilot above and behind him.

Fourteen aircrew and 105 ground crew kept the PRU's five PR9s and two T4 trainers flying. In support were 14 imagery analysts, 25 wet film photo engineers/developers plus four people from the air survey liaison section who made up maps. They all combined to achieve a 95 per cent serviceability rate during Operation Telic in 2003 when two PR9s were deployed to support the invasion of Iraq. Why was the PR9 required over Kosovo,

Afghanistan and Iraq? Simply put, no other reconnaissance platform could carry four different and complementary imaging systems at the same time, as high as 50,000 ft, for up to five hours with a range of nearly 2,000 nm. The PR9 could take panoramic photographs at the same time as EO sensing – the U-2 couldn't do that.

39 Squadron completed 150 missions during the 2003 Iraqi conflict, flying twice daily from its base at Azraq in Jordan. 'Our initial tasking,' recalled one aircrew member, 'was in the western Iraqi desert, Scud hunting. We flew three missions a day, each nine hours solid, looking at 17 "areas of interest". We data linked most of our imagery and the photo interpreters scanned for Scuds, but none were found.' A wet film image taken from 47,000 ft over Basra showed skid marks from a bus crashed on a bombed bridge.

It was a similar story 12 months earlier when the squadron made an unpublicised excursion – Operation Ramson – to Mombasa to look for terrorist threats in Somalia. From an offshore position in international airspace, the PR9's sensors provided good coverage of Mogadishu and other coastal regions. That deployment took place from March to May 2002, only two months after the squadron had returned from Operations Veritas and Oracle. These were the UK's contribution to the defeat of the Taliban regime in Afghanistan, during which 39 Squadron flew out of Seeb in Oman from October 2001 to January 2002. Terry Cairns flew the PR9 for much of the time between 1985 and 2006 and he recalls that, 'the pressure breathing kit was in use during my time in Iraq and Afghanistan'. It was said that the PR9s ranged as far north as Kabul, ending up landing back on fumes on the Seeb secondary runway. It's a great tale but in Terry Cairns' words:

> Apart from one nutter who loitered at altitude over Seeb just to see how long he could stay airborne, and this with the bar open, our average sortie length was four hours and 30 minutes. We certainly did not use the secondary runway because there wasn't one. The taxiway could be used in emergency if the main was blocked.

Regular coverage of Northern Ireland was still required since 'everywhere the army goes, it must have good maps'. During training flights, there were 'targets of opportunity' such as major motorway

Wg Cdr Ken Smith, OC 39 Squadron (1PRU) in 2003. The symbols on the PR9 beside the ejection seat warning triangle are Scud-hunt mission marks from Operation Telic – the superimposed red crosses indicate a fruitless search. (39 Squadron Association)

pile-ups. From time to time, the squadron will be asked to support the police in domestic surveillance operations. A typical request might be: 'Can you photograph the barn at this location? With the doors open? Without being detected?' No problem!

At the entrance to 39 Squadron's hangar at RAF Marham, some comedian placed a copy of the road sign that warned drivers of an adjacent old folk's home. 'Elderly Aircrew Crossing' was the legend beneath, and by the 21st century it could not be denied that the aircraft and the aircrews of the last Canberra squadron were more advanced in years than most of the RAF. The airframes were into their fifth decade, and 11 of the 14 aircrew (seven pilots plus seven navigators) were 40-plus. This brought challenges but also some advantages, according to OC 39 Squadron (1 PRU)'s boss in 2003, Wg Cdr Ken Smith. 'We have some "old" personalities who are used to doing things in a certain way, but they are very experienced and committed. Three of them are over 55, and have signed on for another five years purely because they want to fly the Canberra.' Smith and his two flight commanders served standard 30-month tours, and brought contemporary 'tactical' experience from other weapons systems such as the Tornado.

The final PR9 flight landed at Kemble on 31 July 2006. The total annual cost of operating 39 Squadron in the end was very close to £15million but money was never going to be found to overcome the pressure bulkhead fatigue issue. The last T4 having been retired on 1 September 2005, the RAF couldn't keep relying on old and bold PR9 guys either. The Canberra and its boys had been stars for over 55 years but now it was time to bring the curtain down.

AFTERWORD
TSAR BOMBA

Capt Harold F. Crisler USAF died when the B-57 he was piloting crashed at an Armed Forces Day airshow at Elmendorf AFB, Alaska on 19 May 1962. In the words of his son, **BOB CRISLER:**

> It was typical in the USAF to rotate older aircraft to a utility role as newer, more advanced aircraft enter service. Due to its design flexibility, the subsonic B-57 found itself in a wide variety of utility roles by 1961. The RB-57A was a reconnaissance platform, while the later modification to variant EB-57E was equipped as an electronic-counter-measures platform: in that role it was used in a defence systems evaluation role to probe the distant early warning (DEW) line, a series of radar installations that lined the northern reaches of North America from the Aleutians on the west to Newfoundland on the east. For much of their service in Alaska, Harold Crisler and his close friend Roy Fair were tasked with the rather demeaning job of towing targets for the F-102 Delta Dagger supersonic fighter aircraft, also based at Elmendorf, to shoot at.
>
> In 1961, the Soviets broke the tacit moratorium on nuclear testing that had persisted since 1958. On 1 September, a test series began that would average nearly a bomb a day over 65 days, with a crescendo of 14 detonations over the final four days. Nearly 60 detonations, nearly 60 clouds of fallout drifting east, all with vital clues about the size, makeup and construction of the bombs from which they came. It was the job of the crews at Elmendorf and Eielson Air Force bases to fly through those clouds and gather those clues. ∎

ROY FAIR, in the back on the navigator's seat, operated the sampling apparatus which used a simple five-inch diameter pipe to allow outside air to flow through once the shut-off valve was opened. In Roy's words:

> The operating procedure called for (1) insertion and lock-in of a five-inch pad (sand-wiched in a screen) in the cavity of the airflow pipe, (2) opening of the ram air shut-off valve, (3) monitoring of the nuclear debris build-up on the pad by way of a Geiger counter forward of the pad, (4) removal and storage of the pad in a manila folder when the pegged meter indicated optimum build-up, and (5) repeat the process until fuel dictated return to base. ∎

On 30 October 1961, 1st Lt Fair was again assigned to a sampling mission, one of the 195 sorties flown in support of what was called the 'Team 202/203 Project' by the four RB-57 crews assigned to the sampling task. This one would prove different, however. On that day, he and his pilot would fly through what was left of Tsar Bomba (Tsar Bomb), also known as Big Ivan, the largest nuclear explosion in history with an estimated yield of 57 MT – almost four times greater than the United States' largest, the Castle/Bravo 8MT design which had achieved around 15 MT due to a runaway reaction over Bikini Atoll in 1954. In contrast, Tsar Bomba was a 100-MT design, only limited to its final yield when Andrei Sakharov thought its environmental impact would have increased worldwide radiation due to fallout by 25 per cent. Still, it remains – by far – the largest nuclear explosion in the history of man.

According to ROY FAIR:

It was the only one of the many [detonations] that was visually detectable as it appeared as a brown haze in the otherwise clear Arctic atmosphere. Its strength was quite telling – when the shut-off valve was opened to collect the sample, the meter pegged immediately and never came off the peg. On my crew we stayed in that cloud [visually] for one hour and 35 minutes until fuel dictated our return to Eielson. Another RB-57A took our place soon after departure as we continued around-the-clock sur- veillance of the cloud until it passed beyond our fuel range. When we returned to Eielson, the aircraft was directed to be parked on the far end of the 15,000-foot runway on the opposite end of the field from the 55th Weather Recon Squadron. The squadron technician who checked our aircraft remarked to us that he 'knew we were on the air patch' when he came out of the squadron building and turned on his Geiger counter some 3 miles' distance from our RB-57A. Radiation on that aircraft was so great that it created quite a stir – it was obvious the authorities had not encountered such levels before. How and where to decontaminate the aircraft had no easy solution. We were immediately spirited to the Eielson hospital but feedback was minimal. We were later told that our exposure level was 'only 55 milliroentgens' and that 50MR were 'normal'. There is now nothing in my service medical records to document those numerous visits to the Eielson AFB hospital – I simply don't exist medically from about April 1961 to February 1962. ▪

ACRONYMS

A&AEE Aircraft and Armament Experimental Establishment

ACAS Assistant Chief of the Air Staff

ADIZ Air Defence Identification Zone

AFB (US) Air Force Base

API Air Position Indicator

ATAF Allied Tactical Air Force

BABS Blind Approach Beacon System

CENTO Central Treaty Organisation

C-in-C Commander-in-Chief

DF Direction Finding

DMZ (Vietnamese) Demilitarised Zone

ECM Electronic Counter Measures

EE English Electric

ELINT Electronic intelligence

FAC Forward Air Controller

FEAF Far East Air Force

FRA First Run Attack

FRADU Fleet Requirements and Air Direction Unit

GCA Ground-controlled approach

GPI Ground Position Indicator

IFR Instrument Flight Rules

JARIC Joint Air Reconnaissance Intelligence Centre

LAA Light Anti-Aircraft Artillery

LABS Low-Altitude Bombing System

MEAF Middle East Air Force

NDB Non-Directional Beacon

NEAF Near East Air Force

OCU Operational Conversion Unit

PAR Precision Approach Radar

QGH radio direction-finding let-down procedure

SBB Simulated Blind Bombing

SEATO South East Asia Treaty Organisation

SFOM Societé Française d'Optique et de Mechanique

TDU Tactical Development Unit

VOR Voice Omnidirectional Range

BIBLIOGRAPHY

BEAMONT, R. AND REED, A., *English Electric Canberra,* Ian Allan, 1984

BROOKES, A., *Canberra Units of the Cold War,* Osprey, 2014

CULL, B., *249 At War,* Grub Street, 1997

CULL, B. WITH DAVID N. & SHLOMO A., *Wings over Suez,* Grub Street, 1996

ETHELL, J. AND PRICE, A., *Air War South Atlantic,* Sidgwick and Jackson, 1983

JEFFORD C. G., *The Flying Camels,* privately published, 1995

MIKESH, R. C., *B-57 Canberra,* Ian Allan, 1980

RAF HISTORICAL SOCIETY (RAFHS) Journal 22A, *Royal Air Force in Germany 1945-1993,* 1999

RAFHS Journal 26, *The RAF and Nuclear Weapons 1960-1989,* 2001

RAFHS Journal 39, *Air Aspects of the Suez Campaign,* 2007

RAFHS Journal 43A, *The Canberra in the RAF,* 2009

ROSS, T., *Through Eyes of Blue,* Airlife Publishing Ltd, 2002

THORBURN, G., *A Century of Air Warfare with Nine Squadron,* Pen and Sword, 2014

WILKINSON, P., *Canberra Crusaders, FlyPast,* Key Publishing, June and July 2005

WYNN, H., *RAF Nuclear Deterrent Forces,* HMSO, 1994

INDEX